Working the Woods,
Working the Sea

Empty Bowl is a division of
Pleasure Boat Studio: A Literary Press
201 West 89th Street, 6F, New York, NY 10024

Printed in the USA by Thomson-Shore, Inc.

ISBN: 978-1-929355-40-2
Library of Congress Control Number: 2007940735

New and expanded edition.
First Printing.

Empty Bowl
535 Reed Street
Port Townsend, WA 98368

Working the Woods, Working the Sea

An Anthology of Northwest Writings

Edited by Finn Wilcox and Jerry Gorsline

EMPTY BOWL

For Pat and for Beth

ACKNOWLEDGMENTS / PERMISSIONS

Michael Daley: "The Silver Sea" from *Way Out West: Lyrical Essays* from Aequitas, an imprint of Pleasure Boat Studio: A Literary press, 2006.

John Daniel: "Cuttings" first appeared in *Beloved of the Sky*, edited by John Ellison, Broken Moon Press, 1992.

Richard Dankleff: "First Trip" from *Popcorn Girl*, Oregon State University Press, 1979. "Departure, "Splash," and "Pacific Route" from *Off Watch*, Oregon Sunrise Press, 2001.

Jim Dodge: "Piss-Fir Willie" poems first appeared in, and are excerpted from, a chapbook, *Piss-Fir Willie: A Suite of Poems in Praise of the Northcoast Vernacular* from Tangram Press, 1998.

Erin Fristad: "While You Were Sleeping" from *Blue Collar Review*. (Vol. 8 #1). "Advice to Female Deckhands" from *Stringtown* (Issue #8: 5-6).

Hal Hartzel: Excerpt from "Birth of a Cooperative: Hoedads, Inc." Appeared in the first edition of *Working the Woods, Working the Sea* and later in book form from Hulogosi Press.

Howard Horowitz: "Montana," "Idaho," and "Trying to Reforest a Cut-Over Heart" from *Close to the Ground*, Hulogo's Press, 1986. "Cougar Dam"; reprinted from *Northwest Review Anthology of Eugene Poets*, 1982.

Freeman House: Excerpts from *Totem Salmon*, copyright 1999 by Freeman House; reprinted by permission of Beacon Press, Boston.

"More Than Numbers: Twelve or Thirteen ways of Looking at a Watershed"; reprinted from *A Road Runs Through it*, Johnson Press, July 2006.

Holly J. Hughes: "Working on Deck, Ten Years Later" from *Boxing the Compass*, Floating Bridge Press, 2007. "Point Colpoys, Alaska: Tendering" appeared first in the *Duckabush Journal*, spring/summer, 1993, then again in *The Hedgebrook Journal*, June 2002, Vol. 4 #1. "Preparation Is Everything" appeared in the *Hedgebrook Journal*, June 2002, Vol. 4 #1.

Lynda Mapes (*Seattle Times* staff reporter): "Funeral for a River," originally published in *The Seattle Times* on 03/12/2007 on page A1. Copyright 2007, *The Seattle Times*; used with permission.

Tim McNulty: "Night," "Sourdough Mountain Lookout," "Hub of the Wheel," and "Breath" from *Through High Still Air*, Pleasure Boat Studio: A Literary Press, 2006.

Mike O'Connor: "The River that Is a Deer and the Last Bird Flying," "Kerouac Creek Work Tune," "We Come to Ask for Your Bones: Cutting the Great Fragrant Western Red Cedar," "Elegy for a Log Truck Driver," and "Ray at Tubal Cain Mine" from *The Rainshadow*, Empty Bowl Press, 1983.

Judith Roche: "On The Yukon"; reprinted from *Ghosts*, Empty Bowl Press, 1984.

Gary Snyder: Excerpts from "Tanker Notes": 15: IV: 58 approaching San Pedro," "At Sea 20: III: 58," "At Sea 29: VII: 57," "Kwajalein 30: III," "Midway 1: X: 57," "Off Singapore 6: IX," and "Trincomalee Ceylon 12: IX" from *Earth House Hold*, copyright 1969 by Gary Snyder. Reprinted by permission of New Directions Publishing Corp. "Logging," (1-15) from *Myths and Texts*, copyright 1978 by Gary Snyder. Reprinted by permission of New Directions Publishing Corp. "Smoky the Bear Sutra" first appeared in *The Berkeley Barb*, 1969—"May be reproduced free forever."

Clemens Starck: "Ammo Ship" from *Journeyman's Wages*, Story Line Press, 2005. "At Sea" from *China Basin*, Story Line Press, 2002. "The Pan Oceanic Faith" from *Traveling Incognito*, Wood Works Press, 2003.

Robert Sund: Basho translation and "Salmon Moon" from *Poems From Ish River Country*, published by Shoemaker & Hoard in collaboration with The Poet's House Trust, 2005. Used by permission of The Poet's House Trust.

Philip Whalen: "Sourdough Mountain Lookout" from *On Bear's Head*, published by Harcourt, Brace & World, Inc. and Coyote. Copyright by Philip Whalen.

Richard White: "Are You an Environmentalist or Do You Work for a Living?" from *Uncommon Ground*, edited by William Cronon. Copyright 1995 by William Cronon. Used by permission of W.W. Norton & company, Inc.

Cover photograph: Steven C. Wilson
Design & composition: Shannon Gentry and Nina Noble
Contributing editor: William Bridges
Drawing: Gue Pilon

The editors wish to express their gratitude to the Port Townsend Arts Commission and to Lynn Moser, and Catherine Coates for their generous financial support toward publication of this book. Thanks also to Jack Estes, Ray Greeott, and Alan Polson for their contributions to Empty Bowl.

Three bows to Mike O'Connor—old friend and fellow worker in the woods, whose guidance and faith in this project kept our spirits high when the money was low. Simply put, this anthology would never have been completed without him.

Contents

INTRODUCTION

By Mike O'Connor

"The best poetry is out in the country –
farmers singing
rice-planting songs."
—Basho (1644-1694)
(trans. by Robert Sund)

I.

In the late 1960s with American society under a dangerous and divisive strain of cultural revolution at home and a tragic war abroad, many young people of the counterculture were struggling to find alternative, less alienating ways of life.

They had been initiated into the dark nature of the war, racism and government-police repression, but they were divided themselves, politically and by lifestyle, and the casualties from drug misuse were growing. In time, many extricated themselves from the deepening social malaise, and they struck out on a more hopeful, if uncharted, course.

Where once there had been a flight from universities, the military draft and the provincialism of small-town America, there was soon to be an exodus from the cities, a "movement" known by its imperative: "Back to the land."

The ideas galvanizing this movement had been in the air for some time. Their coalescence, however, suddenly presented a new landscape of possibilities. In the beginning, the movement could be characterized as a yearning to get closer to nature, to simplify one's life and to escape undesirable urban and even suburban conditions. Except for certain advance communes, this was undertaken without much direction or organization. It was as if particular young people were suddenly tuned to a frequency they alone could hear, and to which they responded.

Freeman House described them in an essay, "More than Numbers: Twelve or Thirteen Ways of Looking at a Watershed," reprinted in this collection. He wrote: "There were at the time in American history an extraordinary number of young people who had come all willy-nilly to resist the institutionalization of primary experiences of birth and death, and providing one's own food and shelter. I have no idea why so many people seemed spontaneously to develop the same actualization of this resistance. But like lemmings, tens of thousands of urban people moved 'back to the land' to test a faith unsupported by any evidence or personal experience that they could provide for themselves and each other and thus reclaim their confidence as humans."

For those heeding the call who read contemporary literature (and it was like scripture to many in those days; it did make things happen), the poetry and writings of Gary Snyder proved profoundly important, revelatory, a clue to new terrain whose bounds extended beyond the locus of existing political and cultural paradigms. In 1969, his free and widely distributed "Four Changes" poster-essay alone presented a concise outline of principles and values for those seeking a more spiritual, simple and natural way of life, and his poems, often springing from work in the woods or at sea, gave physical labor a fresh essential character.

Jack Kerouac and Allen Ginsberg, among the very first to awaken a younger generation to the authenticity and richness of their own milieu, put a host of young literary folks "on the road," then Snyder with "skillful means" drew them aside, and pointed out the trail. Once started on it, they joined an extended community of new and rediscovered "whole earth" writers, from Thoreau, John Muir and Aldo Leopold to Wendell Berry, Barry Commoner and E. F. Shumacher. In time, they added their own work and opened further terrain.

14

There were as many ways back to nature—to the countryside, woods or sea—as there were people making the exodus. My own path went first through seaman's union halls and then to trail and firefighting crews of the U.S. Forest Service. Later, I settled on a small rented farm in the Dungeness River Valley on the Olympic Peninsula, Washington State. Early on, I and others realized what Jesse Miller explains in his interview "When You Plant a Tree, Where is the Buddha?" Namely, that to live independently in places close to nature removed from urban centers demanded some regimen of physical labor. To "groove on nature" may have been part of the movement's early billing, but hard work would be much of the show. Most of these neo-pioneers accepted this, even welcomed it.

II.

The present Northwest-North Coast collection of writing from back-country-minded individuals working in the woods and at sea, was written largely during the '70s and '80s, but also more recently. Their descriptions of a variety of work conditions and experiences are drawn with clarity and straightforwardness—there is no art for art's sake here. They are writing out of their direct experiences and not "out of their heads." David Raffeld, reviewing the first edition of this anthology in *Whitney Museum Arts Magazine*, noted: "Water and land are not only the source of their livelihoods but are the resources of their writing." He added that postmodernism has had no ostensible influence on this writing: "There is no division between body and mind, practice and theory. Their sights are on observable reality. The invisible is seen only through the visible . . . ."

Again the ancient, meaningless
Abstractions of the educated mind.
wet feet and the campfire out.
—Gary Snyder, "Logging"

15

Because these young people chose to live as simply as possible, without, in some cases, electricity, running water, a telephone or permanent shelter—many living in trucks, campers, vans, boats and neglected forest cabins—their Waldenesque subsistence living gave them flexible working hours, "dream time" and enough earnings to support personal endeavors. While there had been from the beginning a degree of anti-intellectualism in the movement, and although physical labor was a good antidote to over-education (the province of the abstract rational intellect), in time, physical work and intellectual or artistic work settled closer into balance.

The first existential phase—doing, and then later, finding out what we were doing—gave way to greater conceptual clarity. The evolving idea of bioregionalism, under which re-inhabitation, watershed consciousness and restoration, and the importance of "place" are subsumed, contributed to defining where the back-to-the-landers were and how they should best approach living there. Kirkpatrick Sales, in *Dwellers in the Land, The Bioregional Vision*, defines bioregionalism this way: "Bio is from the Greek word for forms of life, as is biology and biography, and region is from the Latin *regere*, territory to be ruled . . . a life-territory, a place defined by its life forms, its topography and biota, rather than by human dictates; a region governed by nature, not legislature."

The work of the Planet Drum Foundation in bringing bio- and cultural diversity issues together in Peter Berg's formulations of bioregionalism, and the work of Raymond Dasmann and Robert R. Curry, among others, also contributed to the movement's expanding ecological consciousness. Much later, the ideas of bioregionalism began to be applied to cities, with emphasis on soft energy paths and more attention to human scale and wildlife habitat.

For those living on the Olympic Peninsula, the arrival of Jerry Gorsline, co-editor of this anthology, deepened our understanding of ideas of place and enlarged our sense of nature. While he worked along-side us in the field, he also began informally teaching the interconnect-edness of our work and the environment, or "human culture as a form of biological inter-relationship." He and poet Tim McNulty organized and spearheaded a number of hard-fought and mostly successful efforts to defend old-growth forests and expand wilderness boundaries.

Gorsline's trademark was a wooden box filled with books ranging from roadside geology, local botany, bird field guides, to publications such as *Co-Evolution Quarterly, Kuksu* and David Wilk's *Truck Magazine.* The box rode on the floorboard on the passenger side of his van and contained a homemade filing system for environmental articles and reports. Soon, those working on crews with Jerry had assembled their own boxes of books and rudimentary files in their vehicles as well. The motorized camp libraries came later to include such accessories as field glasses and the "William Blake machine," a magnifying lens for observ-ing lichens ("cities of cups" in Lew Welch's term) and for seeing what Blake called "eternity in a grain of sand."

Work on the mountain slopes became part field work, part wage work. In "Treeplanter's Journal," Gorsline writes of "Blue grouse and mule deer on the units. A whole new array of plants and animals to know, and a new geology to unravel. Information that sinks into the daily work routine and enriches it." Jerry also became well known for his declaration: "I'd rather live in a clearcut than anywhere in Los Angeles," a pronouncement that would have endeared him to Piss-Fir Willie (see below).

Furthering this education in re-inhabitation were—and still are—the efforts of Freeman House and Tom Jay, both stalwarts in their commitment to watershed and salmon restoration, the focal work of Northwest re-inhabitation. Through their hands-on experi-ence in salmon restoration and their knowledge of ecosystems, they, like Gorsline, continue to contribute importantly to watershed health and consciousness, showing by example, ways to respond to the natural cycles—specifically salmon migration and spawning—that are respectful, not exploitative, of the resource.

Another instance of the shift of work (and worker) from extractive to restorative is represented by an abridgment of Roger Risley's "Field Journal." While this record of bird surveying in the Olympic National Forest describes the watershed devastation of past forest mismanagement, the very existence of the survey program, implemented by the U.S. Forest Service, points to new ecosystem management practices based on the scientific investigations launched by Jerry Franklin and his U.S. Forest Service colleagues in the 1970s.

When the first edition of *Working the Woods, Working the Sea* was put together, the U.S. Forest Service was on a determined course to liquidate all of its old growth. Today, thanks to Franklin and the work of many conservation activists, the spotted owl crisis and the convening of the Forest Ecosystem Management Assessment Team, made up of top forest ecologists who defined the scientific basis for managing forest ecosystems, old-growth logging has been drastically reduced. Risley's journal and Freeman House's writings have been added to this new edition to reflect such progressive shifts in forest work and management.

Tree-planting

Of the many kinds of traditional woods work, including logging, trail work, lookout fire-spotting and timber cruising (or stand exams)—all represented in this volume—tree-planting enrolled the largest number of back-country participants and, from the months spent by planters in the wilds working the slopes and living in make-shift camps together, it forged lasting friendships. Co-editor Finn Wilcox in his poem "On My Tenth Anniversary as a Treeplanter," thinks back with emotion on the labor of planting nearly a million (that's right, a million!) trees: "No regrets though, / the friends that I love / still work by my side."

In the Northwest, camaraderie, born of shared thought and experience and "the common work of the tribe," spurred creation of tree-planting cooperatives, formed to compete with forest contractors and create economic independence for the band of planters. Food conspiracies and food co-ops took shape about the same time, and small Zendos and cooperative writers' presses also blossomed—Discovery Bay Zendo and Empty Bowl, a writers' co-op in Port Townsend, for instance. The fermenting mix of social-economic influences at the time included the commune, Marxist and Maoist politics, Luddites, the old IWW, Native Americans, transcendentalism, Buddhist economics, organic farming and the Amish—to name but a few. In the Puget Sound area, social radicalism wasn't new. A long history of communitarianism in the form of cooperatives (the town of Port Angeles), communes (anarchists and nudists) and colonies (utopian) dates from before the late nineteenth century.

While tree-planting seemed "right work" to just about every idealist in the back-country, much of the industrial reforestation process, of which tree-planting was the "greening" phase, was actually a war on nature, black magic. Jerry Gorsline writes about it in "Treeplanter's Journal": "Violent patterns of resource management, implemented with war technology: helicopters, defoliants and napalm. One inspector tells me they have a 500-acre clearcut to burn and plant. Site preparation will consist of 'brown and burn,' i.e. spray with herbicides, then 'mass ignition' to burn all 500 acres in one long day (mass ignition: string the unit with primacord fuse, attach cans of napalm at intervals; ignition produces a fire storm which consumes slash) . . . . To prevent brush competition on the 'Whitcom Creek' unit, they're going to apply 2,4-D bound in lignin with a clay bulk carrier over the entire unit, creating a long-duration, low-intensity, plant-toxic environment to 'insure seedling survival.'"

If agreement could ever be reached quickly among a consensus-governed group of individualistic tree-planters, it was on just how hard and all consuming tree-planting could be. Howard Horowitz, who is represented by several poems in this volume, ends his "Montana," with these lines, "Ann when I came / and saw you: / a wild woman, changed in six weeks / your hair and eyes / your sunburnt face. // We lay down / in the hot tent / and cried."

Julia Menard-Warwick's poem, "Treeplanting at Sombrio Creek," ends with the planter hoping new snowfall will shut down the planting (a not particularly wayward hope among tree-planters). "But it [the snow] has all melted by breakfast time, / and as we start up the slopes again in sunlight, / rivulets of water among the skunk cabbage, / all I can think of, not my debts / or future poverty, is throwing myself / off a log, spraining my ankle, / and going home."

Chuck Easton, on the other hand, found a modicum of contentment in tree-planting, thanks to his "Plywood Palace," an ingenious portable shack that he designed and built for cozy living on river and mountain planting sites. His Plywood Palace haiku were penned between practice sessions of jazz guitar.

Fred Miller ("Tale of a Word Planter"), another creative-minded planter, would have us believe that he worked also as a Word Planter, an avocation in which he planted seedlings in intentional patterns. When the trees grew to maturity, they would spell out from the air—like giant coniferous bumper stickers—such statements as THE PRESIDENT IS A LIAR.

Miller, the trickster, is also the romantic: "The work had a beautiful rhythm that intrinsically harmonized with mind, body and external world. I have done no other work before or since that has fulfilled me in the same total sense as tree-planting. It put me in direct touch with the universe. It tied me to our ancestors of the dim primeval past who first worked with nature to produce food and fuel."

Colorful characters—crusty, frayed and immortal—abound in the lore of woods work and in these pages. Pineapple of Hal Gaskell's story of that name and Dodge's Piss-Fir Willie are just two of this cast.

"When I first met Pineapple in Estacada, Oregon, he had a dime in his ear," begins Gaskell's tale. While Dodge gives us the composite ("polymodal") character Piss-Fir Willie. "Never live in a place where you can't piss off the front porch."

Thank you, Willie.

Logging

Richard White, in his essay "Are You an Environmentalist or Do You Work for a Living," notes that "both destructive work and constructive work bring a knowledge of nature, and sometimes work is destructive and restorative at the same time, as when we cut or burn a meadow to prevent the encroachment of forest."

White, an academic historian whose essay provides a sharp perspective on the writing in this volume, argues that work is a "far more intense way to know nature than through play and recreation," and he takes to task those environmentalists who look down on physical labor or see it as only destructive. He also criticizes those who romanticize archaic work and demonize modern machines and tools, and those who invest bioregionalism with a sense of moral superiority. Further, he reminds fellow environmentalists and writers who work in offices that their work only masks similar alterations of nature that they decry in the work of those who labor in nature. "The lights on this [computer] screen need electricity, and this particular electricity comes from dams on the Skagit or Columbia. These dams kill fish; they alter the rivers that come from the Rockies, Cascades, and Olympics . . . ."

John Daniel's "Cuttings" portrays a logger who admits that clear-cutting isn't pretty, "but it's the only way to harvest these trees. It don't pay to go in there just for a few."

Daniel's response to this is sympathetic: "The voice that spoke those words is my voice, too. It's in all of us—the voice of practicality and common sense, the voice that understands that ugly things are necessary. It's a voice that values getting a hard job done and making an honest living."

But Daniel isn't at ease finally with the logger's words. The reality of an ancient forest destroyed by clear-cutting is too overwhelming: "The trees are gone, the creatures are gone, and the very genius of these hills, that gathered rain and changing light for centuries, that grew and deepened as it brought forth a green and towering stillness—it too is leaving. It's washing down in gullies to a muddy stream."

Snyder's long poem "Logging" does not mask the destructive side of logging: "The ancient forests of China logged / and the hills slipped into the Yellow Sea." But he also catches the drama, the aliveness and zing of doing the dangerous work: "Stood straight / holding the choker high / As the Cat swung back the arch / piss-firs falling, / Limbs snapping on the tin hat / bright D caught on / Swinging butt-hooks / ringing against cold steel."

Lookout work, which engenders a good deal of meditation, is playfully recounted in a classic poem by Philip Whalen, "Sourdough Mountain Lookout," the same lookout occupied years later by Tim McNulty and whose poems in this book also sing that wild perch.

Work at Sea

There is a long and rich tradition of writers going to sea, to blue water, and the poets Gary Snyder, Clemens Starck and Richard Dankliff give us a very modern feel of it. Starck's "Ammo Ship" describes the predicament of some young people who shipped out during the Vietnam War and found themselves in morally ambiguous circumstances: "Mostly we hauled asphalt, / tens of thousands of drums of asphalt. / The master-plan / called for southeast Asia to be a parking lot. / If it wasn't asphalt, it was bombs. / The bombs were for the enemy."

Dankliff has four fine sea poems in this collection: "Cargo dis-charged, / we ride high in the water. / Off west, low sun daubs the clouds / blood red, break-glass-for-fireaxe red, . . ." ("Departure.")

Snyder's "Tanker Notes"—technically journal entries, abridged here—is in essence narrative poetry. Snyder weaves strands and snip-pets of observation, poetry, philosophy and amusing crew exchanges. Because he gives his mind over completely to the task at hand, Snyder can coax song from tending a ship's engine: "Reaching through hot pipes to turn nuts—the burned arm—squiggle lines and tiny surprise silver tube running off somewhere to tweet a gauge—box wrench 13/16; eye beam you beam, bulkhead sweat—flange leak and valve drip—old gasket pounder—poke the big bolt through, seek nuts in pocket—whole ship twined about us, where do the pipes go? The engineer cursing and burning his unsteady hand—"

Salmon and Fishing

Holly J. Hughes, who has spent the last 26 summers working at sea in Alaska, is represented by four poems, including "Point Colpoys, Alaska: Tendering," in which she considers a letter telling of theater in New York and wonders "what could be better than this, / watch-ing the fog curtain rise . . . ."

In his prose piece "The Best Day," Paul Thomas describes what it's like to land a big king salmon: "You tug and wait 'til he presents his head, a recalcitrant prisoner full of fear and loathing but more noble in his hatred than you in your greed."

Thomas recalls how fishing, like the woods work of his counterpart back-to-the-landers, created economic independence and commu-nity: "There must have been at least eight boats working that bight, all from our little hippy fleet of 'dock-sixers' as we called ourselves in those days in reference to the transient dock on Fishermen's Terminal, Seattle, where most of us converged during the protest days of the late sixties. We had individually, as couples, and more or less as a group, bootstrapped our way from dockside dreamers into full time entrepreneurs, cognizant of the bottom line, but still given over to the narrative."

In her poem "Advice to Female Deckhands," Erin Fristad, a seasoned fisher, gives us a candid look at the duties that inherently fall to the female on a fishing boat. And in "While You Were Sleeping," she reveals what life without fish for fishers narrows down to, "You can't imagine sitting at a desk . . . ."

Freeman House, a former commercial salmon fisherman, tells (in an excerpt from his book, *Totem Salmon*) how he came to realize that he and his crew were part of an extractive industrial economy and "could only allow ourselves to see the salmon as objects, as product, a product that we hoped would allow us to pay the rent." There was no sense of sacrament in the taking of the fish.

House notes: "By denying ourselves the perception of our relation to the creatures dying on the deck we were in some essential way denying ourselves a wholeness of being." For House, this understanding eventually led to his steadfast commitment to saving wild salmon runs on the Mattole River.

In "Lost & Found"—part diary within a memoir and part philosophic excursion into the theme of place—Mike Connelly speaks of House's salmon restoration effort: "The 'scheme' they [House and friends] developed was to capture live wild salmon, females and males, on their way to the spawning beds. One of the main causes of salmon declines in the northwest has been the degradation or loss of spawning habitat, and this has also been the case on the Mattole."

Connelly adds, "They reached out to everyone—hippies, ranchers, logging companies, fishermen, and everyone else—with respect and humility. They formed the Mattole River Salmon Group."

Whether or not they have been successful is a question, as Connelly points out, that isn't really the issue. What is, according to Connelly, is the realization "that treating the fish problem by itself—without dealing with the "relationship between fish and people—would produce, at best, a temporary fix."

The effort of the people of the Mattole is one of the most enduring developments within the bioregional movement. It's a step beyond just working in nature to working in a healing way over a long period, and requiring strong commitment to place, to community. It's also an example of the actualization of what Arne Naess, a Norwegian and the father of Deep Ecology, called biospherical egalitarianism, the regard for the "rights" of all species.

Tom Jay, inspired early by Freeman House, has long been involved in the grass-roots effort to restore health to watersheds, especially through the renewal and preservation of the wild salmon. For Jay and his wife, the artist Sara Mall Johani, this has included any number of artistic and educational programs to inform the community at large of the importance of salmon and ecological health. Jay, in his sacramental and lyrical essay, "Salmon of the Heart," identifies salmon as "the soul in the body of the world," and "the crown of the Northwest forest biome, the soul of the ecosystem. It is with cedar the paradigmatic expression of this place. If the forests and their waters are healthy, if the sea is clear and uncrowded, then wild salmon thrive."

As will we.

I.

TREEPLANTING

Tales of a Word Planter

Fred Miller

There are words growing in the forests of the Pacific Northwest. Within several years they will be visible, emerging in a pattern far different than the orderly rows of trees growing in our renewable forests (plantations they are called), and quite likely to provoke some controversy.

Using Douglas fir seedlings as a living communications tool, I planted trees in a pattern to form letters that made up words which were part of phrases while I worked as a professional treeplanter.

I have been a Word Planter.

While perhaps not agreeing with the sentiments expressed, you might enjoy the principle involved. Bear with me while I explain.

Planting trees, reforestation as it is called, is a major step in the industrial process of wood production. While still in its infancy relative to other basic industrial processes, great progress has been made by manipulating seedlings as well as the micro-environment that affects their growth.

The techniques used, genetic sleight-of-hand, fungicides, herbicides, monoculture, slash burning, etc., have created enormous controversy and consequent widespread interest in forest management in general.

In any given year, a crew of professional treeplanters may work on several thousand acres of private and public forest land. Those acres may be spread among 100-200 different units in several states. (A unit refers to a designated number of acres from which merchantable trees have been cut and removed and the remaining vegetation and trees burned or otherwise killed.)

An individual worker, man or woman, on a crew may plant 100,000 to half a million seedlings in one season's work.

In the Pacific Northwest, where I worked, the weather was often rainy and cold; the harsh working conditions primitive, as are most types of work involved with extraction or regeneration of natural resources.

Treeplanters, their tree bags strapped to their waists, packed with 300-500 seedlings, tromp onto a unit looking like drab mutant birds with clumps of green feathers rising out of their rump.

Filled, the tree bag weighs 35-75 pounds depending on the size of the seedlings. West of the Cascade mountain range that runs like a backbone through Washington and Oregon, those seedlings are usually Douglas fir. In the drier areas East of the Cascades the seedlings could be different species of pine or other kinds of fir.

A tool called a Hoedad (for which our worker-owned company was named) is sunk into the ground in the manner of a pickaxe, a triangle-shaped slot opened in the soil into which a seedling is dropped, roots down. Soil is tamped to fill and firm the planted seedling. A steady worker will plant from 800-1,500 seedlings a day.

Seedlings are planted on a spacing grid (6' × 6', 8' × 8', 10' × 10', etc.) designed so each young tree is placed in relation to all other planted trees until the unit is covered as close as possible to the designated spacing requirement and the optimum number of trees fills the unit.

Other human beings (although some workers have been known to dispute this) are inspectors. They follow the workers, taking random plot samples to ascertain that there were no open spaces left by the treeplanters. Since amount of pay is based on how well (and how quickly) a contractor can cover the acreage, there are sometimes intense disputes about proper spacing.

The terrain in the Northwest has wide variability. Rock, multi-species vegetation, swamps, streams, clay, ashes, and tremendous piles of forest debris left by the logging operation may be encountered on a typical unit. Finding planting spots is done by clambering over terra not so firma, scuttling sideways on steep mountain slopes while pecking at the ground. Sort of like scratching for grubs.

Treeplanting is among the most arduous types of work in the world. No doubt about it. A productive worker during the work day will swing a Hoedad 3,000-4,000 times, thudding it into the ground with arms, wrists, and upper torso absorbing the shock. Tendonitis and Carpal Tunnel Syndrome are frequent occupational hazards. He or she may bend over 2,000-3,000 times to plant seedlings. Back problems are frequent. Knees, ankles, and feet are continually stressed trying to get a grip on the precipitous slopes.

Sometimes units have been sprayed with herbicides a few hours or days before treeplanters work, creating short-term discomfort and potential longterm reproductive problems or cancers.

Many of the coordinated maneuvers needed to plant a unit in the most efficient manner reminded me of my Navy marching days. Complicated patterns are carried out with workers spread out over 200-300 yards and take a half hour or more to unfold.

Ahhhhh, but the work had a beautiful rhythm that intrinsically harmonized my mind, body, and external world. I have done no other work before or since that has fulfilled me in the same total sense as treeplanting. It put me in direct touch with the universe. It tied me to our ancestors of the dim primeval past who first worked with nature to produce food and fuel.

And, occasionally, when our whole crew happened to hit the same groove, the work became a beautiful dance of life, in stark contrast to the rotting remnants of the rapacious logging operation.

Often, however, like most jobs, it was hard and boring and I was certainly not in ecstatic communication with the natural order. My body went into drone-automatic and my mind drifted along, thinking about the things I like to think about.

It was in one of these periods of disinterest, plodding along, planting a tree here and there when the blinding flash hit me! I began to tingle! I whooped and hollered! I hopped around on one foot (crushing two seedlings in the process). I spiked myself with one of my caulk boots. Sheee-it, I was filled with joy.

Do you remember the feelings of pure excitement you got as a kid? Well, this was one of those times that adults so seldom experience. At that moment I became a WORD PLANTER.

That very next afternoon, after a feverish night of plotting on graph paper, in the achingly beautiful coastal mountains of Oregon, in 1976, I planted FUCK MORE, HATE LESS, in letters 40 feet tall. Now, this was not as odd as you might think sitting there reading this. My immediate condition at the time was quite the reverse. And this particular sentiment was dear to me. It came from two friends who, during the giddy year of 1969, hung a large banner with those immortal words emblazoned on it, over a San Diego freeway bridge for the enjoyment and rumination of the bleary-eyed morning commuters. These folks were rabid Wilhelm Reich fans at the time—early writings of course.

Damn! I felt wonderful as I sat on that slope contemplating my first completed work. I knew in 20 years or so a plane would fly over the mountain, a bored pilot glancing over at the slope, then sitting bolt upright, eyes popping out; "Jesus H. Keerist! What the hell is that?" Word will spread quickly. The U.S. Forest Service people will be quick to deny that they had any part in it. Other leaders of the Vox Populi will put in their two cents. Airlines will make detours to see it; charter helicopter rides will follow. Economic development for the depressed Central Oregon Coast will be built around FUCK MORE, HATE LESS. Laughter and revulsion will reign; investigations demanded; solutions to the "problem" will be suggested. "Well I think we should just clearcut every word, you know like a big eraser."

The overriding question will be: "WHO DID THIS?"

And that is why I am writing this article. I am publicly confessing right now. I did it. I am proud of it. And that is not all.

I have planted many different words throughout the national forests in Oregon, Washington, Idaho, Montana, and California. I even snuck in a couple of words on private property, but I won't tell Georgia Pacific where I did it.

In Idaho's Panhandle, I planted STOP WAR. In Oregon's Siuslaw and Willamette forests, I planted NO MORE POISONS, referring to the tremendous amounts of herbicides sprayed on the forests. The Umpqua forest in Southern Oregon has REBEL AGAINST POISONS. The Six Rivers forest in California has the memorable HELLO OUT THERE! (my greeting to the possible lookers-in from other planets). In the Olympics in Washington, the cryptic BIRD LIVES marks my living tribute to the creative and soulful musician.

All in all I planted some 20 phrases, including: THE PRESIDENT IS A LIAR. (Each succeeding president has been worse than their predecessor. Ronald Reagan is by far the most adept liar in presidential history.)

DO RIGHT! (my advice to the living).

RACISM IS ROTTEN (this ideological sickness of white people permeates our society).

YOU ARE HERE NOW DUMMY (a spoof on mysticism).

HOEDADS ALIVE (my poem to our worker-owned company).

DON'T MOURN, ORGANIZE (more advice to the living from the Wobblies).

WORKERS PRODUCE WEALTH, DON'T FORGET IT! (a reminder to the corporate executives who curiously and erroneously believe they are somehow responsible for material abundance).

TREES ARE BEAUTIFUL (aren't trees wonderful?).

WE SHALL OVERCOME (my optimism about the future drawn from the examples of the past).

PEOPLE AND TREES ARE IMPORTANT (a message to timber corporations).

VENCEREMOS (a lasting appreciation for the examples of the Cuban people).

MEN, NO ABUSE OF WOMEN! (a fervent statement to men to protest violence against women).

TO BE OF USE (the inner drive of working people that my favorite poem by Marge Piercy so eloquently stated).

NEEDLES DROP, SILENT THE SOUND (the influence of Zen on me in the forests).

My most difficult work:

HONESTY, MODESTY, HARD WORK, LOVE, FUN, FORGOTTEN VIRTUES; TIME FOR CHANGES! THROW THE BUMS OUT! 2,500 seedlings, 2 days planting time, 2 acres with a 60% slope turned out to be my last. Soon after, I pulled some chest cartilage from my sternum (ouch), developed psoriasis from the stress of fighting herbicide use (yuck), and was partially hobbled by arthritis (moan). That effectively ended my 10-year reforestation career and my 5 years of sporadic word planting.

One of the neat things about this is the anticipation I have as my work slowly becomes revealed. A joy to grow old. I plan my first visits to the areas in 1989. I figure that the first words will emerge around 1993-95 for other people to recognize. I'll keep you posted.

So that is the story folks, Tales of a Word Planter. Perhaps there have been others out there planting their words, waiting as they grow. Perhaps someone will read this and go do a little woods writing. Who knows. It has been important to me to have secret chuckles. It is even better when they are shared with others. Socially responsible giggles are great.

POEMS FROM THE PLYWOOD PALACE

Chuck Easton

Who says my poems are poems?
My poems are not poems.
After you know my poems are not poems,
Then we can begin to discuss poetry!
—Ryokan (trans. John Stevens)

A month or two every year we get a planting contract from another district. This means we all go on the road with various makeshift living arrangements. I live in the plywood palace, a small, portable house I designed and built that comes apart and travels on the roof of my car. It's built out of five 8' × 4' sheets of plywood reinforced with 1" × 2"s and has a plastic tarp roof. The (dirt) floor space is 8' × 7'. Two 8' × 4' sheets placed long side down form the sides, a 7' × 4' sheet with a small skylight forms the back. The front has two smaller panels, 5½' × 4' and 5½' × 3', an octagonal door with a window in one, a stovepipe hole in the other. A triangular piece with a large Plexiglas window rests on each 8' × 4' side and completes the basic form. The overall shape is saltbox. There's seven feet of headroom at the peak then the roof slopes steeply forward to the 5½' front and more gradually back to the 4' back panel. Inside, a small airtight woodstove and shelves are in the front, the string bed (a design from India) fills up the back. Assembly time is one and a half hours: it goes together with 2½" × ¼" eyebolts and wingnuts. The design requirements were standing headroom and a place to stay warm and dry. In its third season the plywood palace is doing its job admirably.

Just so there is room

for my bed and mats

—T'ao Ch'ien (trans. William Acker)

Nightfall after the first day of tree planting:
In my small plywood shack, I lean forward and blow out the lamp.
The full moon explodes in the glass.

                    *

Just after summer daybreak I lean back next to the stove
playing a Charlie Parker tune.
The rain roars on my plastic roof.

                    *

In the middle of a poem by Tu Fu
a mouse springs the trap.
As death quiets its shaking and rustling
I hear the sparrows sing again.

*

Too hot to stay inside, I go outside and lean against the wall
holding my guitar.
The sound of rock and roll and horseshoes drifts past.

*

The volcano turns white under fresh snow,
gray under falling ash.

*

Watching Koma Kulshan
the coffee beans grind themselves.

*

All day in the rain on summer solstice,
Wet hands, cold feet.
Finally, the hot tea I've been dreaming of for hours
is in my hand.

*

Light showers of rain block out all other sounds.
I drop off to sleep.
At midnight I awake to full moonlight streaming in my window.

TREEPLANTING AT SOMBRIO CREEK

Julia Menard-Warwick

The sea down burned slopes
was silent in its tumult
waves foaming against the rocks
too far away to be heard;
the seals I saw from the beach
too far away to be seen.

They have logged, and they have burned.
We come after, planting new trees:
cedar in the swamps with skunk cabbage,
fir on the dry knolls—
while whining chainsaws topple timber
at the edge of the clearing.

Cursing from the pain in my shoulder
where the weight of trees I plant
has worn a groove in the muscle,
I look out over the straits of Juan de Fuca
over the seals and boats and sea breezes
to the soft blue mountains of the Olympic Peninsula.
And bend again to stab with my shovel and plant.

At the end of the road, in Port Renfrew,
where after work we've driven through hail storms
to make phone calls on Friday night,
the hotel pub is full of women and loggers in party clothes

but every table is nearly silent
and the sandwiches are free.

The faller who died Thursday afternoon,
falling himself from the high rigging,
was only 21.
No one looks at us as we lean against
the wall in the corner, drink beer, and laugh.

I have nothing but respect
for those whose living it is
to drive their bodies like machines
day after day. I cannot
drive myself fast enough, I cannot
really care. I don't want money.
I want only to go home,
to Peter, waiting in Vancouver.

The three men who own land together in Greenwood
make pottery, play guitar,
and have children all the same age,
are sitting on stumps on the dirt floor
of the cookshack by lantern light,
talking softly and singing.
I cannot tell them I wish to leave.

In the morning we awake to snow,
on the mountains, on the clearcuts,
on the tents, in my tree bags.
The straits of Juan de Fuca are as smooth and light
as if snow has fallen there too.
 I think, "Perhaps more will fall.

We will be snowed out.
I can go home."
But it has all melted by breakfast time,
and as we start up the slopes again in sunlight,
rivulets of water among the skunk cabbage,
all I can think of, not my debts
or future poverty, is throwing myself
off a log, spraining my ankle,
and going home.

The end of the day, the pain in my shoulder
much worse, I sit on a huge stump
in the cold wind, looking out across the straits
to the mountains,
the lines of current on the water,
listening to the silence of the ocean.

PINEAPPLE

Hal Gaskell

When I first met Pineapple in Estacada, Oregon, he had a dime in his ear. I was a green treeplanter, anxious for another try at this good earthwork. I'd been laid off after a week in Florence. The boss said it was too tight of a contract and he'd give me another try when they moved to Idaho in a few weeks. The contractor always lost half his crew to the Burnside bars in Portland when they moved a long distance, got snowed out or had any other kind of delay that was long enough for the boys to get started on a bender. I got my call and was the first guy to get into the crummy parked in front of the Stockman Cafe. We'd leave when the crummy was full.

It was getting dark and I was trying to sleep in preparation for the all-night drive to Grangeville and hard day of work to follow.

Suddenly, I heard a ruckus and turned to see two rowdy fellows approaching the crummy. One seemed to be luring the other with a bottle in a brown bag. They were leap-frogging derelict parking meters along the sidewalk.

Jim Brockway had the wine. He was a macho young tramp of about 35. Blue denim with a hickory shirt under his jacket, forester's boots and an Engineer Bill cap. Jim's good looks had been marred by years of alcohol abuse and life on the "Lost Highway." The other man, a whole head shorter than Jim, had on khaki pants, a plain work shirt, Japanese gardener-type cap and lace-to-the-toe boots. He carried a cardboard box bound with twine. Jim carried nothing, save the bottle. Pineapple, Jim called him, was older (58, I found out later), dark skinned, built like a brick and had the hands of a much larger man. He was singing an old Nat King Cole song, "Pretend you're happy when you're blue oo-oohOO . . . !" And when he sang the "oo-oohOO," his squinted bloodshot eyes bulged and his mouth opened enough so that you could see his two yellow teeth, one on top and one on the bottom, both on opposite sides. He seemed reluctant to get in the crummy and after getting in and out several times and after much coaxing by Jim, he climbed back to the rear seat. As others filtered in from the cold night, the crummy filled, the doors closed, and Pineapple was shanghaied. Pointing at the old hoedads, dirty and rude looking, he asked loudly in pidgin Hawaiian, "What are dese tings? Is dis what you use to plant trees?" I thought, oh brother, I'm only 20 and I can hardly hack this work. What are they bringing along this old guy for? Charley, the owner, started the motor and with sober aloofness drove north in the night along the Columbia Gorge. Charley had a crewcut and I sensed that he despised these dregs of society he gathered from the gutters. He used them for his own profit and other than that he gave less than a damn about them.

Now that we were under way, Jim and Pineapple began to pass the bottle they had kept discreetly hidden from Charley, enticing others with it, and now, miraculously, other bottles began to appear. They were having a jolly time and we still had 500 miles to go. Jim was bragging about riding freight trains transcontinental seven times both ways, and telling how gorgeous his first and second old ladies had been and how one of them had been the reason for him smashing his Pimental guitar against a wall. He was playing flamenco on my old beater. Pineapple was singing, "One night the moon was so mellow, Rosita met young Manuelo-oohOO!" I sat shotgun and could see that the rising noise level was getting to Charley. I was amused by the wild craziness of it all but dared not laugh. I needed this job. The others needed it too, just like they needed their next meal or next place to flop. The wine was luxury, and otherwise they seemed to need very little.

The miles rolled by. Somewhere between Pendleton and Lewiston now, the landscape was dark and deserted. It was around 3 a.m. and hatred was coming to a head in the boss. His jaw and lips tensed; the noise level steadily increased. His fists clenched the steering wheel. Suddenly, out there in the middle of nowhere, he screeched to a halt and began shouting that he'd had it and would dump everyone out here if they didn't shut up. Pineapple broke the moment of silence, which followed as he mumbled, "I don't give a shit." Charley ignored it. We got out for a stretch and a leak, then took off again.

I dozed until we arrived at the Spot Cafe in Grangeville where we met Richard, the ramrod foreman of Charley's company, Dangerous Don, the lead man, Dirty Kirk and Buffalo from the old crew in Florence, along with four or five others that they'd picked up along the way. They were finishing breakfast and getting ready to go to work. We had time for a coffee to go and then followed Richard's crummy up the mountain in Chief Joseph country. It was a crisp, beautiful Idaho morning as the sun rose. We drove far into the hills where snow lined the road, I heard Jim grumbling to Pineapple that all these young hotshots would probably leave them in the dust. Pineapple didn't say anything. He just looked bummed-out to be there. Richard took three guys who had not planted before aside and gave them instructions. He reviewed me to see if I still remembered the technique he'd taught me weeks earlier. He led us down the hill to where Pineapple was tamping a nice straight up-and-down 2-0 Doug fir. Richard told them so everyone could hear, "Now there is a perfect tree. That's exactly how everyone on Richard Wilson's crew is supposed to plant trees." By then Pineapple had planted two or three more perfect trees.

MONTANA

Howard Horowitz

The Potluck crummy
broke down
on the way to Montana
and on the way home.

Broke and down:
    pay for a food share
    pay for a crummy share
    pay for a love share
    even if you don't get one.
So few women
and so many men.

Jolie and Ann
tried a short-cut
and got lost.
They didn't need the search party
but that's what can happen
when you follow your heart
down a deer trail.

    Hot
    day after day, hot.
    Sun-baked planters
    scalp the ash
    to mineral soil.

At night
stars and breeze

Red Stars party
Thumbs party
Potluck sulks.

Ann when I came
and saw you:
a wild woman,
changed in six weeks
your hair and eyes
your sunburnt face.

We lay down
in the hot tent
and cried.

IDAHO

It's great
to plant trees
in Idaho, when
snowmelt roars
in the Clearwater
& when frost crisps
the brushfields red
in the Bitterroots.
Steep ridges of shrub
and rock, young larch
and fir, bleached snags:
remember the great fire
of 1910, when Pulaski
   forced his men into a
      mineshaft, to survive;
   when the train got away
   from Wallace on flaming tracks.
 Luck still touches some of us: remember
the crummy, upside-down in a pond (the con-
sequence of driving to camp without headlights
   when the bar closed in Elk City). Good money
   and good times on a Kelly Creek clearcut, in a
   Pierce tavern, in the Grangeville Hotel. Remember
   swimming holes on the Salmon, hot springs baths,
   the log truck driver dancing with his daughter,
   a bear with rose hips scat, a meteor shower in
   Orion, the woman that night in Orofino. Remember
   Idaho is too great to pass nonstop on the freeway.

Hoedads, Inc.:
Birth of a Cooperative, 1970-74:
A Work in Progress

Hal Hartzell

The winter of '74 certainly put the Hoedads to the test. There was one incident, about the second time the Cougar Mountain crummy almost died on the unit, that characterized the winter experience. Cougar Mountain and the Cheap Thrills were working together, about six from each crew. Gerri Mackie, a Cheap Thrill, and me, a Cougar Mountain, collaborated on a true story, since we were both there:

We had worked hard all day. It became clear that with a little extra effort we could finish off the unit. The two crews worked together into the twilight and made it up to the landing in the dark; cold, wet, tired and hungry. More so than usual because of the final push.

Cougar Mountain's green crummy would not start, leaving 12 people in the grasp of the first stages of hypothermia. It was a few hundred feet up, out of the unit, before the road started down hill. It was against government regulations to give rides to treeplanters, so the inspector drove off. There was crankiness, yelling and then depression. But then the collective mind and body began to work.

Rust calmed everyone down, enough to start working together on the problem, which was his talent. While hands held a weak flashlight under the hood and tinkered, voices chanted mechanical deductions. Fire? Electricity? No, the battery was alive, the cables were tight, juice flowed to the dashboard and the lights. Fuel? It was coming through the line, making it to the carburetor. Better check the gas though. Another 20 minutes went by while people searched for a siphon hose or reasonable facsimile. None was found.

Next we disconnected the fuel line and let the gas pump squirt the gas into a jar; soon a quart of amorphous liquid was available for inspection. The problem was clear: the gas was murky. Scrambling for gas from suspicious suppliers in the embargo and too many weeks in the rain forest had produced a fuel mixture that was about one-third water. Knowing the problem and finding the solution were two different things.

Some crummies have a drain plug on the tank for this eventuality. Not this crummy. No siphon, no plug. The cold, dark and hunger dragged on. People shivered and complained, but the greater part of the crew organism was attuned to getting the hell out of there, no matter how stubborn the resistance. Even the stupid suggestions became worthy of consideration. The only way to get that water out of the tank is to punch a hole in the bottom of it with a screwdriver and a hammer; drain the gas and water into a container and then replug the hole. We did that with a sheet metal screw robbed from somewhere on the crummy. We separated the gas from the water, but still the starter motor ground and ground. . . . The fuel would not take. Assumptions were reexamined with anguished deliberation. One thing left to try. "If the gas won't get to the carburetor by itself, we'll get it there ourselves." It had been a dismal two hours up to this point.

A solution was found: fluid was pumped out a quart at a time, allowed to settle, and the nearly pure gas was extracted and set aside. Then it took everybody to get the crummy up the hill. One rode on the front fender and poured small amounts of gas straight into the carburetor, knowing full well that too much could flood the engine or worse. The hood was up and the battery was down, due to all the starting and pumping. The lights could not be used. Someone sat at the driver's seat to work the pedals. Another stood in the driver's door to look ahead and work the wheel. Others were stationed along the edge of the road to provide verbal guidance. The night was pitch black.

It worked. The crummy lurched up the hill, pint-by-pint and foot-by-foot. Another hour passed. We finally reached the top of the hill and another problem arose: the electrical system had drowned because of the open hood in the driving rain. Nothing to do but wait for it to dry out.

Just about then, Lew Melson showed up with gas and food. A couple of Cheap Thrills lumbered in in a housetruck. They had been worried back in camp some 30 miles away and had sent out a rescue party. Most rode freezing back to camp in the pickup. Some stayed in the housetruck. In the middle of the night the crummy's lights started up. Rust fired up the engine and drove the green crummy back to camp. It was waiting for the crew in the morning.

On My Tenth Anniversary
as a Treeplanter

Finn Wilcox

Nearly a million trees older now
I remember when my children
Were shorter than me
And the hair on my head was
Thick as a stand of doghair hemlock.
No regrets though,
The friends that I love
Still work by my side.
But sometimes,
On cold rainy nights,
These stubborn knuckles
Click and hesitate
When I set down the wine.

The River that Is a Deer and the Last Bird Flying

Mike O'Connor

How many days have we
spent on this river,
camped in green willows and sand?

How many trees have we
planted above it,
like alms to impoverished gods?

It is a river
shorn of great trees,
ribboning seaward
in clamorous light

below acres of spruce stumps
and the dust-plumes of trucks.

It's the last thread in the loom,
the one bird from the past
still flying.

The Clearwater…about as
clear as you would ever
want the weather
or the world:

amber, and then around sundown, green.

When we come dizzy
from her slash-choked heights,
we clamber to her side

like fawns to a doe;

and she gives us:
music, swimming holes, water for our tea—
    something of our own clear flow.

When You Plant a Tree, Where Is the Buddha?

Jesse Miller
Interviewed by Mike O'Connor

In the first half, at least, of the 1970s, Jesse Miller was the guardian angel of longhair treeplanters. Through his energy, pragmatism and friendship with Hop Doughee, a small-scale backwoods contractor, he was able to provide enough work on the slopes of the Olympic Mountains to keep the core of the area's counterculture free of welfare offices and cities. Many of the folks who signed on with his crews hadn't been "back-to-the-country" long enough to know the wood to best build fires with or that a hen doesn't need a rooster to lay an egg, but Jesse usually managed to bring the pioneers farther down the country road, not least by securing them an economic foothold.

His crews, in fact, spawned a number of treeplanting luminaries who would in turn go on to form treeplanting cooperatives, which not only created more opportunities for "right work," but also challenged, where it did not eliminate outright, the slave-driving (and that's what it was, folks), wage-shaving forest contractor, and gave women greater prominence in the field.

Aside from being a superlative planter—the fastest for years ("When you fall down, and you will, plant a tree") with a bat's instinct for specifications—he could keep a crew together in the face of the myriad vicissitudes of planting, be it the worse-than-imagined terrain (the Terrible Finger, the Shelton Moonscape, the West End of the World); a change in the wage scale, downward; a snowstorm in June; or the revamped, fantastical specifications from the head office (someone practicing forestry "from a desk map in a distant town").

Camps were full of the laments of the battle-stricken: "Jesse, I can't take this shit anymore, do you hear me!?" "Jesse, I've dislocated my body!" "My tent's on fire!" "I'm hungry, lonely, horny and going bananas, all at the same time!" "Jesse! Jesse! Jesse!" And most menacing of all, the first surfaced thoughts of rebellion: "Yeah, he's got his old lady with him, and lots of firewood, and gets extra pay for using that little calculator." But Jesse's concern for others, and good horse sense, always informed him when it was time to leave the evening tea steeping and the cheese on Swedish rye uneaten, and to venture out among his dispirited troops to talk.

For some of us who survived several seasons to become something like veterans of the treeplanting wars, Jesse often only needed to drop a remark to spring the lock that lifted our morale. Once, for instance, on the steep burned slopes above the Coldwater River near Mount St. Helens, where our crew had been encountering days of freezing rains and unnatural winds, I had fallen into a fairly typical treeplanter's funk, but a funk nonetheless, and I realized that if I didn't get out of my truck and muddy sleeping bag and cook something to eat soon, I was probably going to die. Needing some fresh water, I headed up a cat road in the fog (it was twilight) to a small creek that washed across the spur road for want of a culvert. I got the water from the creek and turned back through the drifting fog toward camp. A figure emerged from the vapors, which, sure enough, was Jesse. At that moment I wanted to unload on him that I was hanging up my boots and taking a long ride with my dog, Rags, back to poverty, when he said, "Hey, man, this is just like a goddamn Russian movie," and then went on to the creek. He hadn't said much, but it was enough to suggest to me that he was not only sharing the crew's discomfort but managing to still joke about it. Anyway, the next day the Russian movie ended and the sun appeared, blazing above the snowy palace of the Fujiyama of the West (which was Mount St. Helens before she blew her immaculate top) and the crew knocked off the unit in royal style.

That was many years ago, but in 1984 I asked Jesse to allow me to interview him for the first edition of this volume. Following are excerpts from that conversation:

Jesse, you ready?

Shoot, kid.

First, how about explaining how you got into treeplanting?

Yeah, in 1969 I arrived on the Olympic Peninsula on an acid cloud from San Francisco. I'd been selling handmade mobiles from a van and was just about broke. So me and a friend of mine named Rich called a West End reforestation contractor name of Hop Doughee, and he hired us over the phone. If he'd seen our long hair and beards at the time, I'm sure he wouldn't have taken us on. So then Rich and I struck out for the West End, and the planting unit turned out to be one of those mountains half gone from clearcutting and erosion, but there were still some magnificent views. I was both intimidated by the place and exalted.

How did your first days go?

Curiously, what I remember most was how one guy right off takes me aside and shows me how to hide trees. We were paid by the tree, you know, and the math is very simple: the more trees you bury or otherwise dispose of, the more bucks you reap. I gotta admit I gave the idea serious consideration, but Rich and I knew very early on we could make really good money without snuffing trees. And though I've been an outlaw all my life, planting was such a good hit for me, I made one-tree-at-a-time my working precept.

So you actually took to planting right off?

No, I wanted to quit the second day. It was a very nasty unit, and everyone kept cutting me off with their lines; but Rich, who had some experience in the woods, gave me a landing to plant and talked me into sticking it out.

Did you have any early precept for quality?

Early on, of course, the planting was helter-skelter, to be sure, but being near Sekiu with all that interminable rain, a tree would grow if you dropped it on a duck.

And later, you continued working for Hop?

Yeah, it's kind of an amazing story, 'cause the next contract was with Crown Zellerbach and Mr. Teagle, their head forester. The site was on the East End, and right off Teagle was real nervous 'cause of our long hair and shit. But because Rich and I were so hungry, we busted our butts and planted over five thousand trees a day between us. No one to my knowledge has done anything quite like that since, and I'm not sure what was going on, but it completely blew Teagle's ass away, I wanna tell ya.

You were holding to the one-tree-per-hole precept?

You can ask Teagle and his inspectors about that. It looked like a massive Easter egg hunt out there, but we didn't bury or hide a single tree. In fact, Hop was so happy with us that he wanted to go out and get an all-hippy crew. In other words, he'd come from wanting none to wanting nothing but hippies. But we clued him in on that one.

Eventually, though, as you began to run Hop's crews for him, longhairs did come to make up the majority of crew members, didn't they?

Yeah, pretty much, because I was soon hiring all my friends. In 1971 Hop got a Weyerhauser contract calling for 1.6 million trees in the Aberdeen region. Big trees, 2.Os at three and a half cents a tree—remember those days? The most anyone could get in the ground in a day was six hundred. Everyone got pretty bummed-out. The groundcover was terrible: sprayed dead alder, sword ferns—a nightmare. Amazing someone didn't die in one of the bogs. Characteristic of Hop, though, he gave us a raise to four cents, and he himself went on to lose his ass on the show.

But the longhairs were now entrenched?

Yeah. Later on we got a contract for four or five months' work, again on the West End. That show really capped the hippy presence in planting. It also had become clear by then that if we of the counterculture, the re-inhabitationists—to use an establishment-smashing term—were going to live on the beautiful Olympic Peninsula, we'd have to work, and work outdoors, and probably in the woods.

So when did you begin running crews?

In 1972. I wasn't keen on being a foreman—we all had a venomous bias against being the "heavy," and for good reason, I might add, but my age, thirty-two, made me a senior-citizen hippy, and I'd had experience as an assistant manager in a grocery store in San Francisco, so it was a natural, if a reluctant, transition.

At this time you're speaking of, what was your impression of forestry and reforestation on the Peninsula?

As I recall, there wasn't any Forestry Practices Act, and plunder and pillage was pretty much the code of the timber industry in the West. Reforestation only happened when logging companies had their noses rubbed in certain ecological disasters, or were simply required to do it. Landings were always huge garbage piles with big lakes of oil drained from cats.

What kind of people were the planters, the longhairs?

I'd first off characterize them as tough—this despite all the stereotyping of longhairs as flowers-in-the-hair peaceniks, and such. They were also well or over-educated, for the most part. On the other side, the compliance people were pretty good folks, too, mostly sympathetic to the plight of the planters.

Planters, as you know, were viewed early on as being at the bottom of the forestry stick. Loggers, for example, would have shot themselves first rather than become planters.

How about women, what was their percentage on the crews?

The ratio was about one-to-five or one-to-six. As you know, several women were not only the fastest planters, but also later played instrumental roles in founding the treeplanting cooperatives.

What was the lifestyle of the planters?

Most lived in the woods and when they weren't working for a wage worked on their own projects, everything from boatbuilding to music—or they just hung out. Most felt very good about doing planting, a job which largely was positive, healing. Also, treeplanting allowed you to keep your beard and long hair, or, in other words, to be yourself; you couldn't work at Shop-rite, for instance, but you could plant. In truth, I became a kind of counterculture employment bureau. It was lots of work, but also a privilege. I never fired anyone. That was probably a weakness. One guy on our crew, for example, stole the goddamn door from a neighbor's house and put it on his own. He was finally pressured out of the community and gave up planting, but by all rights, I should have canned him . . . he had a beautiful old lady, though. Also as foreman, I'd have to deal with the effects of drugs on the crew. One planter, a woman, got real stoned one morning and, not knowing this, I sent her over the edge of a mountain to plant. It was mountain goat country, and this gal gets stuck on a rock, and everyone leaves her, everyone thinking, "I gotta get these trees in the ground, so long." I had to perform a rockface rescue mission, and then found her some flat ground to hallucinate on. I myself never worked stoned—you could fall down and get killed. It's amazing there were so few injuries.

You mentioned Hop Doughee several times; could you talk about who he was?

Well, Hop really proved to be the vital link—hell, maybe the only link—for the counterculture to the straight world, where the bucks were. He himself was a total country boy, the genuine bumpkin, perhaps, and was born and raised in Humptulips—Humptulips, for Chrissakes! He picked brush and ferns, and lived in the woods. On the wages he earned from brush, he bought a cabin and three or four acres, then started doing a little contracting.

Actually the first year, he hired a lot of hippies, but they fucked him. So he would never have hired Rich or me, except over the phone, as I said.

Hop is a very truthful and—to some extent, naïve—individual. He said once, for example, that he didn't like to go to Seattle because all the people looked at him. But if he trusted you, he'd do anything for you. For a long time, he was the best wage deal on the Peninsula for planters.

What's Hop doing now?

He's back doing brush and some cedar. He got rich during the cedar boom with his shake mill. Got married and has kids and a semi-tame cougar. For a while, he even had three helicopters for his cedar salvage operations, but one that he leased was wrecked and when he read the fine print in the insurance policy, he discovered he had to write it off as a total loss. He is still the babe-in-the-woods in many respects. You know, there are always sharks when the money starts.

Hop had a brother working with him also, right?

Sure did. Ron. He's quite a guy, too. Get Hop and Ron together laughing and it's downright devastating, something like a duet by a hyena and a jackass. You only learn to laugh like that by never going to schools and by living in the sticks. Once on a planting show in Shelton, ole Ron draws us a map to reach a unit by. I lead a convoy of vehicles miles and miles into the heart of the Olympics until we come to this landing at the top of a mountain half in snow. Everyone gets out of their cars, trucks and crummies and surveys the scene. Then we all just cracked up. We were completely lost. Later, Hop said, "Oh yeah, never trust Ron; he draws bad maps."

By the way, that was the contract during which one planter began to factionalize the crew, leading a rebellion against Hop, whom he deemed an ogre, for Chrissakes. That was heavy, and we lost of lot of the crew and momentum.

So when did the treeplanting cooperatives begin to take off?

59

Well, first about the same time there was a group called the Hoedads, then later Olympic Reforestation (ORI). A lot of people who were fed up with working for greedy contractors got the cooperatives started and working right. For personal reasons, I stayed with Hop, though, at least through the formative years of the co-ops. Later, with friends, I formed another cooperative.

What cooperative was that?

R & R, Resource Renewal. Shitty name. But a good group of people, and it's still growing.

In forming the co-ops, there must have been some very complicated ideological battles?

You ain't kidding. When you consider that at any one crew meeting you might find feminists, Buddhists, Marxists, musicians, photo-journalists, anarchists, nudists, chemists, drug addicts—you name it—why sometimes seeking a consensus was like pissing against the wind.

What about the future of the cooperatives?

The Peninsula has always harbored interesting folks, utopians, collectives, cooperatives—Port Angeles, you know, was a town founded by a co-op. I don't know the reason for this, unless the natural beauty of the place inspires dreams, which I'm sure it does, and the relative isolation, experimentation. But today, the co-ops have got to diversify their work. There's tremendous economic pressure being put on treeplanting by the importation of alien labor, which has forced wages way down. Immigration isn't really backing the planter on this. I see co-ops moving into more specialized activities, such as fire suppression, although for treeplanting there still is a large demand because of the timber industry's backlog of unplanted units. Also, because of the Forestry Practices Act now in place, everything cut, theoretically, must be replanted.

Of course, what the forestry industry needs to do is go back to selective cutting, but with its Herculean equipment, it's just too easy and profitable (in the short term) to rip down hundreds of acres at once. You could even get more natural seeding with selective cuts, but the industry won't do it. The industry tries everything, even shooting trees from helicopters, but nothing is very cost-effective.

Let me also add, the co-ops could begin to diversify by cottage industries, such as furniture-making or producing tofu. With a cooperative, I think there are many possibilities for "right work."

What do you see as the biggest changes in the planting game?

Well, shooting trees from helicopters is certainly one of the most bizarre. Actually, the emphasis on quality control is an important change, and that includes micro site planting, shade blocking, etc. Second, the growth of the cooperatives. And third, getting paid by the acre.

Another change has been the increased number of women planting; they even have their own crews, in some cases. It was the cooperatives that encouraged this.

Aside from the bucks, what was important to you about tree plantings as compared to other forms of livelihood?

Planting always took you into wilderness, to some extent, to places you probably never would have ventured, really some incredibly beautiful sites. The connection with the land, the earth, has always stuck with me wherever I go. I didn't know I was, and didn't set out to be, a country boy. I'd lived in cities thirty years, damn near. Planting, you experience every kind of weather imaginable, from freezing white rain to sun that beats on you like a hammer on steel. I always thought the neatest month was March because you never know what the hell kind of weather will come, hour by hour. And to be able to watch spring arrive at different elevations, to watch things grow: it's midspring at two thousand feet, but still winter at four thousand. There are wild cherry blossoms at two thousand and the first trillium at four. Planting gave us work as a tribe and a yoga to reconnect us to the land. You plant a thousand trees in the day, and at night the earth shapes all your dreams. I think treeplanting was the perfect vehicle for us to test out the ideas we'd inherited from the cultural revolution of the sixties—of religion, economics, political science and ecology. And after testing them in the field, so to speak, we installed them, however imperfectly.

Anything you'd like to add?

You know, the truth is I still like the feeling of strapping on a bag of 2.Os and flying up a fucking mountain, but I'm getting too old for that now.

Note: "When you plant a tree, where is the Buddha?" is a Zen koan given to Jesse Miller by Roshi Sazaki in 1973.

Excerpts from: Piss-Fir Willie: A Suite of Voices in Praise of the Northcoast Vernacular

Jim Dodge

Introduction & Dedication

This suite of poems is offered as homage to the vernacular of northcoast working people, particularly loggers, restoration workers, commercial fishers, ranchers, and those, like my father, in the building trades. I've tried to capture the idiom—the diction, cadence, and phrasing—as well as that combination of aesthetics and attitude, the turn-of-mind, that constitutes style. To my sense of it, I've been successful enough that I can't honestly claim these poems as my own. Whatever virtues of language, wit, or wisdom you might find, praise should accrue to the speakers; any liabilities, alas, are likely mine.

When I've read these poems in public (for me, an essential part of revision) I was commonly asked if Piss-Fir Willie is a real person, or at least based on one. I always have difficulty with questions containing the word real, but my short answer is this: Piss-Fir Willie is a suite of voices drawn from many decidedly real men (and a few women) whom I've worked, partied, and gambled with most of my adult life on the Pacific northcoast, a region roughly equivalent to the range of redwoods from Big Sur to Coos Bay, though the vernacular is probably applicable to all the big timber country of the Pacific Northwest. Much of Willie's speech is quoted verbatim, or as accurately as I recall it, and the rest of what he has to say is more or less closely paraphrased.

I chose the name Piss-Fir Willie for sentimental reasons. During a poker game at the S&K in Eureka in the late '70s, I was pursuing the etymology of Piss-Fir Willie with an old timber faller across the table when one of the other players, in a tone of clear reprimand for deflecting attention from the game, snapped, "What're you doing, kid, writing a book?" Sounded like a good idea to me.

For those interested in etymology, as nearly as I can determine a Piss-Fir Willie was first used as a slang term for a timber-cruiser jacket manufactured by the Filson Company of Seattle (a cruiser's jacket is a nifty piece of apparel, with many pockets for packing tools of the trade, and Filsons are noted for both their design and durability). Nobody I asked could give me the source of the name, though a few old loggers suggested that in the '50s a Piss-Fir Willie took on a sense of mild opprobrium because, as one explained it, timber cruisers don't do the grunt work of logging, felling, setting choker, yarding—and thus it became associated with someone who looked good but didn't get dirty. More recently, in some places it has become a term for Forest Service employees, perhaps because many favor cruiser jackets as part of their uniform, and lately I've heard USFS and CDF workers called simply "Piss-Firs." It should be obvious that the Piss-Fir Willie of these poems is not a Forest Service employee. I should also note that piss-fir is a common name for grand fir (*Abies grandis*), also called white fir, whose sap wood emits a urine-like stench.

Although Piss-Fir Willie was conceived as a traditional persona, he ended up with a polymodal personality and a braided blend of identities. Moreover, unlike the first-person address traditional in persona poems, Willie just as often speaks in the third-person, as a character rather than narrator. Finally, I'm not speaking through him, employing him as an agent for my imagination; in an odd way, Piss-Fir Willie has made me his persona—as noted earlier, I served the work more as recorder than creator.

Part of my impulse to celebrate northcoast vernacular was a desire to preserve it, and that happily suggested working on another chapbook with Jerry Reddan, publisher, designer, printer, and janitor of

Tangram Press. For my taste, Jerry is among the best letterpress print-ers and book designers in the northern hemisphere, and I'm always gratified when our work finds a common occasion.

Piss-Fir Willie is dedicated to those who gave him to me.
French Hill, 1998

GETTING AFTER IT

All the planters on our crew
Packed double tree-bags.
Piss-Fir Willie harnessed three,
And stuffed another 20 bare-root stock
In a day-pack with his lunch.
When Timothy ragged him one morning
"Jeez, Willie, you could probably get
Another six down each pants-leg
And dozen between your teeth"

Willie turned to him and said,
Loud enough for us all to hear,
"I'll tell you what my daddy told me:
  Son, if you're gonna be a bear, Be a grizzly."

What It Takes to Be a Tree Planter

Crazy Jack Fraser, my first planting boss,
Claimed unless a man's collar size
Was triple his hat size,
He wouldn't hire the guy.

But if you aim to plant trees
Only two things you really need to know:
Green side goes up,
And ain't no raingear in this world'll keep you dry.

How to Catch the Biggest Fish

Pouring December rain, the crummy's windows all steamed up,
Our tree-planting crew was talking salmon fishing during lunch
When Piss-Fir Willie matter-of-factly announced,
"Due to my natural modesty I didn't mention it to you boys,
But I caught me a 30-pound chinook on Thanksgiving morn
Hit a big silver spinner in the Ten-Ten Hole."
J-Root Johnny immediately hooted, "Hey, dude,
Throw that fucking minnow back!
I nailed one in the gorge last week
That went 38—" But before we could ask him on what
(A pitchfork was rumored his favorite lure)
Pete Tucker honked, "Put it in Glad Bag, Johnny,
And set it out on the curb. I landed one
From that little pool behind the Ulrick Ranch
That weighed-out a hair over 42
On the Hiouchi Hamlet scales."
At which Willie threw up his hands and wailed,
"Shitfire! On this damn crew
The first liar don't have a chance."

HARD WORK

Boys, I've listened to your horseshit enough.
You want to know what hard work is, listen up:
I've rode a misery whip; carried hod;
Pulled green-chain; broke big rocks into little rocks;
Whupped a hundred miles of picket fence;
Set choker in country so rough
You were doing good if you could crawl downhill.
I've fought wildfire; lugged sandbags against floods;
Bucked hay till I was tripping on my tongue;
And made so damn much split stuff
I plumb wore out a sledgehammer head
And a couple o' pairs of elk-hide gloves.
So you boys can write it down as gospel when I tell you
The hardest work you'll find in this world
Is digging the grave for someone you loved.

His Response When Matt Wilson Suggested He Needed to Get in Touch with His Feminine Side

Pardner, I'd rather get in touch
With the real thing.
But fact is,
I haven't had anything feminine
By my side or anywhere else
Going on eight months now,
And I'm so horny
The crack of dawn ain't safe.

Basic Precepts and Avuncular Advice for Young Men

Don't eat a roadkill you can bounce into your pickup.

Don't bare-ass the Highway Patrol.

Long odds on short money is usually a loser.

Don't confuse the gospel with the church.

Never snitch on family or friends.

Avoid living any place where you can't take a piss off the front porch.

Just because it's simple doesn't make it easy.

Don't write a check with your 'gator mouth that your lizard ass can't cash.

If you don't want her, don't whistle.

Don't get between two dogs kicking dirt.

Anybody can mash potatoes; takes a chef to make gravy.

You're never too poor to pay attention.

Don't mumble around paranoids.

Never sleep with a woman who is doing you a favor.

If you're struck by a bully, turn the other cheek. If he whacks you again, shoot the sumbitch.

Keeping it is always twice as difficult as getting it.

Never drive through a small town at 100 mph with the Sheriff's drunk fifteen year old daughter on your lap.

Never draw against the drop.

If you're not confused, you don't know what's going on.

Love is always harder than it feels.

On Hearing Some Young Tree-Planters Discussing Reincarnation in the Crummy on the Way to Work

Now that's about the goddamnedest thing
I ever heard of, this "recarnation" crap—
But you know,

If I gotta come back as something else,
Wouldn't mind being a bird.
Yeah, a goose would be good . . .

One of them huge Canadian mothers
You see come November, way up there
On wings that must feel thirty miles wide.

'Cept this goose would haul-ass straight for the moon.
Yes! Right straight the hell outa here.
Stretch that neck out and put them wings in pronto.

Well, maybe slow down every now and again
Just long enough to look back
And give this mess a big ol' honk good-bye.

GREEN SIDE UP

Kid, there's only two things a treeplanter needs to know: the green
side goes up, and ain't no raingear in the world that'll keep you dry.
—Piss-Fir Willy

Once you're soaked
it doesn't matter
if it's raining.

The trees go in,
one by one by one,
and you go on

borne and lost in
that mindless rhythm,
bent to the work.

No time at all,
you forget the rain,
blur into its

monotony.
Between root and breath
no difference:

it's all hard work.
Your wet body burns
from the bones out.

SONG 5

Michael Daley

Planting Silver Fir above Silver Creek,
the ground has broken out in stone.
Boulders lie crooked and cracked in the basin at the creek.
Their formation spells the word
we must never speak.
Glacier water, ice white, falls
and in incessant sighs
runs the slipping ledges
past crackling runt rocks,
soft firemoss, red, orange.
The water's is the only sound
unless our tools sing metal to the ground.
Then work stops. The snow gossips
for a minute with our clothes.
This high, money should be pebbles in the boot.
But it's not. We count the hours
till we drive down 4,000 feet of cloud
to a wave battering the dream
beneath our bed. How I long for you.
But we have to work. We dig again
in something that has made us. We curse it.
A buzzard's shadow hums in brief sun and we go on.
We do this in the tracks of deer.

After Losing the Bid on a Season's Treeplanting to an Out-of-Work Fisherman, We Take a Hike up Barnes Creek and Reflect on the Nature of the Times

Tim McNulty
For Kevin & Finn

In the frozen shade of an old forest
we cut through stiff winter brush, and climb
to the base of the oldest tree we can find.

Its deeply furled bark is charred
by centuries of fires, and looks almost
rock-like beneath its pale gray-green lichens.

All the out-of-work treeplanters in two counties
stacked up on each other's backs (which
isn't far from the truth)
couldn't match its height.

"It's good to be around someone
who's lived through harder times than these."

Out on 101, no log trucks or tourists,
but Barnes Creek moving its quiet stones,
building its delta incrementally into the lake,

like a ghost crew of Chinese coolies,
or an old tired CCC gang
who never got the news about Roosevelt.

CONVOY

the close-spaced truck
headlights
the long line
climbing the valley road
at dawn
looked like some old war movie
& us
camped high on the ridge
in our trucks
& smokestacks
could have been a guerrilla band
but for the fact that
the cover of trees was conspicuously
absent
and we were working for the bastards

TREEPLANTER'S JOURNAL:

Jerry Gorsline

North Fork Toutle River

A few miles distant Mt. St. Helens looms, glaciers shining in sun. As far as the eye can see, thousands of acres stripped of forest; continuous clearcut; barren ridges, choked streams. Nutrient capital accumulated by forest ecosystems over thousands of years draining away. Our inspector tells me that, at the present rate of cut, there is less than seven years of old growth left in these tributaries of the Cowlitz River.

Pysht River

Storm in last night from the southwest, bringing rain and gusty winds. buffleheads and goldeneyes at the mouth of Deep Creek; a lone wood duck on the Pysht River.

Delicate pink-white bloom of springbeauty against the scorched earth and blackened slash of our planting unit. At timber's edge, a stand of alder, stems white, canopy glowing purple with new spring catkins; a vine maple thicket, end twigs and buds vivid red and shining from rain; white fluffy catkins on Scouler willows.

Realized last night this is the aboriginal territory of the S'Klallam Nation, from Discovery Bay west to the Hoko River. Lush lowlands around the Pysht River. Deep loamy soils. The original forest reportedly some of the finest Douglas fir on the Olympic Peninsula, logged by McMillan & Bloedel, Ltd., circa 1900. Natural regeneration produced this dense stand of hemlock and spruce. There is a study plot on our unit designed to test hybrid Sitka spruce for resistance to the sprucetip weevil. Larva from galls eat the interior of stems, then emerge as caterpillars in phase with bud-burst to defoliate in spring.

Big River

No drought here on the west end. Wave after wave of rain fronts drenching the coast. Crossing the Big River Bridge: a large hemlock sagging over swollen and turbid water; waves and foam on the shores of Lake Ozette; huge wind and sheets of rain. Images of storm.

Wessler Ranch

The crew strung out in a loose line, scalping away sod for each tree planted. Hoedads thudding into heavy sod, we resemble Neolithic farmers. Coyotes yipping and howling in broad daylight. Roger says this is part of their February mating pattern. Sexual madness everywhere. Bud-burst and bloom: on the way to Seafield Lake, Oxeye daisy, coltsfoot and salmonberry flowers. Hiked along the beach, two pairs of gaudy Harlequin ducks along shore. Point of Arches far to the north, ancient rocks pre-dating coast range geology: a tectonic puzzle. Evening, back to the Big River camp. At sunset, Venus, Jupiter and the first quarter moon.

Ellis Mountain

Woke up to a snowstorm. We pull camp hastily and try to escape down the mountain, but the road is already too hazardous. Three trucks and a tent, perched on an exposed landing. Silver fir zone and deep snow. Storm after storm moves in from the southwest, across the Dickey watershed, the Hoko valley, then sweeping against Stoltzenberg and Ellis mountains, rattling tent flaps and rocking the trucks.

Goodman Creek

A coastal watershed between the Hoh and Quillayute rivers in the Sitka spruce zone. Selective grazing of hemlock seedlings by elk is said to be one factor contributing to spruce dominance. Planted down a steep side hill this morning to the creek bench bounding the north side of the unit. Next to timber, I found elk shit everywhere and browsed hemlocks (their leaders clipped) next to intact fir and spruce seedlings.

The white "mold" visible on the roots of our seedlings is actually Mycorhiza, structures combining plant root and fungus in ancient, symbiotic association. Without Mycorhiza, seedlings would die. The fungus protects against disease, assists in the assimilation of micronutrients (particularly phosphorus) and water, and receives in exchange food from the outer cells of the host roots.

"The life of the tree dignifies the worker," says Roger.

Boulder Creek

Stew is a soils scientist working for the Forest Service. As the crew moves from unit to unit, he follows, monitoring seedling physiology (moisture stress and photosynthetic rates), temperature and moisture variables, wind velocity, etc. The object is to correlate survival rates on each site with objective physical and biological conditions.

The Boulder Creek watershed was heavily damaged by roading and harvest, with massive slope failures on the east side of the drainage. On one occasion, a plugged culvert initiated a debris torrent that swept 100,000 cubic yards of silt into the Hamma Hamma River, then out to the estuary where it buried shellfish beds.

We stand around in the rain after work one evening, talking about erosion from forested watersheds, while soil sloughs off the cutbank behind us with a hissing sound. Stew delivers up clichés about the need for toilet paper and 2×4s to justify this business. Erosion is natural, he says, pointing to slides on the steep rocky slopes of Mt. Pershing.

Four Streams

Last night parked on a high windy landing, truck buffeted by heavy wind gusts all night. Today we worked four hours in sideways rain and hail. After lunch, no one got out of the crummy. Camped on the same landing tonight, looking north towards Six Ridge white with snow and moonlight; the North Fork Skokomish angling east; dark, turbulent weather, mist lofting up from the valley walls.

Elk Creek

An extremely steep unit on the west sidehill of Elk Creek, with only one road into the top. A toehold necessary at all times. The kind of unit that makes a treeplanter sick. We single line across the top, floating our lines down to the bottom, then hike out along Elk Creek through the timber, back to the mainline and the crummy for a fossil-fuels assist back to the top. Repeat tactic tomorrow. Dick is pushing the crew hard, anxious to get on to his Oregon contract.

Baker River

Camped directly above Lake Shannon, looking northeast to Shucksan, the top of Mt. Baker looming over the next ridge west of here. Clear, crisp nights. The moon and Jupiter rising together over Shucksan Ridge.

"Bear Flat Slashing" is an eight-acre planting unit, high-graded in the past, now being "rehabilitated" under DNR management, i.e. converted from a stand of mixed ages and species to one of pure Douglas fir. Prescription: clearcut, burn and hand plant. The patient, however, is too fragile for this treatment, with unstable, alluvial soils on very steep slopes. The old-timer's method, which amounted to selective cutting, was kinder, and the watershed was healing. Now, with vegetation gone, the slopes fail and slide into creek-beds, bound for Lake Shannon and the hydroelectric dam. Some drainages literally flow with mud. "Rehabilitation" has set the patient back irreversibly. And things will get much worse as stump root systems holding soil in place give out over the next three to five years. The crew is appalled. This is the worst management we've ever seen, creating a hostile environment for our seedlings, which will surely be buried and overturned, or die of moisture stress in this exposed sandy soil. And this is the state agency that is also charged with enforcement of the state forest practices regulations!

Upper Sekiu River

Usually a site is burned by the time we reach it, but this 120-acre clearcut had no site-prep whatever and it's incredible to see the volume of wood left behind and usually burned! Somehow we're going to have to plant seedlings in this heavy concentration of hemlock slash. No streamside buffer; draws and streambeds choked with slash from cross-stream yarding. Streambanks caving in everywhere; heavy siltation. All of this justified by "Type 4" stream classification under Forest Practices Regulations (meaning no fish population or direct domestic utility). In this legalized disregard for upper tributary streams, the total lack of watershed consciousness that stands behind present forest practices is starkly evident.

Willipa Hills

Last unit of the Chehalis contract: 71 acres marked originally for thinning, then clearcut because of mistletoe infestation. Attempts to burn the unit, using helicopter with suspended driptorch, were thwarted when a front moved in and extinguished the fire. At the bottom of the unit, seen through a strip of timber, the Willipa River curls out of the hills, clear gravel bottom, hemlock forest touching both sides.

Violent patterns of resource management, implemented with war technology: helicopters, defoliants and napalm. Our inspector tells me they have a 500-acre clearcut to burn and plant. Site preparation will consist of "brown and burn," i.e. spray with herbicides, then "mass ignition" to burn all 500 acres in one long day (mass ignition: string the unit with primacord fuse, attach cans of napalm at intervals; ignition produces a fire storm which consumes slash).

To prevent brush competition on the "Whitcomb Creek" unit, they're going to apply 2,4-D bound in lignin with a clay bulk carrier over the entire unit, creating a long-duration, low-intensity, plant-toxic environment to "ensure seedling survival."

I'm more and more fascinated by the use of plant indicators to read out site characteristics: fertility, moisture and temperature relations, successional patterns, etc. This method can be used to divide up areas within a given site into classes based on environmental characteristics. These classes would determine management. Researchers call this "habitat typing" or "site stratification." Currently, management units are given universal treatment (clearcut), ignoring differences in slope, aspect and soils within the unit. Actually, climate, topography and soil characteristics may change drastically within a few yards within any given area, creating several microsites. Treatment should vary accordingly: regulating canopy density to control moisture/temperature relations, managing each site for nutrient budgets and sediment yields. Modern forestry will have to work within these parameters, no matter how uneconomical they may seem by short-term accounting. Sustained yield depends on long-term maintenance of site productivity.

Baker River Ranger District

We're camped on the South Fork Nooksack, facing the jagged ridgeline and snow-filled cirques of the Twin Sisters Range, ten miles southwest of Mt. Baker. Strange rocks up there. Thirty-three square miles of dunite outcrop, described as an "unaltered piece of the earth's mantle emplaced by faulting sometime in the early Tertiary." Rich in olivine and with such high levels of magnesium, nickel and chromium that unique plant communities inhabit the slopes.

Planting is tough. Elaborate and difficult hand site preparation to establish Douglas fir in the hemlock zone, burrowing through hemlock roots and duff, look for good dirt, a red-ochre soil which blossoms sudden and beautiful against the back duff layer when you strike it.

Chelan Ranger District

The reforestation we do here is primarily aimed at rehabilitating watersheds burned in a catastrophic fire eight years ago that destroyed 120,000 acres of forest. I suspect the destructive magnitude of this fire is related to fuel accumulations resulting from years of misguided fire-exclusion policies.

Actually, the natural vegetative cover—ponderosa pine/bitterbrush/ceanothus/pine grass—is shaped by periodic fire (15- to 25-year intervals, according to one forest ecologist). Even now you can see the healing mechanisms. We have to wade through thick stands of Snowbrush ceanothus, a typical post-fire ground cover which restores lost nitrogen. Heat generated by burning triggers germination of its seeds, which can lie dormant for years.

Our hoes sink easily into the sandy pumice soils generated by a series of eruptions from Glacier Peak 12,000 years ago. Beneath layered pumice and ash, ancient igneous rocks of the Chelan Batholith. The effects of fire are everywhere in time and space.

Work is intense, with frequent meetings (since this is how contract administration is done in cooperatives). Camp consists of two big yurts and a number of multi-colored tents scattered on a creek bench in a narrow canyon. Burned snags cover the slopes. The bloom cycle is just beginning, with balsamroot showing bright yellow over the hills; a waterleaf species named "cats paws" with a misty lavender flower head that dazzles the eye and seems to resonate in my psyche. Blue grouse and mule deer on the units. A whole new array of plants and animals to know, and a new geology to unravel. Information that sinks into the daily work routine and enriches it.

II.

WORKING THE WOODS

KEROUAC CREEK WORK TUNE

Mike O'Connor

After three days of summer rain,
I'm back splitting cedar
            in the hills.
The horse skidtrail
               is muddy
          and rainclouds dapple
                  the peaks.

But work goes well,
    the saw and truck run fine;
    cedar splits
        into fifty
      sturdy rails,
    and by evening
  —truck loaded, tools packed away—

the moon and stars
    jingle in the sky
      like wages.

We Come to Ask for Your Bones: Cutting the Great Fragrant Western Red Cedar

for Steve Conca

The first thing we do:
clear the brush and wiry limbs
back from the flaring butt and look up.

I tap the trunk with my axehandle
and the top answers
200 feet in the blue,
then hugging it, reckon the lean.

I stand back and ask you who to cut;
you grin and say, so I reach around
and make the lower portion of the undercut
straight in till I think I might hit rot;
then the upper portion at 45 degrees
and kick the wedge-shaped block out;
stand back, look up,
kill saw and figure the backcut.

Now this is a big tree for the Rainshadow,
and a 36-inch bar is nice to have,
and a powerhead that blows your ears off
 (use a little wax or cotton).
That distant top is barbed like devils club
and non-regulation caps are crazy
(forgot my hardhat, thought we were going fishing).
Tap the tree, make sure it's still one piece.

You got the wedges—what am I doing here?—
put the saw across the swell and go
through blue exhaust that floats among the maples,
through jets of sawdust warm as blood.
Jam the plastic wedge in deep;
I'm where the rot must start.
She tips a little;
click off saw and find a place to run.

She's talkin', she's crackin'
in the check but will not fall.

We freeze, like game in someone's sights,

Back under her again, you tap the wedge
and give it one firm bust
and then another:

slower than a rising star
the butt begins to turn across the stump,

and then she's free!

Chainsaw and sacklunch and find a place to fly,
we've cut the ridgepole that supports the sky.

And the brittle Goddess—after standing dead
and silver fifty years—like a wave
begins to break upon the rocks.

Barbtop whipping like a fly pole
splinters into stars; the accelerating stem explodes

the crown of a maple; pauses momently
in the whirl of greenry, slams a big Doug fir,
blazes down its side, pounds into the earth,
recoils, lurches sideways and falls still.

A clap of thunder echoes through the hills.
A conky chokecherry floats out from the shade
and bursts beside us.

Limbs, sprays . . .
then only thousands of needles
raining in our hair, on the fern
and honeysuckle earth, on the silent cedar hulk.

We get to our feet. The sun streams through
the thinned canopy. Steve is making
one of his wide-eyed, Holy Jesus-what-was-
that-all-about faces,
then says, "Holy Jesus, what . . ."

laughs and hands me the Copenhagen.
"Except for the maple, Doug fir,
woodpeckers, squirrels, etc., I think
you dropped her just about right."

We clamber up the high and hollow stump to look:
lots of taper wood and nothing serious in fractures.
Then a short leap, and we are walking,

walking the length of her lovely bones.

ELEGY FOR A LOG TRUCK DRIVER

I know that swooping place
in the downhill curving grade,
after snowy Koma Kulshan
skeets up like the moon
through the trees, after
a last thistled clearcut
gives you the eagle's view
over Juan de Fuca waters
into Canada, distant mountains, into blue . . .

And there,
with your speed-splitter transmission,
king-of-the-woods heavy duty clutch,
high in your brand-new Western Star truck,
switching down through your gears
like a man dealing cards,
easing r.p.m engine whine
with each bite of the brakes . . .

> "Maybe there is a way to get ahead
> in this cock-eyed land; have
> Vivian come home with the kids,
> build a little better place
> down by the river
> and have horses . . ."

BUT THE GODDMAN BRAKES ARE GONE

And the valves of your heart
thumped and fired like pistons
diving at your gears
trying to hold a dragon by its tail.

"Last year, tested by the storm of recession,
we prioritized our efforts, and as a result,
cut our overhead costs,
while maintaining our ability
to serve the basic corporate needs."

Dragon of timber, dragon of steel,
plunging down a mountain road
with a tin-hat hero in your jaws.

"Our profits are the primary
determinant to add to our asset base."

O driver in the terrors
of the shadow of death,
free-wheeling past a last
thinned stand of fir—a
squirrel skittering out a
bough—snapping off a whanging
guard rail section, dispersing
rubber tread like shrapnel
in a long squeal of tires and smoke.

And then with the final curve
at the foot of the hill before you—
brain burning like a welder's torch—
you knew the way of escape:

"At the curve go straight
through the split-cedar fence
and on toward the river
through the fields;
then back onto Salmon Road,
or even left
along the river into wheat."

Out from the shadows of trees,
descending to the gentle river valley
with the seagulls dove-white in the sunshine
over the river like angels,
and the long trim pastures, sparsely
cattled, green vibrations in the heat.

That's when some extolling spirit
sprang into you heart,
as you began blessing farmers
for their lush fields of clover,

Jack Philips and Butterfly Pete,
who gave you your first chance to drive.

YOU REACHED THE CURVE

And the extolling spirit sprang again,
as you blessed without reason:

lumber executives
and their tennis-court wives,

caterpillar mechanics
in jumpsuits of grease,

drunken commissioners
and the builders of road.

> YOU BURST THROUGH
> THAT SPLIT-CEDAR FENCE

And began blessing every which way:

hippies for their feminine hearts
blackmen for their funny talk

> YOU PLOWED THROUGH THAT FIELD
> OF FLEABANE AND CHICORY

blessing like a tickertape:
  union leaders,
    suspenders
     squirrels
      women
       bar-tabs
       lice

and the Lord;

            speeding toward the river like a curse.

But the irrigation stream—cool
sweet water of the Dungeness,
channeled off to a slow blue ditch

that gives the cows to drink
and the fields to ripen—

you couldn't see it till you hit!

The farmwife turns from her oven;
the farmer looks out from the barn;
a postman wavers by a mailbox;
fishermen see fire in the trees.

Instant repeat gasoline explosions!

Forty crashing tons of you
bursting like a nightmare
above stunned waters,
clanging and crackling
    upward
higher than a man could ever bless,
    upward
            into ash-blossom
                    whirlwind
            and the sun.

"When the Lord toucheth the hills, they smoke."

And then, O driver,
you awakenend
on a hillside

with a bird book
in your hand.

RAY AT TUBAL CAIN MINE

Twelve years ago,
on this very hillside—
the same open view
to the sea, and the longest
switchbacks that ever reached a pass—
you beat the earth
down around a charge
with your dynamite bar,
while the pocket radio
spluttered "Que Sera Sera."

Now as then Copper Creek
flows cold and clear
over the broken cedar dam,
built by miners circa 1910,
and the snows have beaten flat our cabin.

You were a refugee of school,
conventional hygiene
and tailgate safety meetings.

Sixteen and practically feral,
taking an hour that time
to read a single page
of *Studs Lonigan*
I'd loaned you, never owning
your own toothbrush, tamping
dynamite to build
a smooth piece of trail

to Buckhorn Pass,
through bedrock and meadow,
in sun and thunderstorm,
rock 'n' roll on that tiny transistor,
camels to smoke every break—
in the endless dew of morning,
in the purple light of dusk.

"What I remember about Ray
is how in the friggin'
night—everyone asleep in their bunks—
he'd whip out that hootin' big revolver
and start blastin' packrats off the walls.
It got Arnie so mad one night, he reached out,
grabbed Ray's gun, slipped off the goddamn
bunk and shot himself in the foot.

"That's when I got permanent hire, remember?"

I recall when we woke
to the first light of snow of September,
hiked up from the alpine lake,
and, from chill heights
of the whitened pass,
saw elk still in summer
grazing by the river far below.

You liked to dance atop
that purple-stumping. Laughing,
non-clinging, ready to blow
us all to scree.

The ranger finally took your gun,
so you spent off-hours contriving
packrat traps: peanutbutter bait
on narrow paper bridges
over pots and tubs of dishwater.
Needless to say, come dawn,
we let you rise first,
start the fire,
empty the catch.

A week later,
you married a girl from home.

On the second page of *Lonigan*,
you had to show me
where the text reprints
in Studs' hand
two pen-book exercises—
up and down and oval—
and taking them for
scratched out errors,
said you'd never seen a book like that,
and liked it when an author
left some proof of his mistakes.
"On their wedding night," swore Elmer,
"sleepin' in the backyard at her parents' place,
Gus and me snuck up and cut all the guylines
on their tent. Turned out he had his wife's sister
in there with 'em."

The day my time was up
was the start of Indian summer.

Lupines and hare bells
shimmered like streams
along the fresh cut trail,
and the Queen Anne's lace
and yarrow were as melting snow.

At the last rocky go before the pass,
I shook hands with the crew all around:
Jim, Elmer, the two young seamen
and Ray. "Now we don't havta really
tell you what's what with them shakey-Leo
college girls," confided Elmer, "but
the crew here thinks you ought to know
something about the cookie jar."

He told me. And then Ray, wanting to add
something original of his own, said,
"You take the chain off the chainsaw,
and then from behind,
slip the bar between his legs
at full throttle!"
To hasten my exit, I dropped
off the trail and glided
down through meadow
and clusters of young fir.

By the time I reached Copper Creek,
I could just barely pick them out
in the glare of rock outcropping;

and, as if timed for my departure,
a puff of smoke appeared above them

in the rock, followed by a rip of thunder
and echoes from Iron Mountain.

I ~~sloshed~~ splashed across the creek
and went up the bank into the cool trees.

THE BRIDGE

Bill Shepherd

He stands legs apart, each boot on a different timber of an old high-mountain timber-cutter's road bridge that's coming down this after-noon—way down, 100 feet down, to a thrashing and jagged river that's blinked up at this bridge for decades. He wants to finish dismantling the bridge today, right now; then rebuild it in the coming months. He wants to cut the next-to-last bracing timber of all the old square creosotes that are ready to go, every bolt and spike carefully loosened the last six weeks, ready to fall. He wants to cut that next-to-last brace just enough to let the near part of the bridge sag, slow and graceful, so he'll be already running with the saw.

It's not far, 15 feet to safety, or four strides. His more experienced mates are just trotting back from the cook fire, muttering, and now yelling, trying to talk him out of it. There are other ways, there is no real hurry.

The bridge could fall overnight. Or they can toss a stick of dyna-mite out there in the morning. It's time to finish cooking supper. The evening lanterns will soon be on in the five tents. Five tents for this band of blood brothers and for Troy—all young, all here for 35 weeks of Forest Service contract work.

They throw him a line.

"Take this rope, Troy, c'mon!"

His sharp and railing chain saw is chanting a little war song as he steps from bare timber to bare timber. He wears handmade, worn and costly high-heeled logger's boots. Steady, watchful.

Like the others, grease and dirt and sawdust cake his clothes. The chain teeth, lit by the late sun, roll slow around the bar, and come to a stop. The teeth are filed, brushed, curried, and fashioned every day to rip, shaped for high speed, to wreak splinters and to loose life's blood where it's pointed, to make ends of things, to make whole things fragment. The teeth roll snickering along the bar; the dusty engine, all nicked and scratched and smeared with creosote, gnars and whispers about kerfs and deep slicing, about sawdust, that good smell. Or about flesh and blood mistakes, legs and ankles and toes, that smell. Plenty of daylight left to see the yellow crayon marks. He crouches, looks around, sensing. He has felt with his feet how the bridge trembles now with most bolts gone, most bracing timbers taken.

He says, "I'm glad I'm not a heavyweight."

"Shit!!" say his mates.

He says, "Aw, I'm all right, we know this bridge y'know."

"We know it's fuckin' heavy and it's ready Troy, goddammit!!"

The bridge squeaks where he walks; it gives under his boots just a little, and rises some behind him. He shifts his weight side to side, listening, sensing. Everyone's quiet now, attentive to the bridge that sounds more like some unknown live thing than it ever has before.

As the heavy heat of day lessens, the timbers of the bridge pop and sigh, expanding and contracting as the cold air from the river rises and cools his brow.

He feels the cold now that he's stopped talking and moving and gone to listening. This bridge whispers and rubs its beams together a hair at a time, with weight behind every whisper.

He thinks he's right for this. He looks at his mates and wishes he were their real brother, a member of this respected mountain family. A year he's worked beside them, wishes he had been born one of them to live always in these mountains. If asked, he talks of ideas, politics, literature, but can't match their snapping humor, or their ease with horses, tools, sweat. So he's worked hard, tried to learn, and that's why he's here today, right?

He's used to taking chances.

He says: "It's easier than you think, guys."

He wants to show no hesitation.

He wants to get started.

He triggers and rattles his saw and reaches it between the timbers.

The shout of the saw startles everyone in the quiet, sends a shriek into the air.

He is cutting the right one, from the top of it down, so when he cuts through the critical strength of it, there should be a little sagging, but the saw goes so fast he barely sees timber move as it rips the saw from his hands. The whole bridge howls and groans and is louder than the saw ever was, squeals, roars as the timbers bend to breaking and he wastes one quarter second grabbing for his saw, but it's gone already, snatched and twisted, crushed, spit out, falling, and that timber broken in one motion.

He turns, tries to run uphill against a falling mountain; he makes one labored step, reaches toward the outstretched hands of the brothers, but the bridge drops behind him, timbers snapping and flying. He tumbles backwards, swallowed in a twisting chaos that strikes and batters him, breaking his bones on the way down.

Logging: from Myths & Texts

1.

The morning star is not a star
Two seedling fir, one died
                    Io,Io,
Girdled in wistaria
Wound with ivy
                "The May Queen
Is the survival of
A pre-human
Rutting season"

The year spins
Pleiades sing to their rest
                at San Francisco
                dream
                dream

Green comes out of the ground
Birds squabble
Young girls run mad with the pine bough,
                                    Io

2.

But ye shall destroy their altars,
    break their images, and cut down their groves.
                    —*Exodus 34:13*

The ancient forests of China logged
     and the hills slipped into the Yellow Sea.
Squared beams, log dogs,
     on a tamped-earth sill.
San Francisco 2×4s
     were the woods around Seattle:
Someone killed and someone built, a house,
     a forest, wrecked or raised
All America hung on a hook
     & burned by men, in their own praise.

Snow on fresh stumps and brush-piles.
The generator starts and rumbles
                         in the frosty dawn
I wake from bitter dreams,
Rise and build a fire,
Pull on and lace the stiff cold boots
Eat huge flapjacks by a gloomy Swede
In splintery cookhouse light
                         grab my tin pisspot hat
Ride off to the show in a crummy-truck
And start the Cat.

"Pines grasp the clouds with iron claws
like dragons rising from sleep"
250,000 board feet a day
If both Cats keep working
& nobody gets hurt

3.

"Lodgepole Pine: the wonderful reproductive
power of this species on areas over which its
stand has been killed by fire is dependent upon
the ability of the closed cones to endure a fire
which kills the tree without injuring its seed.
After fire, the cones open and shed their seeds
on the bared ground and a new growth springs up."

Stood straight
   holding the choker high
As the Cat swung back the arch
   piss-firs falling,
Limbs snapping on the tin hat
   bright D caught on
Swinging butt-books
   ringing against cold steel.

Hsü Fang lived on leeks and pumpkins.
Goosefoot,
  wild herbs,
    fields lying fallow!

But it's hard to farm
Between the stumps:
The cows get thin, the milk tastes funny,
The kids grow up and go to college
They don't come back.
   the little fir-trees do

   Rocks the same blue as sky
Only icefields, a mile up,

                           are the mountain
Hovering over ten thousand acres
Of young fir.

                    4

Pines, under pines,
                    Seami Motokiyo
                    The Doer stamps his foot.
                    A thousand board-feet
Bucked, skidded, loaded—
(Takasago, Ise) float in a mill pond;
A thousand years dancing
Flies in the saw kerf.

Cliff by Tomales Bay
Seal's slick head
                    head shoulders breasts
                    glowing in night saltwater
Skitter of fish, and above, behind the pines,
Bear grunts, stalking the Pole-star.

Foot-whack on polished boards
Slide and stop; drum-thump.

"Today's wind moves in the pines"
                                    falling
And skidding the red-bark pine.
Clouds over Olallie Butte
Scatter rain on the Schoolie flat.
A small bear slips out the wet brush
                           crosses the creek
Seami, Kwanami,

Gone too.
Through the pines.

5.

Again the ancient, meaningless
Abstractions of the educated mind.
   wet feet and the campfire out.
Drop a mouthful of useless words.
—The book's in the crapper
They're up to the part on Ethics now

   skidding logs in pine-flat heat
   long summer sun
   the flax bag sweet
Summer professors
   elsewhere meet
Indiana? Seattle? Ann Arbor?
   bug clack in sage
Sudden rumble of wheels on cattle-guard rails.
   hitching & hiking
   looking for work.

"We rule you" all crownéd or be-Homburged heads
"We fool you" those guys with Ph.D.s
"We eat for you" you
"We work for you" who?
   a big picture of K. Marx with an axe,
"Where I cut off one it will never grow again."
   O Karl would it were true
   I'd put my saw to work for you
& the wicked social tree would fall right down.

(The only logging we'll do here is trees
And do it quick, with big trucks and machines)
        "That Cat wobbles like a sick whore"
So we lay on our backs tinkering
                                    all afternoon
The trees and the logs stood still
It was so quiet we could hear the birds.

6.

"In that year, 1914, we lived on the farm
And the relatives lived with us.
A banner year for wild blackberries
Dad was crazy about wild blackberries
No berries like that now.
You know Kitsap County was logged before
The turn of the century—it was easiest of all,
Close to water, virgin timber,
When I was a kid walking about in the
Stumpland, wherever you'd go a skidroad
Puncheon, all overgrown.
We went up one like that, fighting our way through
To its end near the top of a hill:
For some reason wild blackberries
Grew best there. We took off one morning
Right after milking: rode the horses
To a valley we'd been to once before
Hunting berries, and hitched the horses.
About a quarter mile up the old road
We found the full ripe of berrytime—
And with only two pails—so we
Went back home, got Mother and Ruth,
And filled lots of pails. Mother sent letters

To all the relatives in Seattle:
Effie, Aunt Lucy, Bill Moore,
Forrest, Edna, six or eight, they all came
Out to the farm, and we didn't take pails
Then: we took copper clothes-boilers,
Wash-tubs, buckets, and all went picking.
We were canning for three days."

7.

    Felix Baran
    Hugo Gerlot
    Gustav Johnson
    John Looney
    Abraham Rabinowitz
Shot down on the steamer Verona
For the shingle-weavers of Everett
      the Everett Massacre November 5 1916

Ed McCullough, a logger for thirty-five years
Reduced by the advent of chainsaws
To chopping off knots at the landing:
"I don't have to take this kind of shit,
Another twenty years
      and I'll tell 'em to shove it"
      (he was sixty-five then)
In 1934 they lived in shanties
At Hooverville, Sullivan's Gulch.
When the Portland-bound train came through
The trainmen tossed off coal.

"Thousands of boys shot and beat up
For wanting, a good bed, good pay,

decent food, in the woods—"
No one knew what it meant:
"Soldiers of Discontent."

8.

Each dawn is clear
Cold air bites the throat.
Thick frost on the pine bough
Leaps from the tree
      snapped by the diesel

Drifts and glitters in the
      horizontal sun.

In the frozen grass
      smoking boulders
      ground by steel tracks.
In the frozen grass
      wild horses stand
      beyond a row of pines.
The D8 tears through piss-fir,
Scrapes the seed-pine
      chipmunks flee,
A black ant carries an egg
Aimlessly from the battered ground.
Yellowjackets swarm and circle
Above the crushed dead log, their home.
Pitch oozes from barked
      trees still standing,
Mashed bushes make strange smells.
Lodgepole pines are brittle.
Camprobbers flutter to watch.

A few stumps, drying piles of brush;
Under the thin duff, a toe-scrape down
Black lava of a late flow.
Leaves stripped from thornapple
Taurus by nightfall.

9.

Headed home, hitch-hiking
leaving mountains behind
where all Friday in sunlight
fighting flies fixed phone line
high on the lake trail,
dreaming of home,
by night to my girl and a late bath.
she came in naked to the tub
her breasts hung glistening
and she scrubbed my back.
we made love night-long.
she was unhappy alone.

all Sunday softly talked,
I left, two hundred miles
hitching back to work.

10.

A ghost logger wanders a shadow
In the early evening, boots squeak
With the cicada, the fleas
Nest warm in his blanket-roll
Berrybrambles catch at the stagged pants
He stumbles up the rotted puncheon road   .
There is a logging camp
Somewhere in there among the alders
Berries and high rotting stumps
Bindlestiff with a wooden bowl
(The poor bastards at Nemi in the same boat)
What old Seattle skidroad did he walk from
Fifty years too late, and all his

                  money spent?

Dogfish and Shark oil
Greasing the skids.
"Man is the heart of the universe
the upshot of the five elements,
born to enjoy food and color and noise . . ."
Get off my back Confucius
There's enough noise now.
What bothers me is all those stumps:
What did they do with the wood?
Them Xtians out to save souls and grab land
"They'd steal Christ off the cross

               if he wasn't nailed on"
The last decent carpentry
Ever done by Jews.

11.

Ray Wells, a big Nisqually, and I
            each set a choker
On the butt-logs of two big Larch
In a thornapple thicket and a swamp.
            waiting for the Cat to come back,
"Yesterday we gelded some ponies
"My father-in-law cut the skin on the balls
"He's a Wasco and don't speak English
"He grabs a handful of tubes and somehow
            cuts the right ones.
"The ball jumps out, the horse screams
"But he's all tied up.
The Caterpillar clanked back down.
In the shadow of that racket
            diesel and iron tread
I thought of Ray Wells' tipi out on the sage flat
The gelded ponies
Healing and grazing in the dead white heat.

12.

A green limb bangs in the crotch
Of a silver snag,
Above the Cats,
            the skidders; and thudding brush,
Hundreds of butterflies
Flit through the pines.
"You shall live in square
            gray houses in a barren land
            and beside those square gray
            houses you shall starve."
—Drinkswater. Who saw a vision

At the high and lonely center of the earth:
Where Crazy Horse
            went to watch the Morning Star,
& the four-legged people, the creeping people,
The standing people and the flying people
Know how to talk.
I ought to have eaten
Whale tongue with them.
            they keep saying I used to be a human being
"He-at-whose-voice-the-Ravens-sit-on-the-sea."
Sea-foam washing the limpets and barnacles
Rattling the gravel beach
Salmon up creek, bear on the bank,
Wild ducks over the mountains weaving
In a long south flight, the land of
Sea and fir tree with the pine-dry
Sage-flat country to the east.
Han Shan could have lived here,
            & no scissorbill stooge of the
            Emperor would have come trying to steal
            his last poor shred of sense.

On the wooded coast, eating oysters
Looking off toward China and Japan
"If you're gonna work these woods
Don't want nothing
That can't be left out in the rain—"

13.

T 36N R   16E   S 25
Is burning. Far to the west.
A north creek side,
              flame to the crowns
Sweeping a hillside bare—
              in another district,
On a different drainage.

Smoke higher than clouds
Turning the late sun red.

Cumulus, blowing north
              high cirrus
Drifting east,

              smoke
Filling the west.

The crews have departed,
And I am not concerned.

14.

The groves are down
                    cut down
Groves of Ahab, of Cybele
Pine trees, knobbed twigs
        thick cone and seed
        Cybeles tree this, sacred in groves
Pine of Seami, cedar of Haida
Cut down by the prophets of Israel
        the fairies of Athens

the thugs of Rome
          both ancient and modern;
Cut down to make room for the suburbs
Bulldozed by Luther and Weyerhaeuser
Crosscut and chainsaw
     squareheads and finns
     high-lead and cat-skidding
Trees down
Creeks choked, trout killed, roads.

Sawmill temples of Jehovah.
Squat black burners 100 feet high
Sending the smoke of our burnt
Live sap and leaf
To his eager nose.

                    15.

Lodgepole
          cone/seed waits for fire
And then thin forests of silver-gray.
               in the void
               a pine cone falls
Pursued by squirrels
What mad pursuit! What struggle to escape!

Her body a seedpod
Open to the wind
"A seed pod void of seed
We had no meeting together"
               so you and I must wait
Until the next blaze
Of the world, the universe,

Millions of worlds, burning
   —oh let it lie.

Shiva at the end of the kalpa:
Rock-fat, hill-flesh, gone in a whiff.
Men who hire men to cut groves
Kill snakes, build cities, pave fields,
Believe in god, but can't
Believe their own senses
Let alone Gautama. Let them lie.

Pine sleeps, cedar splits straight
Flowers crack the pavement.
   Pa-ta Shan-jen
(A painter who watched Ming fall)
   lived in a tree:
"The brush
May paint the mountains and streams
Though the territory is lost."

REGARDING "SMOKEY THE BEAR SUTRA"

It's hard not to have a certain amount of devotional feeling for the Large Brown Ones, even if you don't know much about them. I met the Old Man in the Fur Coat a few times in the North Cascades, and once in the central Sierra, and was suitably impressed. There are many stories told about humans marrying the Great Ones. I brought much of that lore together in my poem, "This Poem is for Bear," which is part of Myths and Texts. The Circumpolar B—r cult, we are told, is the surviving religious complex (stretching from Lapland to Utah via Siberia) of what may be the oldest religion on earth. Evidence in certain Austrian caves indicates that Neanderthal ancestors were practicing a devotional ritual to the Big Fellow about 70,000 years ago. In the light of meditation once, it came to me that the Old One was no other than the being described in Buddhist texts as having taught in the far distant past, the one called "The Ancient Buddha."

So I began to see, not without some pleasure, the USFS "Smokey the Bear" project as the devilishly clever re-surfacing of our ancient benefactor as Guide and Teacher in the twentieth century, the government not even knowing it.

During my years in Japan I had kept an eye out for his traces in folk religion and within Buddhism, and it came to me that the patron of the Mountain Yogins, the Yamabushi, namely Fudo Myoō, the "Immovable Wisdom King," was one of those traces. I cannot provide an academic proof for this assertion—it's an intuition based on Fudo's most common habitat—mountains. Fudo statues (a wickedly squinting fellow with one fang down and one fang up, a braid hanging down one side of the head, a funny kind of gleam, wreathed in rags, holding a vajra sword and a lariat, standing on rough rock and surrounded by flames) are found by waterfalls and deep in the wildest mountains of Japan. He lurks in caves. Like the Ainu Kamui,

Kimun, Lord of the Inner Mountains (Ursus Arctos Deus), he has the surpassing power, the capacity, to quell all other lesser violence, he is an aspect of Avalokitesvara the Bodhisattva of Compassion, and consort (and other self, animus) of the beautiful lady Tara, She Who Saves. This is the kind of compassion that is needed to quell the fires of greed and war, the countless scary campfires lit by dumb-assed military boy scouts who are burning their wienies at this very moment, all over the globe, and at any time any one of them could escape and turn into planetary holocaust. It takes Fudo/Smokey to deal with that.

So with those thoughts in mind for several years, on my return in February of '69, noting the announcement of the Sierra Club Wilderness conference at some San Francisco downtown hotel the next day, I was seized by the power of the chance and sat down and the Sutra composed itself. Those who notice such things will note that it follows the structure of a Mahayana Buddhist Sutra fairly faithfully, and that the power mantra of the Great Brown One is the mantra of Achala, or Fudo, the Immovable, also known as Chandama-haroshana, Lord of Heat.

We got it printed that night. At opening time the next day I stood in the lobby in my old campaign hat and handed the sheets out, say-ing "Smokey the Bear Literature, Sir," BLM and Forest Service offi-cials accepting them. The geologist Robert Curry and I met that way that morning. And the Underground News Service then took it up; it was never copyrighted; it went first to the Berkeley Barb and then all over the country. It has a life of its own now, as intended.

G. S.

SMOKEY THE BEAR SUTRA

Once in the Jurassic, about 150 million years ago,
the Great Sun Buddha in this corner of the Infinite
Void gave a great Discourse to all the assembled elements
and energies: to the standing beings, the walking beings,
the flying beings, and the sitting beings—even grasses,
to the number of thirteen billion, each one born from a
seed, were assembled there: a Discourse concerning
Enlightenment on the planet Earth.

"In some future time, there will be a continent called
America. It will have great centers of power called
such as Pyramid Lake, Walden Pond, Mt. Rainier, Big Sur,
Everglades, and so forth; and powerful nerves and channels
such as Columbia River, Mississippi River, and Grand Canyon.
The human race in that era will get into troubles all over
its head, and practically wreck everything in spite of
its own strong intelligent Buddha-nature.

"The twisting strata of the great mountains and the pulsings
of great volcanoes are my love burning deep in the earth.
My obstinate compassion is schist and basalt and
granite, to be mountains, to bring down the rain. In that
future American Era I shall enter a new form: to cure
the world of loveless knowledge that seeks with blind hunger;
and mindless rage eating food that will not fill it."

And he showed himself in his true form of

SMOKEY THE BEAR.

A handsome smokey-colored brown bear standing on his
hind legs, showing that he is aroused and watchful.

Bearing in his right paw the Shovel that digs to the
truth beneath appearances; cuts the roots of useless attach-
ments, and flings damp sand on the fires of greed and war;

His left paw in the Mudra of Comradely Display—indicating that
all creatures have the full right to live to their limits
and that deer, rabbits, chipmunks, snakes, dandelions,
and lizards all grow in the realm of the Dharma;

Wearing the blue work overalls symbolic of slaves and
laborers, the countless men oppressed by a civilization
that claims to save but only destroys;

Wearing the broad-brimmed hat of the West, symbolic of
the forces that guard the Wilderness, which is the Natural
State of the Dharma and the True Path of man on earth;
all true paths lead through mountains—

With a halo of smoke and flame behind, the forest fires
of the kali-yuga, fires caused by the stupidity of those
who think things can be gained and lost whereas in truth all
is contained vast and free in the Blue Sky and Green Earth
of One Mind;

Round-bellied to show his kind nature and that the great
earth has food enough for everyone who loves her and trusts her;

Trampling underfoot wasteful freeways and needless
suburbs; smashing the worms of capitalism and totalitarianism;
    Indicating the Task: his followers, becoming free of cars,
houses, canned food, universities, and shoes, master the
Three Mysteries of their own Body, Speech, and Mind; and
fearlessly chop down the rotten trees and prune out the
sick limbs of this country America and then burn the leftover
trash.

Wrathful but Calm, Austere but Comic, Smokey the Bear will
Illuminate those who would help him; but for those who would
hinder or slander him,

            HE WILL PUT THEM OUT.

Thus his great Mantra:
        Namah samanta vajranam chanda maharoshana
        Sphataya hum traka ham mam

   "I DEDICATE MYSELF TO THE UNIVERSAL
DIAMOND BE THIS RAGING FURY DESTROYED"

And he will protect those who love woods and rivers, Gods and
animals, hoboes and madmen, prisoners and sick people, musicians,
playful women, and hopeful children;

And if anyone is threatened by advertising, air pollution,
or the police, they should chant SMOKEY THE BEAR'S
              WAR SPELL:

DROWN THEIR BUTTS
CRUSH THEIR BUTTS
DROWN THEIR BUTTS
CRUSH THEIR BUTTS

And SMOKEY THE BEAR will surely appear to put the enemy
out with his vajra-shovel.
Now those who recite this Sutra and then try to put it in
    practice will accumulate merit as countless as the sands
    of Arizona and Nevada,
Will help save the planet Earth from total oil slick,
Will enter the age of harmony of man and nature,
Will win the tender love and caresses of men, women, and
    beasts,
Will always have ripe blackberries to eat and a sunny spot
    under a pine tree to sit at,

AND IN THE END WILL WIN HIGHEST PERFECT
ENLIGHTENMENT.

Thus have we heard.

SOURDOUGH MOUNTAIN LOOKOUT

Philip Whalen

Tsung Ping (375-443): "Now I am old and infirm. I fear
I shall no more be able to roam among the beautiful
mountains. Clarifying my mind, I meditate on the
mountain trails and wander about only in dreams."
—in *The Spirit of the Brush*, tr. by Shio Sakanishi, p. 34

For Kenneth Rexroth

I always say I won't go back to the mountains
I am too old and fat there are bugs mean mules
And pancakes every morning of the world

Mr. Edward Wyman (63)
Steams along the trail ahead of us all
Moaning, "My poor feet ache, my back
Is tired and I've got a stiff prick"
Uprooting alder shots in the rain

Then I'm alone in a glass house on a ridge
Encircled by chiming mountains
With one sun roaring through the house all day
& the others crashing through the glass all night
Conscious even while sleeping

Morning fog in the southern gorge
Gleaming foam restoring the old sea-level

The lakes in two lights green soap and indigo
The high cirque-lake black half-open eye

Ptarmigan hunt for bugs in the snow
Bear peers through the wall at noon
Deer crowd up to see the lamp
A mouse nearly drowns in the honey
I see my bootprints mingle with deer-foot
Bear-paw mule-shoe in the dusty path to the privy

Much later I write down:
    "raging. Viking sunrise
    The gorgeous death of summer in the east"
(Influence of a Byronic landscape—
Bent pages exhibiting depravity of style.)

Outside the lookout I lay nude on the granite
Mountain hot September sun but inside my head
Calm dark night with all the other stars

HERACLITUS: "The waking have one common world
But the sleeping turn aside
Each into a world of his own."

I keep telling myself what I really like
Are music, books, certain land and sea-scapes
The way the light falls across them, diffusion of
Light through agate, light itself . . . I suppose
I'm still afraid of the dark

      "Remember smart-guy there's something
      Bigger something smarter than you."

Ireland's fear of unknown holies drives
My father's voice (a country neither he
Nor his great-grandfather ever saw)

A sparkly tomb a plated grave
A holy thumb beneath a wave

Everything else they hauled across the Atlantic
Scattered and lost in the buffalo plains
Among the trees and mountains

From Duns Scotus to this page
A thousand years

(" . . . a dog walking on his hind legs—
not that he does it well but that he
does it at all.")

Virtually a blank except for the hypothesis
That there is more to a man
Than the contents of his jock-strap

EMPEDOCLES: "At one time all the limbs
Which are the body's portion are brought together
By love in blooming life's high season; at another
Severed by cruel Strife, they wander each alone
By the breakers of life's sea."

Fire and pressure from the sun bear down
Bear down centipede shadow of palm-frond
A limestone lithograph—oysters and clams of stone
Half a black rock bomb displaying brilliant crystals

127

Fire and pressure of Love and Strife bear down
Brontosaurus, look away

My sweat runs down the rock

HERACLITUS: "The transformations of fire
are, first of all, sea; and half of the sea
is earth, half whirlwind. . . .
It scatters and it gathers: it advances
and retires."

I move out of a sweaty pool
          (The sea!)
And sit up higher on the rock

Is anything burning?

The sun itself! Dying

Pooping out, exhausted
Having produced brontosaurus, Heraclitus
This rock, me,
To no purpose
I tell you anyway (as a kind of loving) . . .
Flies & other insects come from miles around
To listen
I also address the rock, the heather,
The alpine fir

BUDDHA: "All the constituents of being are
Transitory: Work out your salvation with diligence."

(And everything, as one eminent disciple of that master
Pointed out, has been tediously complex ever since.)

There was a bird
Lived in an egg
And by ingenious chemistry
Wrought molecules of albumen
To beak and eye
Gizzard and craw
Feather and claw

My grandmother said:
"Look at them poor bed-
raggle pigeons!"

And the sign on McAlister Street:

"IF YOU CAN'T COME IN
SMILE AS YOU GO BY
L♥VE
THE BUTCHER

I destroy myself, the universe (an egg)
And time—to get an answer:
There are a smile, a sleeper and a dancer

We repeat our conversation in the glittering dark
Floating beside the sleeper.
The child remarks, "You knew it all the time."
I: "I keep forgetting that the smiler is
Sleeping; the sleeper, dancing."

From Sauk Lookout two years before
Some of the view was down the Skagit
To Puget Sound: From above the lower ranges,
Deep in forest—lighthouses on clear nights.

This year's rock is a spur from the main range
Cuts the valley in two and is broken
By the river; Ross Dam repairs the break,
Makes trolley buses run
Through the streets of dim Seattle far away.

I'm surrounded by mountains her
A circle of 108 beads, originally seeds
     of *ficus religiosa*
       Bo-Tree
A circle continuous, one odd bead
Larger than the rest and bearing
A tassel (hair-tuft) (the man who sat
        under the tree)
    In the center of the circle,
     A void, an empty figure containing
     All that's multiplied;
     Each bead a repetition, a world
     Of ignorance and sleep.

    Today is the day the goose gets cooked
    Day of liberation for the crumbling flower
    Knobcone pinecone in the flames
    Brandy in the sun

Which, as I said, will disappear
Anyway it'll be invisible soon
Exchanging places with stars now in my head
To be growing rice in China through the night.

Majestic storms across the solar plains
Make Aurora Borealis shimmy bright
Beyond the mountains to the north.

Closing the lookout in the morning
Thick ice on the shutters
Coyote almost whistling on a nearby ridge
The mountain is THERE (between two lakes)
I brought back a piece of its rock
Heavy dark-honey color
With a seam of crystal, some of quartz
Stained by its matrix
Practically indestructible
A shift from opacity to brilliance
(The Zenbos say, "Lightning-flash & flint-spark")
Like the mountains where it was made

What we see of the world is the mind's
Invention and the mind
Though stained by it, becoming
rivers, sun, mule-dung, flies—
Can shift instantly
A dirty bird in a square time

Gone
Gone
REALLY gone
Into the cool
O MAMA!

Like they say, "Four times up,
Three times down." I'm still on the mountain.

Sourdough Mountain 15:viii:55
Berkeley 27—28:viii:56

Note: The quotes of Empedocles and Heraclitus are from John Burnet's Early Greek Philosophy, Meridian Books, New York.

Cougar Dam

Howard Horowitz

The rhythms
that shape this land
proceed with little regard
for human considerations—
    angle of the sun, nine months of rain
    the piling up and melting off
    of mountain snowpacks,
    the growth cycles of alder and fir.
Our efforts to control them
leave monumental scars—
Cougar Dam
to drown the South Fork,
poison in the hills,
another road carved into the mountainside.

The storms that visit every winter
no longer cause floods
but the exceptional storm
still leaves its mark—
    gravel bars swept clean of alder
    banks caved in, logs
    jammed up against trees,
    bridges washed out.

The personal storms
that visit every winter
pass unnoticed
but the major shocks

(they strike as suddenly
as lightning strikes old snags up on Deathball)
    —Patty unable to get out
    of her burning house
    —little Aly fallen in
    and carried away by the river
    —Lane crushed under his log truck
are felt like a jolt in Blue River
putting creases, worry lines
on the faces of storekeepers
and drinkers in the tavern
    like ripple marks
    left in the reservoir
    after drawdown, to remain for a season
    before fading in the rains and mist.
At the Cougar Room
too much to drink
rain beats on the pavement
Jim don't try to make it home . . .

My reservoir of love
—so deep and blue this summer—
is once again drained
to a sea of stumps and mud.

THE BLUE RIVER HIGHWAY

Love
makes impossible demands.
Love for the river
     and the giant trees
has made crusaders of us.

It's just that highways
chainsaws & paychecks
may be stronger than lovers:

     jobs
     are scarce here;
     you can't eat
     trees.

Blind in our passion
crusaders and lovers,
have been sold down the river
time and again

     (or since rivers
     were first sold).

The clouds over the river
seem darker than usual.
It's just a storm
coming in from the west,
     but the wringer

is on: that squeeze
of people against land.

After the announcement,
you and I head for the meeting
at Blue River:
      we open the car
      in a driving rain.

FINNEGAN'S FIR

(dedicated to another, the Clatsop Fir,
flattened by storm on Columbus Day 1962;
now just a hole with root hairs of memory . . .)

1.

One hundred years
of mowing down old growth,
transforming the coast range
into a tree farm,
could be counted
on the edge of its rings:

  a giant
  tucked away in a canyon
  about fifty miles from Remote.

This is logging country:
square mile checkerboards
cut out of the forest.
Gravel roads dead end at landings
or stop abruptly at washouts.
One view is another view
from the Eel north to the Skagit
and all the way up the coast
to Alaska:

  below, broken logs and duff
    drop off a thousand feet;
  above, a snag appears, then is gone
    in a rain-whipped patch of fog;

beyond, a ragged slope, edges of trees,
a gale-swept sea of ridges.

2.

The great fir was overlooked
in the crosscut-and-springboard days,
though a scar on the butt
shows a rock slammed down
when Old Dan Melton Road was built.

In 1974 BLM forester Lance Finnegan
"discovered," measured, and gave the tree
his name. Declared official champion
Douglas-fir, like old Clatsop before the blow,
a 25-acre patch was set aside
from logging.

(Perhaps shock waves
vibrated to the heart
of the crusty old king.
Cyclonic currents
began to stir over Asia ...)

weeks later a storm howled in
with 140-mile gusts.
Ten thousand trees blew down,
And one was Finnegan's Fir.

The crown was shattered,
but the great trunk
spans the canyon—

a bridge
into silence.

3.

We gather boughs
for tea—a delicate infusion
of needles in water,
a ceremonial sip.
    Molecules of the great fir
    reach to our feet
    as we drink up substance
    from below the horizon;
may we absorb a little
of the weathered earth,
the 800 years
of sun and snow.

Only the sky does not change:
    rain comes in fits;
    green limbs drip, and drop
    clumps of Lung Lobaria
    to the forest floor.

At night, hanging from fallen branches
above the ravine,
    the Old Man's Beard
    bathes in fog, combed
    by shafts of moonlight.

TRYING TO REFOREST A CUT-OVER HEART

This heart
is like a hundred others:
rocky & steep,
gullies washed out by erosion
veins choked with debris
    from old loggers,
      old lovers.
The view from the landing
is a full-color map of hell.

Don't be too trusting on the way down:
the old log may give underfoot.
Watch out for boomer holes, bouncing rocks,
hornets. Should you stop to loosen
that heavy bag cinched around your waist,
be ready to run if a limb cracks overhead.
The brush can overtake you,
rise in your throat,
enclose like a ribcage.
    Look up—hard to see!
      climb out—hard to move!
    The thorns cut and sting
but oh! those sweet little berries!

Down at the bottom
is a place even hunters avoid
where deer trails go nowhere
from nowhere, and you won't know
which way you are going. In these thickets
your best bet is to follow the moon.

In some places the land sinks
beneath the vastness of its own weight:
the Great Wall is visited by fishes.

We never know what to expect on this job:
downpours, windows of sunlight,
shafts of darkness, onrushing logs
caves etched by years of corrosion
a land of green stones . . .
In the middle of these worked-out spoils,
in the shade of an old stump
    look!
    A plantable spot!

Climbing back out is the hardest part:
a ledge in the crag to hold onto,
overhanging limbs to pull oneself up with.
I have to rest awhile
as my heart pounds in my chest
  and the tongues of silence
    gather in my throat

POEM FOR A FORESTER

Ru Kirk

See how the alder
bring to the full sun
leaves gray and green
to dance supple
in this healing wind.
Leaves brighter
than a thousand
thousand dreams of salmon
flashing toward home;
leaves brighter
than the last patch of ice
on the mountain
whose name sounds like
constant
but isn't/is something else
is something forgotten.

See how the alder
speaks the one
word of the earth
gray and green
the last rhyming
of transformation
gray and green
the alchemist's cloak
flashing

toward union/reunion
gray and green
whose voice is constant/is nothing else
is something forgotten.

Invited to the wedding feast
we murder the messenger
burn the vineyard
and sow the land with
something worse than salt.

Life's minute and eternal
messages spoken backwards
inverted
turn dark.

Night, Sourdough Mountain Lookout

Tim McNulty

A late-summer sun
threads the needles of McMillan Spires
and disappears in a reef of coral cloud.

Winds roil the mountain trees,
batter the shutter props.

I light a candle with the coming dark.
Its reflection in the window glass
flickers over mountains and
shadowed valleys
seventeen miles north to Canada.

Not another light.

The lookout is a dim star
anchored to a rib of the planet
like a skiff to a shoal
in a wheeling sea of stars.

Night sky at full flood.

Wildly awake.

HUB OF THE WHEEL

Fingers of smoke from wildfires
reach down Big Beaver and Pierce Creek valleys
and cover the deep blue of Ross Lake
like a quilt.

The drift mingles with other smokestreams
from Ruby and Thunder creeks,
where mountains, too,
have been touched by the sky.

Smoke clouds curl around Sourdough Mountain,
where I sit in the clear blue center
of this gesture: *mudra*
  of the mountain Buddhas.

Waft of incense from a world renewed,
             forests / meadows
    rained into soil.
The teachings come round again.

BREATH

Into the clear morning air, the radio
crackles with a med-evac call.
Sheriff's deputy from a small town
in the valley:
Street address. Time of report.
An "individual" overdosed on sleeping pills,
"still breathing."
Later, "a female, 21 years old."
She's rushed to the E.R. in Sedro Woolley.

Morning sunlight on the cliffs
and snow-blue glaciers of Colonial Peak.

Timeless beauty and human grief—
between these poles
the world's suffering wakes anew
with each striking sunrise.

THE QUEETS

We worked through dinner
on windfall spruce above Pelton Creek,
a tree thick as we were tall.
Wedging our cuts, edging peevee & shim,
wheel after slow turning wheel
to near dark.
Smoothed out the trail tread,
packed our tools and started back
seven miles downriver to camp.

Past Bob Creek the last light
was loosening itself from the grass,
falling from the moss shoulders
of maple and alder.
A doe and her yearling browsed
the far riverbank, and somewhere nearby
a flicker tapped randomly.
The river
carried with it its own light
and coursed slowly through the late summer bottom.

The tools lay in a pile
where I'd dropped them at the trailside;
my partner hadn't yet caught up.
All I knew
at the worn and frazzled end of that long day
was the last light slipping from us,
the chill air
troughing down dark timbered slopes,
and the lucent voice of the river
telling me it no longer mattered.

THE RIDE HOME

for Jay Sisson

Summer leans its borrowed leaves
toward Solstice—a year now
since the morning you left
to finish yarding a cut over on Cabin Creek
and didn't come back.

A month's overcast has just lifted
and the high meadows are opening again.
Creeks all noisy and ice-green in sunlight,
goldenrod and thistle in the uncut hay:
the time of year you'd lead the Clydesdales
from Leland Valley, up past the cabin
and down to fresh pasture on the other side.

I still see the great hoofprints at the crossings,
their small wells filled with night,
and an old shirt you left on a peg by the door
hung there most of a year.

Too many things
we don't let go to each other
washing down the taste of exhaust and sawdust
Quilcene paydays after work. Jay,
you were too young and quick-footed
to have to pay so dearly for the ways
of this mean and greedy land.

Rain to willowbloom, ashes to grass;
but yours is the always joy
of having the old truck running good
and filled with a load of freshly-poached cedar,
and a bottle of Jim Beam for the long ride home
by dark.

COYOTE AT THE MOVIES

We've all seen it before—Weyerhaeuser, Georgia Pacific, Simpson Timber, Crown Z.—the same forestry promo film, rundown of the industry from forest tree to suburb box; but when Coyote got hold of the lost film can and took a look at the end of the reel, *he* knew immediately how to run it, and invited all his friends.

So—the finished tract houses and tormented lawns and shrubs, that so upset and displaced all the animals there, became the beginning.

"Here we are," said Coyote, and all agreed.

But suddenly there appeared a whole crew of human workers who carefully and quickly began taking the houses down—shingle by board by window by door, and loading the pieces into large flat trucks. In a flash the trucks had delivered the lumber to a great lodge Coyote told them was the Lodge of Many Healing Wheels, told them he'd been there himself, at night, and seen it all. Inside, the great wheels, with teeth sharper than Beaver's, spin all the boards back into logs again. No one had ever seen anything like this. (Even Coyote was taken aback at the sight.) And in awe they watched the logs be carried by huge machines larger than elephants and loaded onto long trucks which—driving backward so the trees could steer them to exactly where they wanted to be—carried them through many small towns far into the mountains on special roads built just for them. It was such a wonderful sight even the old man himself had to smile. All those old trees going back home.

Once there, there were huge towers as high as a Douglas fir, which carefully lowered the logs down to just their precise spots on the hillside. The squirrels were beside themselves! But who are these blue-shirted workmen who wait in the brush? Coyote says they are shaman who possess magic wands of smoke. And if everyone watched closely, they would see them placing all the limbs and branches back onto

151

the broken trees. Amazing! They were even joining and healing the cut trunks back together! Everyone agreed these must be powerful priests (and marveled at the special herbs they kept in small tins in their pockets, and kept adding to endlessly from behind their lips).

"They all work for me," Coyote said, but no one was listening. Instead they were watching the shaman wave their wands over the stumps and the trees would leap into the air amid great clouds of needles and dust and noise—everyone ducked, and when they looked again, the trees sat majestically back on their stumps unscratched!

Now there were such great cheers from the crowd that Rabbit had to place his forepaws into his ears, and Mole hurriedly dug his way underground. Coyote, he decided right then and there that was just the way he was going to work things. And that he was going to start the very next day, "even if it takes awhile," he thought out loud, "yes, even if it takes a good long time."

THE WHITE LINE

Greg Nagle

Timber stand exams are God's gift to aging treeplanters. I turned to them after planting for many years. They involve walking over stands of timber and noting various characteristics such as height, growth, species and disease. This story takes place in Montana at the edge of a million-acre wilderness area. Often we'll be miles from the nearest road. It's a good feeling to be out there although it's also depressing to realize that we're little more than the first scouts for the eventual logging of an area. From the data we collect, preliminary logging plans are drawn up.

As you walk you hang plastic ribbon along your route of travel. Usually you'll know where your partners are working so you can find them. But there're times when the details get lost in the morning rush. This story comes from these times I've sat in the evening waiting for my partner's return. –G.N.

It was fall and getting late in the year. You never knew from day to day what the weather would bring. The Forest Service kept saying we didn't have more than a few days before snow-out but we'd been going like this for almost two weeks. Some days it would be raining, that kind of mean, cold rain that almost falls as snow. Those days we usually stayed inside. After working together three months we'd already said all we could and on those long, wet days we usually sat by the stove. We'd been friends a long time but everything gets old after a while.

The work involved measuring forest conditions. Every 600 feet on a grid spread across the face of the mountains we'd measure and note the health of six trees. Wherever the compass pointed, that's where you went—up and down hill, into deep canyons, across high exposed ridges. Sometimes we'd come to cliffs and have to work our way around them and somehow get back on the same compass bearing. In gentle terrain it wasn't so bad, but this was some of the roughest country I'd ever worked. It was dangerous and we were pushing ourselves too hard at the end of a long season.

The Forest Service came behind us and checked the measurements on a random 10% sample of our work. Although we worked separately, our plots were averaged together and we were paid based on the results of that inspection. It was usually a breeze but a few mistakes that took less than a minute to make could cost hundreds of dollars. We were tired enough as it was and getting sloppy and fast. The Forest Service put up with it for a while and then they clamped down.

We came back to the cabin one night and read the note they left with the latest inspection results. We were down $400, almost a week's wages for each of us.

"Damn," he said. I could see him grimace in the half light of the kerosene lantern.

"Who in the hell do they think they are? I'd like to see them humping it week after week up those goddamn hills. Hell!"

He threw his vest against the wall and slumped down in a chair. He sat there a moment and then kicked the wood stove, the echo reverberating off the narrow walls.

I was mad, too. We both had our problems but this time the mistakes were his.

"Whose plots were they?" I said, knowing damn well whose they were.

"I don't want to talk about it."

I didn't say anything and made a show of looking over the inspection sheet.

A hard, cold silence settled over us.

"Lemme see that," he said and grabbed the paper out of my hand. I bit my lips to keep from smiling.

He looked at it a long time and then he leaned over and lifting the lid of the stove dropped the paper into the fire.

"Hey, that's our only copy." I grabbed the lid. He pushed my hand away, happy now to have it out with me.

"So, big deal. You know what it says, I know what it says. So big deal."

"Big deal hell, they were your plots."

"Oh yeah? Well, what about two weeks ago with your plots up North Derby?"

"Those plots passed."

"Passed, hell. They gave you those plots. So they didn't give me these. They came down on me but they're no worse than yours." He grabbed me by my shirt and pushed me back against the wall.

I wasn't one to indulge in violence and besides, he was bigger than me so I decided to let it slide. I sat down on the far side of the room and began shaving wood for kindling. I figured that if I sat quiet it would all pass, but it had already gone too far for him.

"I'm sick of this. I don't want you getting down on me. The only way we can finish this is to work separate items. I'm going up to Gold Hill tomorrow and get those plots by the road. I'm sorry about my plots but working with you is too much of a hassle. Next inspection we won't have to deal with whose fault it is."

I'd thought of that. We could always have split up but in the weeks before, our company hadn't been quite so old. Gold Hill was eight miles as the crow flies but 35 by road. It was up at the head of a long ridge that dropped sharply down on both sides into steep, rugged canyons, and it was 2,000 feet higher than where we were. Going there this late in the year was just plain stupid. So I said, "Look, I'm sorry I gave you trouble about the plots. You're right, mine haven't been much better."

He didn't say anything for a while and just sat slouched by the stove staring at his feet. Finally he looked up. "Yeah, no big deal. I'm sorry, too, but I just want to work alone for a while."

"Listen, we'll work it out. It could snow any day now. What if you get snowed in up there?"

"No way, I'll come down if the weather gets bad. There's no way I want to sit up there in the snow."

"But what if you get hurt?"

"Hurt, bullshit, I've been in the woods alone for years. I walked all the way from Livingston to Dubois once, and no one knew where I was for seven weeks."

I'd heard that one before. It was a point of pride with him. "Yeah, but you said yourself that you always stayed on the trails in case you did get hurt."

"Look, I'm not worried, I can handle it," and he got up and started rummaging through the food boxes, dividing up the food and stacking his in the corner.

The next morning he left. We parted on good terms but I had to admit I liked having him gone. I enjoyed the solitude of the cabin and my time alone by the stove. I thought of him up there on Gold Hill crouched by a fire or rolled up in his sleeping bag, the only two ways to stay warm. If he wanted it that way it was his business. I'd let him be.

The weather held another five days. Then it began to snow, not heavily at this elevation, but I figured up where he was it must be getting pretty grim. Next day the snow tapered off and the sun came out, and I expected him down any time.

On the seventh day I came home from work in a steady snow that began at noon. I felt sure he would be there, but the cabin was cold and empty when I returned in the waning light.

I started up a fire and sat down to wait, expecting any time to hear the sound of his truck coming down the hill and his boots on the porch. But the hours dragged on. He might have gotten stuck in the snow on the way down. I'd have to head up there in the morning. There was nothing I could do tonight.

The next morning was cold and windy. The snow was more driven than falling. A hard Montana winter was finally setting in. I emptied the extra five-gallon gas can into the truck and headed up the hill. The road was covered with shallow, drifted snow. After a while I had to chain up and pushed on slowly. I was pissed at the hassle. Why hadn't he come down, and why did he have to go up there in the first place? His stupid truck was probably stuck somewhere, and I didn't want to get stuck with him. At each corner I expected to find him, but I drove three hours all the way to the head of the ridge before finding his truck parked by his empty camp.

The tent had drifted snow in it and the sleeping bag was damp and cold. Water was frozen solid in a pot on a small camp stove and there were no tracks anywhere, not even deep under the crusted new snow. He hadn't been there since before the first snow and he'd been out there for three days with no cover. He must have been hurt bad or he'd have made it back by now, unless he was dead. I felt a tingling up my spine and looked into the blowing snow that blotted out the sky.

"Oh Christ," I whispered, "oh, Jesus Christ."

When we were together we always had a general idea of where the other was on a certain day. All you had to do was find the point where he started from and follow his route, which was marked with pieces of white plastic ribbon. But it wasn't always so easy as that and it depended on knowing exactly where he started from.

In the days he had been up here he might have done 60 plots and started from any one of four or more places.

His maps and papers were thrown together in a sodden, half frozen pile in a corner of the tent. He always was disorganized. I began to go through them looking for the plot sheets of stands he'd already completed. I had to somehow figure out where he had gone the last

time he went out. But I couldn't. I ripped a number of the sheets trying to pull them apart. I needed time to dry them out, and the snow
was driving down harder now, blowing through the flapping door of
the tent and creeping in cold rivulets down my neck. I'd be no help
to him if I got snowed in up here, too. I had to move.

I got up and left camp, looking for any sign of his passing, or for
the telltale white ribbons that might point to his route. I found an old
trail off to the side that cut through the dense timber and dropped
rapidly into the canyon that flanked the ridge. I walked down about
a mile, slipping on the icy rocks buried under the snow. I wrenched
my ankle once but kept going, surmising that this would have to be
at least one of his routes if he entered the canyon. Halfway down I
stopped. I was cold and the wind cut through my clothes. I hadn't
come prepared for this, my ears ached and my sodden mittens felt
like ice on my fingers. I decided to turn back.

Climbing back out I saw one, a ribbon I had missed off to the side,
almost invisible in the snow. I rushed over to it and looked around
for another. I found one and waded off into the knee-deep snow in
that direction. I found two more, strung fifty yards apart, and finally
came to the flags that marked the center of a plot.

Running as hard as I could through the snow-covered boughs of
trees, I followed the flags where I could find them, finding two more
plots with a ring of white flags on the trunks to mark the trees he
had measured. I came to the end of that line of plots in the bottom
of the canyon.

Ahead the ground grew rockier and steeper and in the distance I
could just make out another flag line that ran down deeper into the
canyon. The flags fluttered in the breeze and were almost invisible
through the haze of falling snow. I looked over the surface of the
drifted snow that covered numerous mounds and protrusions but
there was no sign of him.

I called as loud as I could. There was no answer. I heard a low thump behind me and looked around, my heart pounding, but it was only a clump of new snow blown from a tree. The tingling in my spine started again and I felt the trees closing in around me, the dark canyon walls somewhere overhead. What it must have been like those days he lay out there in the deepening snow, the time drifting by, alone like he had always wanted to be in these mountains, and maybe waiting for me.

The snow was quickening, coming down hard and lashing in the cold wind at my face. I could barely see 100 feet ahead of me, and it was getting dark. I didn't have time; the road might already be too snowed in to make it back down. I called again into the wind, hearing the echo of my voice reverberate off rock walls that hung above me and disappeared into the dark blowing snow. I waited for an answer and only heard the rise and fall of wind in my ears.

I looked for my last time at the white flag fluttering in the wind on the edge of the darkening timber ahead and I knew I had to go back. It was 40 miles to town and I'd be lucky if I made it back tonight.

THE ANGOON WITCH

Leonard Davis

So that makes three stories. Slim Akers told me you got married same day you got out of Firlands. Living somewhere in Seattle. Pokey Tvieght said you went back to the bars of Ketchikan, and your demoniac laughter echoes along Creek Street like in the old days. Now Marvin Crummy says that's all bullshit. Says you never left Firlands at all. Just shriveled up and died. Marvin's no bullshitter.

The last time I saw you, you clung to the screen like a kitten in an animal shelter, huge black eyes begging, ninety-pound body trying to strain itself through the wire.

"Lornie, sneak me out. Other guys do it. I'll show you how."

"Can't Winnie. I'm flying out to Ketchikan in a couple of hours. I hired out for Sinclair's. I'll tell Slim I seen you."

Jeez, cold up here on Deadhorse in the morning. And fancy meeting Marvin here. I haven't seen him since I quit out at Cape Pole in '61, same night I ditched you and went off with Lola. Now here he is with the cutting crew, swinging his gear out the back doors of the bushellers' crummy.

"So ol' Winnie she's dead, uh Marv?

"That's what I heard, Lornie."

"What happened to the rest—Dale Petersen, Gordon Alexander and Tinears?"

"Tinears got busted up. Flipped his yarder over on hisself. I hear he runs a tavern down in Portland. Dale got killed on a cold deck out at Edna Bay. Big spruce rolled down and smashed him all to hell." Marvin sucks his cigarette and squints for another recollection.

"Gordon cut hisself out of a tree up by Sitka. Fell ninety feet and run a stob through his chest. Died on the plane, I guess."

"Jeez, I hate to hear that, Marv. Whole bunkhouse gone except you and me—and Slim. I seen him out at Twelve-Mile arm last fall. He said Winnie was married in Seattle."

"She ain't."

I think of Dale, blonde and beautiful, shoulders wide as a suitcase, drifting like a stag beside his tiny Tlingit woman in a soft evening on Koskiusko Island. And Gordon, gaunt and disheveled, his eyes peering bleak and humorous out from the savage jut of his brows and cheekbones. It was Gordon who gave me the name "Lornie." Couldn't seem to pronounce it without an "r." When I spoke of my fear of having gotten the clap from you, he consoled me. "You got to diddle something first, Lornie. You don't really get it from toilet seats."

I think of Tinears squat like a toad at the levers of the yarder. Known as a wild donkey puncher, his whipping haulback and flailing chokers had busted up many a brush ape. He put me in Ketchikan General for two weeks back in '62. His highball habits had developed back in the Depression when men were cheap. They piled the dead and injured behind the yarder, and took them out at night when the log train cleared the tracks. But he and Gordon were a team. When Gordon was in the tree, Tinears would ease the tons of rigging into place so gently they wouldn't crush a mosquito.

"So, Marv, what brings you down here?"

"They shut down the camps, Lornie. Almost no camps in southeastern Alaska anymore. All homeguards. A tramp logger can't make it up there without a camp."

Marvin swings his Homelite over his shoulder on the flat of its bar, stubs out his cigarette, and walks off up the ridge, bucker's tape swinging from his hip and hip pockets full of falling wedges bobbing with his stride. He enters the slash and shifts to an undulating sidestep motion—Marvin always reminded me of a rangy black bear—as he angles to the timberline a thousand yards off.

Me, I'm still a rigging slinger. My chokermen cluster around me like sheep about to be shoved into a dip tank. These cold wind-rainy days it's hard to get them over the bank and into the wet brush. One young chokerman who just got married still sleeps in the crummy. Says he feels cold and wet even in bed with his wife.

We talk a little over the beller of the yarder warming up on the landing. I say, "Jeez, fancy meeting Marvin out here." The chokermen just shrug. They're all homeboys never been off the North Olympic Peninsula. Names like Marvin Crummy and Pokey Tvieght and Gordon Alexander and Packsack Thompson don't mean anything to them. Names like Saginaw and Sheaffers and Long-Bell conjure up no sentimental hankerings for lost worlds. Neither of course do the Arctic Bar and Creek Street, Firlands TB Sanitarium and a Ketchikan kloochie called the Angoon Witch.

Toot-toot! The whistle on the yarder asks do we want the rigging back. Scanning the forty acres of fallen timber and logged-over slash below me, I see the whistle punk has reached the end of his signal wire and huddles in the shelter of a stump, the whistle bug cradled in his rain jacket. We've got radio whistles so the rigging slinger can punk whistles for himself, but they're on the fritz now. So we've gone back to a whistle punk, like the old days.

"Whoo-hoo!" I holler, and the whistle punk squeezes off my reply to the yarder. Toot-toot! Go ahead on the haulback. Below us a half mile of seven-eighths-inch steel cable snakes to life, snapping branches and whipping viciously as it straightens itself. Up ahead, the buttrigging awakens clanking, rises from a bed of slash and hangs between the haulback and mainline, shuddering a bit as the steel forgings work out their kinks. From the yarder the squeal of frictions and howl of the diesel tells us the engineer has eased the mainline brake and poured all his power to the haulback. The buttrigging gallops back toward where we knocked off Friday, now collapsing into the slash with a gnashing of steel, now rising from the wreckage with a flail of thirty-foot chokers.

"Whoo!" The rigging halts in mid-gallop and crashes to the ground. Fucking mainline brake's still wet. "Whoo!" The rigging rises from the brush as the engineer brakes the haulback and goes ahead on the mainline. "Whoo!" The engineer dogs both brakes and the chokers dangle above the logs buried in the wreck of trees they once were.

For a moment we stand at the edge of the road and look out over our world in the ravines below. "All right girls, over the edge. Get sleeping beauty out of the crummy. Ah, there he is. Bruce, you work real hard today and I'll come warm up your bed tonight. We got other holes to feel for now." Steel caulks crunch on the crushed rock as we scramble down the bank and onto the slash, bodies teetering on the angled logs, frantic for balance. "Dammit Hank, if you can't walk lay down and roll. Bruce, bonus them two hemlock pecker poles. You two get that big fir."

I'll slap the number three choker on a mid-sized hemlock.

"Whoo-hoo-hup!" Slack the haulback. Rigging crashes. "Told you guys to stay clear of that rigging. Can't find no hole? How you guys get children like that? Get down under there and feel. Work the kinks in the choker. If you can't poke it under, screw it under. Everybody clear? Bruce, you're standing on one of the logs you just choked. Stick around, your old lady's got business with the milkman. Whoo!" The buttrigging stirs and lunges, chokers tighten, yarder engine lugs into the load. I'm Captain Ahab on a hemlock stump of a quarter deck, the show surging around me in a symphony of whipping lines, smashing limbs and humping and grinding logs; the spar tree bucking in its guys, the yarder howling and growling as the load eases and burdens. That big fir lunging on the end of number two choker, that's Moby Dick. Three hundred yards through a gauntlet of stumps and he's mine. Ten thousand board feet of number one peeler safe on the landing.

"Ho! Hang up, you sonofabitch!" Jeez, solid against a cedar stump. "Who-hoo!" Skin 'er back. "Hup-ho! Tight line that bastard." That's my baby, let the choker pull the rigging to the low side of that stump. Now, "Whoo-hoo-hup-ho!" Slack the haulback and let the rigging drop to the low side. "Ho! Jeezus jeezus jeezus. Hare-brained donkey puncher, I wanted you to keep going ahead on the mainline. Now you draped the choker right over the stump!" The engineer can't hear me of course, but he knows somebody's cussing back here. Let's try that again. Slack the mainline and skin 'er back. That's it, let the log roll to the low side. Now, "Whoo-hoo-hup, hup-ho!" Slack the haulback and go ahead. "Whoo-hup!" Now tight line that bastard or it'll hang up again. There she goes, just like it had eyes.

Hallelujah! My world is in motion, the lines keening out from the spar in a tilted Andromeda of stumps and logs on the edge of being. If anyone seeks to know why a man serves the rigging, let him feel through his caulked boots the shudder of a mountain, let his nerves wed themselves to the shriek of lines though the shives, let his soul guide the paths of logs through stumps to the landing.

* * *

I remember when I was growing up on a stump ranch the other side of Port Angeles. We moved there in '49, bought the place from a family of itinerant cheap land developers named Schlichting who lived on the hill above us. On the lower side of the hill, down by the Milwaukee Railroad tracks, lived a tribe of Okies and Arkies—the MacFarlands and Turneys—who lived by horse logging the second growth for pulpwood. I don't know what the Schlichtings lived on, besides the very occasional sale of a twenty-acre patch of swamp and brush land. The grown boys were always cutting down old military six-by-sixes for logging machines, but I don't recall them doing any logging. The oldest son died in the war, swallowed a chicken bone in boot camp actually, and I think they ate on his government money.

Anyway, we kids, Elwin and Nora Lee Schlichting and too many little Okies to name, used to cut through the second-growth woods on our way home from Fairview School. Elwin, who was the oldest and had a knack for inventing mysterious games, would yell, "Watch for flying cables!" We young ones would drop to the ground and the older boys would duck off into the bushes with the McFarland girls.

Now, no flying cables had disturbed the squalid repose of that place since the Swedes came through in the '20s with their whipsaws and steam donkeys. But once having come, the spirit of the rigging hangs over a region like a living scythe. In a boy's imagination, those cables were bodiless arms from nowhere. A sudden hiss and they had you. I used to wonder how they got through all those trees. Now I know.

I think of Elwin, a homely runt with a hatchet face swiveling like a weathercock, keen for anything that could be put together to make anything. He was a Steller jay's alertness for value in all things aban-doned—buggy wheels, axle rods, bicycle parts. Neither he or Nora ever had anything new. And Nora Lee, an equally homely wisp of a girl, a high-pitched whooping and pantyless cartwheeling in the dusk beneath the circling nighthawks. What Elwin was to junk she was to us, a bird-eye appraisal of possibilities, an eye-flashing invitation to all sorts of trifling mysteries and naughtinesses.

* * *

Lunchtime, and the rigging hangs silently. My chokermen huddle around the whistlepunk's fire below a big stump. I stand atop the stump munching my horsedick sandwich and looking out across the waves of ridges going down to the Straits of Juan de Fuca. The marine wind tugs at my rain jacket, breathes on my face. On it comes the bawl of Marvin's power saw down from the ridge above us. On it comes the breath of the whole northeastern Pacific archipelago streaming off toward Asia. Rosenblad. Winifred Rosenblad. Buried somewhere beyond the Urals, there was a Caucasian ancestor, Slav or Teuton or Jew maybe, for the Angoon Witch. If he ever made it home from Alaska. Angoon, a Tlingit village on an island somewhere off Juneau. The Angoon Witch. Slim told me about you one night in a floating bunkhouse out in Rodman Bay, west of Ketchikan.

"Inbreeding, I guess. Some of them Injuns way out on the islands get inbred. Living on government money, they don't get around like in the old days. Almost her whole family was deaf mutes. Winnie, she wasn't deaf but she had to use sign language with her people. Came to Ketchikan, we all thought she was a witch, talking with her hands and eyes and all. Whole fucking body. "Ever notice that, Lornie, how she talked witch-like?"

"Yeah, Slim, I noticed that." Vast luminous eyes in the gloom of a Ketchikan bar, laughing, taunting eyes that spoke of fathomless mysteries about nothing but themselves. A high, tinny, insinuating voice ("You buy me a drink, Lornie?") that clustered around your frail body like a swarm of mosquitoes. Disembodied hands wove the space between our eyes into a web of forbidden communions with darkness. It was quite a performance. If ever a woman became the spirit of a place, you did. You became the lights and obscurities, the bottles and mirrors, the clink of glasses and rumble of taxis on the boards of Creek Street. There was nothing else, but it's not often a man can spend half the night humping the queen city of a region.

"So you actually snuck her out of Firlands, huh Slim?"

"Yeah, hell yes. Snuck her out and fucked her the same day you went to see her. I missed the plane, remember?" Probably bullshit, but I liked the idea of that spirit uncaged just one more night.

"You know, Slim, I never realized how intelligent that girl was until she got sent to Firlands and started writing me letters."

Slim scowled and sucked on his jug of V.O. "Fuck a bunch of fat intelligence." To him you were just a skinny body. The closer to the bone, the sweeter the meat. I couldn't even feel your body that first night. That's why you got out of bed after I sweated away for an hour or so and asked me for some money to buy hamburgers and went out to the all-night beanery and told all the other kloochies what a great lover I was. Eat your heart out, Lola. When you got back it took me another hour to finish up, and all I could feel was hamburger crumbs. Next morning early you walked me down to the float plane and asked me for money to buy breakfast. Hungriest girl I ever knew.

Even then the bug must have been sucking away at what there was of your body. About a year later I heard you had been sent to Firlands and went down to the clinic for a skin patch test. Then I wrote you a letter. You needed cigarette money so you wrote right back. Like you, your letters hinted and wheedled, but they had something articulately musical and dignified in them. There was finishing school primness in the way you spoke of your longing for Ketchikan and the good times with the boys, almost as if apologizing for deserting your post, and as if the calling of a barfly were of equal dignity with that of a teacher or nurse.

* * *

Toot, toot-a-toot-toot, toot-toot! The engineer blows the evening slack-off as the last turn of logs breaks over the rim of the landing and sags to the log deck. The chaser unhooks the chokers and the engineer gently guns the haulback drum to clear the rigging from the landing. He dogs his brakes and shuts down the engine. We file up to the landing, trudging the muddy trenches gouged by the logs. After ten hours of throb the silence seems unnatural, but with a hiss of air pressure bleeding off from the yarder, the landing settles into a peaceful repose.

Now the rigging hangs dormant in the belly of the lines, the mainline slack against the bole of the spar. One of my college-boy chokermen up on his Freud called it phallic, a macho symbol of the western he-man's rape of the wilderness, or some such pigshit. It's a shaft all right, one hundred feet from the log deck to the mainline lead block above the top guys. But the spar always seemed female to me, bridal in her regalia of lines and blocks, maternal in the spread of her guylines over the squalid landing.

In the old days, when the cutting crew got done, the spar was the only tree of any size left standing, right in the center of a forty-acre cut. Then came the topper with his belt and spurs, climbing axe and topping saw, limbed her all the way up to a twelve-inch taper, and cut the top out of her. That's how Gordon Alexander killed himself. You'd think a man been topping for thirty years would know better than yank the starting cord of his power saw with the blade laying across his climbing rope. But a man gets savagely suicidal, sweat running in his eyes, fighting the woods. Inseminate the bitch and die. I do things like that all the time.

Then would come the yarder, the itinerant scow of the wilderness, winching along on its mainline choked to a stump up ahead, scudding the hillocks and hummocks on its twin spruce sled, deck house lurching, deck piled with all the rusting junk that forms a high lead show—blocks, shackles, straps, chokers, butthooks, marlin spikes, railroad spikes, guy lines, haywire and gear dope. Not pretty, I guess, but she was the queen of the rigging crew, the rigging shop of our hearts.

Then would follow a nightmare of screaming and cursing and hauling on lines as the fabric of the show formed about the crown of the tree. The high rigger howled like a demon a hundred feet up, struggling to force, fit and coax the tons of plates, straps, shackles, guys and lead blocks into a hymeneal girdle for the tree. The ground crew gaped upward as a chaos of lines snaked and tautened to a web of intent.

These new logging machines aren't like that. The telescoping steel tower is hinged right to the yarder, which mounts on a rubber-tired carriage. Just drive it into the landing, drag out the guylines and choke some stumps on the compass points, pull the levers on the hydraulic valves, and the whole show pops up like a big umbrella. No need for high riggers anymore. No quivering nose for the hover of possibilities over the junk of a more heroic age.

We lean back against the tires of the yarder, crank our heads upward toward the lead blocks, yawn, and wait for the engineer to back the crummy into the landing. The march of clouds against the radiating guys makes the world wheel in the evening. My mind drifts back a year in time, and 750 miles to the north.

* * *

The wind sucked on the stovepipe, rain pelted the windows, and seawater slurked around the raft. Sinclair had the whole camp mounted on rafts and anchored in a bay of Prince of Wales Island. These little A-frame operations were usually that way. Just yard the timber straight off the slopes and into the water. Then hook the whole shitteroo to a tug and tow it to another bay. It beat building roads on the muskeg. Sprawled on his bunk, Slim sucked the V.O. I brought him from town and scowled at the label. He preferred Canadian Club. A gust of wind rocked the bunkhouse, and the woolen socks and long handles hanging over the stove jiggled in the draft.

"Yeah, hell yeah. The An-goon Witch." He liked the reverberations of that name. He swung up to a sitting position. His hatchet face brooded on the darkness between his knees where the bottle hung limp from his wrist. Slim's narrow, receding cranium was not given to profound reflections, but I could feel a rumination forming. That business about your letters set it off.

"You ever notice how the older women up here talk, in that phony baby-doll voice? Most of them came up as whores in the '20s and '30s when the big copper mines were running. Lot of them from Chicago and St. Paul, which is why they sound like babes in the old gangster movies, I guess. Some of the ones that stayed on after the mines went down are waitresses and receptionists now. You ever hear the radio dispatcher for the logger's association? Sexy voice, ain't she? Must be pushing sixty.

"The kloochies picked that up from them. Kloochies ain't whores, of course. They pick up cigarette money off kickbacks from the drinks the loggers and fishermen buy them. You order them a screwdriver and the barkeep gives 'em orange juice. Government takes care of the rest. If they get caught whoring the Feds ship them back to whatever village they run off from and tell the pilots not to bring them back. Kloochies don't give a shit about money, though, long as there is some. They just like being queens of the bars, and going home with whatever logger or fisherman strikes their fancy."

Slim scowled at this and looked over at me. "Lornie, how did you come to get tangled up with the Angoon Witch? Tight-ass bastard, you never spent enough money in them bars to draw flies. But all them kloochies talk like you was their kid away at medical school or something. Lola and Gladys, too. Winnie, all she talked about was you and them hamburgers in the Knickerbocker Hotel. I come close to slapping the shit out of her for that."

"Jeez, I don't know, Slim. It was my first night in Ketchikan. Maybe they just wanted to mother my tender young body, make a man out of me or something. Maybe it was Lola. She was with Cougar Martin, but you know Cougar, just sits in a corner and grins. I was dancing, wrestling actually, with Lola because Cougar wouldn't. I guess Winnie thought I was with Lola. You know how those kloochies compete with each other."

Slim picked right up on this with a story about how you caught him slipping the meat to Lola in a dark corner of the Frontier Bar. "Jumped her like a cougar squalling and scratching and yarding her by the hair. They went crashing over tables, booze flying everywhere, and down in the sawdust, pussies winking like horse clams. All the loggers egging 'em on and laying bets and me down on the floor trying to get 'em apart . . . ." Bullshit, Slim, but he was so grateful for the opening that I let him talk.

The stove muttered, the Coleman lantern flickered and hissed and the bunkhouse shuddered in the March wind. I stepped out the door to the edge of the raft and stood, bottle in one hand, peter in the other, watching the piss light up the phosphorus in the black water. I could see a faint glow on the ridges off toward Ketchikan to the east. Ketchikan without her Angoon Witch. When I came back Slim was brooding again.

"You know, Lornie, I tramped this whole fucking coast from Eureka to Afognak, and it's all the same. It presses down on a man—the ridges press in, the trees shut out the sun, the fog sucks all the heat out of you. It's like a cold fucking womb, you know? Tourists yammer about how beautiful it is, but all this scenery bears down on a man. I got to get out of this country, go back to North Carolina maybe, before I get busted up or killed, or wind up huddled in newspapers down on skid road. You know what I mean, Lornie?" he whined.

"I know, Slim."

* * *

The crummy whines and rattles toward the crest of the ridge, lugs in third and downshifts to second, pulling us out of the darkening hole where we serve the rigging. We top the ridge and hang for a moment before dropping into the valleys of the outer slope. Our eyes follow the abandoned railroad grade down to the slender sprawl of the coastal shelf and out across the straits to the pelts of the islands streaming softly off to the north, 700 miles to Ketchikan, and then curving off to the west almost to touch the other continent. Who really wrote them letters? I wonder.

CUTTINGS

John Daniel

1.

Sometimes the fallers would be working on a distant slope where we could see them, and when I wasn't wrestling a choker around a log I'd watch them drop the Douglas firs. As a tree toppled and then fell faster, its boughs would sweep back, the whole trunk would flex a little just before it hit the hillside, a flash of wood showing if it broke somewhere. Across the distance the sound came late, and small. The saws sounded like hornets.

The fallers worked in pairs, and they worked slowly. It's a dangerous job—the trees are big, the hills are steep. On any one day they never seemed to advance very far against the front of forest, but they worked slowly and steadily, and day by day they got the job one. They drove the back roads every morning, they laid the big trees down, they bucked them into standard lengths. All across Weyerhaeuser's Northwest empire, they turned the forest into pickup sticks.

2.

There are forests on the rainy side of the Cascade Range where the best way you can walk is on the trunks of fallen trees. Some of them are thicker through than you are tall. They make a random pathway through devil's club and thimbleberry, one to another and another, leading you nowhere except to more trunks with upthrust roots, more standing moss-coated stubs and skeletal snags, more bigleaf maples and western hemlocks and tall Douglas firs. The bark of the big trees is pocked and charred, and most of them lean, already beginning their eventual fall. The filtered light is clear and deep. The only sound you hear is the stepping of your feet among ferns and seedling trees that grow out of softening sapwood. And when you climb down from the pathway of trunks, your feet sink into a yielding matrix of moss and needles and rotting wood—trees becoming earth, earth becoming trees, the forest falling and gathering itself, rising from the abundance of its dying.

3.

Up on the landing the steel tower stands a hundred feet tall, a diesel yarder at its base with a reel of heavy cable. When we've set the chokers and scrammed out of the way, the rigging slinger sounds his whistle. The yarder roars, the chokers cinch, and two or three logs start stubbornly up the hill like things alive, plunging and rolling, snagging on stumps and lurching free, dragging and gouging the ground, then dangling in air as they approach the landing, where they're deftly dropped in a neat deck for the waiting trucks. Everything goes to the landing—butt-cuts ten feet through, mature saw logs, buckskin snags, measly pecker-poles, even half rotted slabs and splintered chunks. Nothing is wasted. The operation scours the hillside, as far as the cables can reach, and by the time we lower the tower and trundle along to a fresh show, only stumps and sticks and boughs are left, patches of sun-struck fern and sorrel, long raw furrows in the barren ground.

4.

Like the sea, like the streams full of salmon, the ancient forest gave plenty—totem poles, tool shafts, bows, fishing floats, baskets, dishes, robes, roots, tubers, medicine. A good red cedar might be felled by storm, or they'd bring a tree down themselves by burning into its base. They hollowed the trunk with adzes, heated water in the cavity with hot stones, stretched out the softened sides with posts, lashed stern and bow-spirit to the hull with cedar rope. For their houses they split cedar logs into wide boards, tapping horn or hardwood wedges with a hammerstone. And sometimes they split large planks from standing trees and let the trees live on. They still live on. Here and there in the silence of the rainy forest you can find them, you can stand inside those spaces that yielded good wood, where human hands selected a careful portion of what the trees could give.

5.

We started out from Bagby Hot Springs in Mount Hood National Forest. As I remember the trail, it climbed along a stream bed and topped out on a sunny ridge, then turned north along the far ridge flank, easy ups and downs through fir and hemlock, gray cliffs on the right. We walked a day like that, then camped in thicker woods where patches of old snow remained and small sounds stirred around our sleeping bags. In the morning after breakfast we walked on, following the trail toward no certain destination. We climbed for a while, still in trees, and then saw light ahead—a meadow, we thought, or a small lake. We walked into a glare of stumps and piled boughs, sap-smell heavy in the air. We worked around the far edge of the cut, trying to pick up the trail. We found the logging road, of course—dry and dusty white, unearthed boulders by its side—but we never found the trail. We sat on stumps a while and walked back the way we had come.

I was new to the Northwest then. I'd been hearing about multiple-use on the public lands, and now I knew what multiple-use was. I decided that even a college drop-out could find better things to do than set chokers for a living.

6.

The rain shadow east of the Cascades is the native home of the yellowbellies, ponderosa pines that can measure up to eight feet through and a hundred sixty feet tall. Where they've been left alone they tilt from the earth like great orange arrows, fletched with green, parceled out in a spacious array contrived by shallow soils and periodic sweeps of fire through the centuries. Logging here is usually called selective, like the fires, and sometimes that's exactly what it is. But clearcuts aren't too hard to find. The Forest Service has called them "group selections," and little blowdown patches sold for salvage have a way of expanding into sheared squares. The pine forest stands on gentle terrain. It's easy to get at. By the thirties many of the old yellowbelly groves were gone—clean-cut, in the usage of the day, the fat logs hauled out under ten-foot wheels. Now they're skidded out on chokers behind big Cats, and in most of ponderosa country, selective logging means that every thirty years or so the Cats drag out the biggest trees. It's called creaming, or high-grading, and it doesn't take everything. But the forest any kid sees is lesser than the one her father saw, diminishing toward little trees and big stumps, the ancient woods gradually brought down to human scale.

7.

Junipers are stubby trees full of branches, and they often have several trunks. In most of them the grain is twisted, a natural tendency accentuated by the big Great Basin winds. He had to walk many dry hills and search many canyons to find a straight-grained tree, or a tree with one straight-grained trunk inside a thicket of outer trunks. He carefully stripped a length of bark to inspect the wood. With chisel-stone and hammerstone he notched the top and bottom of the stave he wanted, about four feet long, two-and-a-half inches wide. He went away then, for a few years maybe, while the stave seasoned on the tree. When he came back, if it had seasoned well, without weather checking, he split it from the tree with a tool of stone or antler. He carved and steamed and worked the stave until it curved in a deep belly and recurved at the ends. He boiled horn for glue, and glued on sinew fibers for strength and spring. He glued on rattlesnake skin to protect the backing, fashioned a grip of wrapped buckskin. He strung the bow with a length of sinew.

One juniper, a huge tree with several great trunks and limbs, shows scars of twelve staves removed. A scar heals as the tree lays in new wood, straight-grained wood laid down where straight-grained wood was taken. One scar shows clear evidence of having yielded four staves in sequence. The harvest interval was probably longer than a human life. In a crotch of one of the tree's big limbs, a hammerstone remains where it was placed.

8.

Mount Adams, Mount Jefferson, Three Sisters, Diamond Peak—it doesn't matter which Cascade mountain you climb. From any of them you see a few singular volcanoes ranging away to north and south, studding an expanse of rolling green going blue in the distance. From most of the peaks you can see a lake, or several lakes. And always, more each year, on both flanks of the range and sometimes high up toward the crest, you can see the white squiggles of advancing roads and the bare geometric patches of sheared ground. From the highways you see mostly trees. From the summits you can see where all those trucks are coming from. And almost every acre in your view is public land, retained in the ownership of the American people, part of a national forest system established a hundred years ago to hold good woodlands in reserve against the aggressions of the timber barons.

Some of the cuts are greening up with a growth of genetically selected Douglas firs, which will yield a forest of identical clones, which will be cropped in sixty or eighty years and the clearcuts planted again, to raise another forest if they can. But many of the cuts are bare and brown, flecked with silver whiskers of culled wood. From this elevation they look neat and trim. Whenever I look down at them I search for a new metaphor. They aren't a quilt, not yet at least, but their clustered patchwork does suggest a farmer's fields. "Cascade crew cut" is a term you sometimes hear. Mange is the best I've been able to do, a mange spreading through the mountains. But mange is scraggly and uneven. These clearcut barrens are too regular, too geometrical and clean-sided. Whatever is making them is working surgically, with fine precision. Mange doesn't know what it's doing to the animal. What's working at these mountains knows exactly what it's doing.

9.

As my friend grows older he feels himself turning from a farmer to a forester. He walks his wooded hillside, which about the time that he was born was cleared and planted in crops. The topsoil ran away, the fields were left to scrub, and now he walks among the young trees that have reclaimed the hill. He names their kinds, delighting in their company. "Look at that oak there, isn't it pretty? That'll be an oak for a long time." He tells a story about a neighbor who swung his dog on one of the wild grape vines, a story that ends badly for the dog but brings laughter to the hillside decades later. Stories grow here like the trees. My friend comes to walk and talk sometimes, and other times to work. Low stumps are visible where he's thinned, the poles and logs hauled out behind his horses, seasoning now in neat piles below. In his mind he sees the cut wood forward to its good uses—fence posts, rafters, fuel for the winter—and the standing forest grows on in his mind, too. "If I cut that sassafras," he says, "the little oak might grow." He opens such small spaces for the sun, opens and raises his hillside forest toward the beauty of the big hardwoods that once stood here, sunlight playing in their broad leaves, their roots grown deep in the rich soil of their making.

10.

"No, it ain't pretty," a man said to me once, "but it's the only way to harvest these trees. It don't pay to go in there just for a few." We were standing in the rainy morning outside the Weyerhaeuser time shack. His tin hat battered by years in the woods, a lunch pail and steel Thermos of coffee in his hands, he spoke those words with a certainty I remember clearly—just as I remember what a good man he was, how he cussed beautifully and told fine stories and was friendly to a green choker setter, how he worked with an impossible appetite that left me panting and cussing unbeautifully behind him. I don't remember what I or someone said that drew his response, or whether he was answering some doubt he himself had raised. I only recall the authority of his voice, the rain dripping from his tin hat, and the idling crummies waiting to carry us out the muddy roads from camp, out through the stripped hills to another day of work.

The voice that spoke those words is my voice, too. It's in all of us—the voice of practicality and common sense, the voice that understands that ugly things are necessary. It's a voice that values getting a hard job done and making an honest living. It has behind it certain assumptions, certain ideas about progress, economy, and standard of living, and it has behind it the evidence of certain numbers, of payrolls and balance sheets, of rotation cycles and board footage. It is not a heartless voice. It has love for wife and children in it, a concern for their future. It has love for the work itself and the way of life that surrounds the work. And it has at least a tinge of regret for the forest, a sense of beauty and a sorrow at the violation of beauty.

I must have nodded, those years ago, when a good man spoke those words. I didn't argue against his experience and certainty, I had only a vague uneasiness. Now, I suppose, I would argue, but I know that arguing wouldn't change his mind, just as I know that he wouldn't change mine. As he defined the issue, he saw it truly. Many of us define the issue differently now, and we think we see it truly, and all of us on every side have studies and numbers and ideas to support what we believe. All of us have evidence.

The best evidence, though, is not a number or idea. The land itself is not a number or idea, and the land has an argument to make.

Turn off the highway, some rainy day in the Northwest, and drive deep into a national forest on the broad gravel roads and the narrow muddy roads. Drive in the rain through one of the great forests of Earth. Drive past the stands that are left, drive past the gentle fields of little trees and big stumps. Pass the yellow machines at rest, the gravel heaps and sections of culvert pipe, the steel drums here and there, a rusting piece of choker in the ditch. Drive until you come to a steep mountainside stripped of its trees—you will come to it—where puke-outs have spewed stone rubble across the road, where perhaps the road itself, its work accomplished, has begun to sag and slide.

Stand in the rainfall, look at the stumps, and try to imagine the forest. You will have to imagine it, because on this steep slope no forest of that scale, very likely no forest at all, will stand again. The great trees, and the creatures that wove their countless strands of energy into a living, shifting tapestry, from deep in the rooted soil through all the reaches of shaded light to the crowning twig-tips with their new cones . . . . The trees are gone, the creatures are gone, and the very genius of these hills, that gathered rain and changing light for centuries, that grew and deepened as it brought forth a green and towering stillness—it, too, is leaving. It's washing down in gullies to a muddy stream.

THE MOUNTAIN POEMS OF STONEHOUSE

Translated by Red Pine

Stonehouse was a 14th-century Chinese Buddhist monk who spent over forty years living in a hut on a mountain one hundred and fifty kilometers southwest of what is now Shanghai. At the emperor's request, he once came down the mountain and served as abbot of a prominent monastery for a few years, but he preferred his hut. At some point someone gave him some paper and ink and asked him to describe such a life. He sent down a scroll of nearly two hundred poems and prefaced them with these remarks: "Here in the woods I have lots of free time. When I don't spend it sleeping, I enjoy composing gathas. But with paper and ink so scarce, I haven't thought about writing them down. Now some Zen monks have asked me to record what I find of interest on this mountain. I've sat here quietly and let my brush fly. Suddenly this scroll is full. I roll it back up and send it down with admonition not to try singing these poems. Only if you sit on them will they do you any good." He called his collection Mountain Poems. *This selection is from those poems.* The Mountain Poems of Stonehouse *was published by Empty Bowl in 1986 and was later incorporated into* The Zen Works of Stonehouse, *published by Mercury House in 1999. Both works are currently out of print.*

#41

the ancients entered mountains intent on the Way
their constant effort depending on themselves
adding stones to their belts to hull rice
carrying hoes in the rain to plant pines
hauling mud and rocks of course
or water and wood they worked
the slouches who beg for a living
don't come near an old zen monk

#99

a clean patch of ground after rain
an ancient pine half-covered with moss
we all see what's before our eyes
but how we use it isn't the same

#87

a stand of pines behind the house
a few mounds of taro in front
a mountain recluse doesn't have many schemes
his conversation is about cooking

#54

the sun rises east at night falling west
the bell sounds at dusk the rooster at dawn
Yin and Yang have turned my head to snow
over the years I've used a hundred crocks of pickles
I plant pines for beams where there's room
spit out peach pits for shade along the trail
tell hunted birds throughout the realm
head for the mountains and choose any tree.

#11

my hut's on Redcloud Summit
few visitors brave the cliffs
I haul wood to market and slip where there's moss
drip with sweat lugging rice back up
with no end to hunger less is better
and limited time why be greedy
I don't want to spoil your fun
only make you let go

#13

I live far off in the wild
where moss and woods are thick and plants perfumed
I can see mountains rain or shine
and never hear market noise
I light a few leaves in my stove to heat tea
to patch my robe I cut off a cloud
lifetimes seldom fill in a hundred years
why suffer for profit and fame

#16

this old monk's lived so long in a hut
the wind's blown my robe into rag
leaves for my stove I rake by the stream
covers for orange trees I weave when it frosts
basic reality isn't created
ready-made koans aren't worth a thought
all day I sit by an open window
looking at mountains not lowering the shade

#18
my zen hut leans at the summit
clouds sail back and forth
a waterfall hangs in front
a mountain ridge crests in back
on a rock wall sketched three buddhas
for incense there's a plum branch in a jar
the fields below might be level
but can't match a mountain home free of dust

Field Journal: Olympic National Forest

Roger Risley

May 6, 2000: *Quilcene Ranger Station*

First day on the job. The district ranger gives a pep talk. He's good at setting the tone. In his background remarks, he says we can't judge what happened in the past, that those people were doing the best job they could. Some of those people are in the room, in uniform.

June 6: *Big Quilcene River*

Today we're going to walk through a typical field day, surveying for birds in late successional stands. Our surveys must be completed by 1000 hrs. because the birds are the most active and therefore detectable in the hours just after dawn.

Birds in the canopy can't be seen from below so that most of our sampling is done by ear. Once we reach our station, we sit down for five minutes, and list by species all of the birds we hear. We only occasionally see bird species and tally these also.

Three of us—the wildlife biologist and two technicians—drive up to where there are two survey routes laid out. We stop at a large rockslide and proceed on foot for another mile or so. Apparently there is little funding for road maintenance, now that the harvest has been cut back and the cash-flow has dried up. I'm of the opinion that damage to watersheds by unmaintained logging roads within the entire coniferous forest biome constitutes an emergency of the most urgent sort.

We reach the "trail" to our route. From the road, the way is marked by white flagging (for maximum visibility in dim light) and heads more or less straight down the hillside. It goes thru an old shelterwood cut from the seventies. These stands have a reputation for blowing down a lot but it's not bad going. Then we enter a smallish late successional stand made up of cedar and fir and hemlock. The period of stand-leveling fire events is on the order of 200-300 years on this side of the mountains, and most of this stand appears to be half that age with scattered older firs.

The biologist told us that it was a matter of debate as to which way was quicker to the next route, to go sidehill or return to the road to reach the next five stations. So we—the two technicians—hiked the half-mile back up to the road, then up the road another mile where we picked up a flagged route back downslope to an elevation similar to the previous route. The biologist beat us by ten minutes. We located the first station and then started to hike out, since we had a long walk back.

June 7: Big Quilcene River

Today is the technicians' turn to survey. We get out of the truck at the rockslide and are greeted by the calls of marbled murrelets coming from directly below in the valley bottom. It's about full daylight and the birds are probably headed back to Hood Canal. Until we get to where we can find all the routes and achieve comparable results, we are working together and comparing notes on species identification.

On the second route we passed a stand where much of the cedar appeared to be pretty heavily used by cougar. The bark was all fuzzed up to at least the lowest branch from heavy climbing

June 8: South Fork Skokomish River

We meet at the Quilcene Ranger Station at 0330 hrs. and drive down to the S. Fork of the Skokomish River. We reach the Pine Lake road a little before 0600. It's more than a bit overgrown and pretty soon we have to park the truck and get on the bikes. Wearing our caulk boots around our necks and our hardhats instead of our bike helmets, we pedal the remaining two and a half miles up to Pine Lake. We have to dismount for several debris avalanches that have come out of the clearcuts above. This is very steep country. Near the lake we enter tall timber. Our routes are on opposite sides of the valley and a couple of hundred ft. up. The north-facing route has a bad devil's club hazard and the route on the other side proves hard to find. There's also a marbled murrelet survey route flagged in white and we're not sure which is which in places. We pedal back down with wet alders slapping at us, get back into the truck and drive up to the South Fork trailhead and make camp. We try to radio out to the Hoodsport R.S. as agreed, but we can't reach anyone. We find out later the radios don't work from remote areas.

Later that evening I scout out the next two routes and hike up the Skokomish a few miles toward Sundown Pass, which takes you over to the Quinault side. The trail runs along the edge of the Wonder Mt. Wilderness. All four square miles of it. That's all the roadless area that was left between the forks of the Skok. The late setting sun lights up the cloud deck from below and the pink light of evening pours through the pass above.

June 9: South Fork Skokomish River

We sleep in until 0600 knowing that we're only a short mile by bike to the first station. Rain, blisters, fatigue, sleep deprivation are clearly taking their toll. The second route up Rule Creek heads into some of the wilder and more remote terrain in the Olympics, a jumble of waterfalls and avalanche debris and rock outcrops. At the last station I peer into the gloomy beyond where only Sasquatch and owl surveyors dare to tread. We don't hear much for birds. Even though the rain is holding off, there is nowhere to escape the sound of running water and we don't hear well or for very far. White noise. Acoustic claustrophobia.

June 13: Travel Day

We're on the road again, headed west for the Soleduck River and beyond. Our next two routes are on Rugged Ridge, east of the town of Forks; but nobody's been there since '96 and the routes may be missing.

June 14: Sitkum River

Next day raining. Too much drip noise to survey. We sleep in. Later we head up to locate our routes. It takes a long time to get to the top, then find exactly where we drop off the ridge to reach our route. Most of the flagging has disappeared but we're following the Park/ Forest boundary, which is marked. I find a piece of faded blue and white striped ribbon on the ground about a mile in. This must be where we drop off the ridgeline. The slopes are thin soils over scree and we're doing the two-steps-forward, one-step-back a lot on the sidehill. We find the first three stations, reflag the route and head back. The last two stations shouldn't be that hard to find.

June 15: West Fork Humptulips River

Up at four, looks like a nice day. We hike up to the Pete's Creek trailhead, then hike into the Colonel Bob Wilderness where the route is laid out on a steep slope with large down timber on the ground, most of it pointing straight downhill. We lose a lot of time getting around, over and under big logs. At one station there is water running everywhere, with no defined stream course anywhere. Sheet flow. It's been raining a lot. The ranger station measured six inches in the last six days. The noise of water trickling all around us makes it hard to hear the birds.

June 16: Quinault River

I headed back to the Humptulips. The road was cleared and I found a pretty good size log on which to cross the river. It was so big I had to shinny up a small alder to get on to it. The other side was easy going. A narrow bottom that rose abruptly to give it a walled-in feeling. This is our only route that's flat. Much elk browsing. It smelled like a feed lot. Even the skunk cabbage was browsed. You thought spinach was bad! Maybe there's some essential micronutrient there that elk need. This is the second day in two weeks without rain. I'm walking on moleskin and don't it feel good!

June 17: Sitkum River

Dawn stretches her rosy fingers across the sky...

The last mile I can't keep up with my supervisor on the bike as the road gets steep and I run out of gears. He's taking the far route, which is now well marked, and I'm headed into the Park to lay out new stations. The other surveyor has been dispatched to the Hoh and we'll all meet back at the office in Quilcene later in the day.

I'm in the upper S. Fork of the Calawah River, on the south side of Rugged Ridge, north of Indian Pass. I'm looking for acoustic space between streams to establish "easy-listening stations."

Nothing exciting to report birdwise. These late successional stands have fairly depauperate avifaunas and we seldom detect anything interesting. These aren't exactly the kind of places you'd go to look for birds. Although there are no sweeping views of spectacular mountainscapes, the trail affords intimate glimpses of waterfalls and small slides full of wildflowers. The forest itself is extremely interesting with its variety of understory communities that change sometimes subtly with aspect, moisture gradient, canopy condition, and the soil profile which is evident everywhere the trail cuts into the slope.

June 22: South Fork Skokomish River

Just before daylight low clouds and fog roll in. Lots of murrelet traffic overhead. We're only hearing murrelets on cloudy days. On clear mornings they appear to leave for the breeding grounds early.

On the way out we see a bobcat cross the road in front of us. The fur looks reddish in the bright sun, like a fox.

June 29: Quinault River

Marine air moves in and clouds with it. Marbled murrelets heard everywhere in the valley. I get the Zeigler Creek routes. Ten stations on the trail from 1,000 to 2,200 ft. in elevation in the Mt. Col. Bob Wilderness. We can't borrow a second truck this time so I get dropped off with a bicycle, while the other surveyor drives up to do the route on the Hoh.

The trail allows me to move silently through the forest and it's as if the birds are not affected by my presence. I hear murrelets all the way up the trail and the fog is thick above the canopy. Lots of warblers here. The calls are similar to what we hear in Quilcene and I suspect more hybrids although I have no other data on that. At one of the last stations a hairy woodpecker flushes a spotted owl. The owl comes down and checks me out, flying past at eye level. After these birds have been handled a few times they may become very tame.

I'm thinking about marbled murrelets a lot. We know that they occupy stands on the lower halves of their respective slopes. They have been found occasionally above 4,000 ft. But that is probably less than optimal habitat at that elevation. I think that the murrelet is altitude limited.

A wing used for swimming underwater must be reduced to be more efficient. The best wing underwater is a flipper, as the penguins know. Such a wing would increase loading in the lower viscosity medium of the atmosphere. Since air pressure decreases with elevation, the bird would fly with difficulty at higher altitudes. We see geese and ducks and gulls—birds with typically high wing loadings—adjust their height of flight with changes in the barometer. Few seabirds are found to fly at any great elevation, certainly no diving birds. These murrelets are flying uphill carrying food, so wing loading may be an issue. The murrelets nesting farther up the Quinault are much closer to Hood Canal than the Pacific, but nonetheless return to the ocean twice daily for feeding rather than making the trip over Anderson Pass, the shortest route to salt water on Hood Canal. Besides that, the murrelet is also reported to be fairly site faithful, returning to the same stand to breed each year.

The implication for stewardship of the species is that we need more lowland old growth to preserve the species. The other implication is that for purposes of population viability analysis in the Olympics we may need to look at smaller metapopulations, possibly like the salmon which are also site faithful and confined to their watersheds for breeding purposes.

Historical records indicate that murrelets used to be found on salt water in flocks occasionally numbering in the thousands. Seventeen is the largest flock I've ever seen. We don't know enough about this bird to understand the changes in genetics, social structure, and behavior caused by such a drastic reduction in population. It is suspected that the murrelet nested in colonies formerly. All other birds in this family *Alcidae* are colonial nesters, and the habit is common in seabirds of other families as well.

What we know about the marbled murrelet on land depends on the study method. Like the blind men and the elephant we have radar studies that tell us how fast they fly, radio telemetry to tell us where they go. Surveys in the dark that tell us where and when their voices are heard, a relatively few visual detections of their flying beneath the canopy in dim light. We have videotape of nesting behavior during daylight. But for all of this, the picture we get is fragmented and incomplete.

The fog and low clouds are an inseparable feature of the habitat. The same landscape that traps the fog also holds the murrelet between its steep sides. The fog allows the birds to come and go in daylight without being seen by predators. This probably enables multiple feedings. It provides the ambient canopy moisture that encourages the epiphytic mosses that the murrelets nest on. It may reduce fire danger on lower slopes. It may reduce overheating in flying birds, which reach speeds of almost 50 miles an hour up valley and over 60 mph downhill. It's interesting to speculate.

In northern California the loggers in redwood country heard the murrelets much the same way we do on foggy mornings and called them fog larks.

Could fog also present a denser medium for flight? We hear their contact calls for hours after dawn flying in the low cloud on foggy mornings. From this we may infer only that they call more on foggy or cloudy days.

Off to the Skokomish we go in the late afternoon after long naps, driving by way of Wynooche Dam. When we reach the dam there are two ways to go to get to the Skok. Over Dusk Peak or up Spoon Creek, a tributary of the Satsop. Seems like there's always rocks in the road going over the high route. There's a rain gauge up there for the reservoir and it averages over 200 in. of rain a year, the rainiest spot outside the National Park. So we prudently take the Spoon Creek road. The road prism forms one bank or the other of the creek most of the way up, another artifact from the bad old days. The way I remember it, this was a mainline thirty years ago. I haven't been this way in a long time. The road looks kind of like the Oregon Trail in places. Two narrow tracks with damage and debris in more than a few places.

When we get to the top and look down into the Canyon River, it's what the forestry texts euphemistically refer to as a managed landscape. Slides everywhere there are roads, their edges eroding back, sloughing into the clearcuts below. A lot of this was too steep for roads, but was logged with a skyline instead. The skyline is admittedly a less invasive harvest technique, but on steep slopes, where there is little topsoil accumulation and a high risk of erosion, it enables har-

191

vest where it would be prudent not to harvest. What wasn't removed was burned off, leaving the thin soils exposed. The replanted trees are small, chlorotic looking and the coverage is thin in many places. Rock outcrops are protruding everywhere and there's few mature stands in sight.

These are the places nobody sees, where greed and criminal forest practices raped publicly owned forest lands with impunity for decades. And lost taxpayer money doing it. Looking from the top down, there is little watershed health in evidence.

The road is patched in places, only eight feet wide in spots and runs over the top of some of the bigger slides that couldn't be removed and when we get to the bottom there is a big sign facing the other way that says ROAD CLOSED.

July 8: Hoh River

The trail traverses a wide river terrace. At the far end of the terrace, at the base of the backslope, all the trees are blown down east and west as far as the eye can see, an area about the width of a powerline right-of-way. This stand is no longer unfragmented. This is some 25 miles from the ocean, but the wind gets its way. Uphill the forest is a '21 blow stand that came up in doghair hemlock and fir and appears to be growing slowly. It could be an '04 blow stand. It appears to be extensive, but I have a long day ahead of me so I don't survey any farther. There is some debate as to whether '21 blow stands count as late-successional or mature coniferous forest, and the decision was that if they were extensive enough and unfragmented, to survey them. One of the routes included in the study but surveyed by the state may be such a stand. It's the pair to this route and located to the west a couple of miles, but I've never visited it. Until we do vegetation surveys (next year) we can't do any habitat-based analysis of the bird database. This will present a big limitation to my summary of the survey.

Grazing by elk has a huge effect on plant species composition on river terraces. Even in the canopy, because selective grazing spares the spruce seedlings which are prickly and selects for hemlock seedlings. Wind throws hemlocks over much easier than spruce also, but this close to the ocean it appears to all blow down the same. Selective grazing has been demonstrated by elk exclusion plots, areas that are fenced off from elk to study ungrazed vegetation for comparison.

There should be more birds in evidence here, but the season is getting very late. This is our last survey day, we've completed all the routes three times each, even if a little late. This is the first year since 1996 that all the routes were surveyed. I leave a note at the office in Forks on the way thru town to let my supervisor know everything went OK. He'll be through before noon, back from Rugged Ridge, and will be eager to know that we're finished with the field work.

III.

WORKING THE SEA

KWAWIYA
(Steelhead)

Silver fish, run leaping
Through the riffles
        Gleaming.
      Power of my people.

Tagged now. Stapled with the wires of unbelievers.
Leap against weirs, stripped of
                new life.
      Not their own beginnings.
Eggs in a bucket.

Akil take them
Pixt'adax dive screaming
My canoe is empty—you must
            fish for me.

My grandmother weeps.

          (Anonymous Quileute)

Note: If one wishes to read the poem aloud, the pronunciation of
these Quileute words in the poem are more or less as follows:
    akil, "bear"—AH-kill
    pixt'adax, "eagle"—PICK-tuh-duck
    kwawiya, "steelhead"—KWAH-wee-yuh

Sea Bloom

Paul Thomas

Don't ask how to predict it. It doesn't happen every day, but when it does, it comes at tide change. The tide books won't help. They don't tell about the waters five, ten or twenty-five miles offshore where the vagaries of wind and light make their own appointments with the tides; nor will they mention the deep ocean currents, set in motion by forces thousands of miles away, that tug along the edges of the continental shelf and stir the sea into soupy clouds of protein.

Don't ask where. There are charts which show reefs, canyons, and pinnacles, all likely settings for an underwater feast; but a sea bloom is fathered by a west wind and born in an upwelling that, like a volcanic plume that shifts directions as it rises through the stratosphere, can spiral to the surface miles away from its source and tear the water into long bands of smooth and leaping water.

The secret may lie in the interplay of lunar and solar tides that sweep around the globe and reverberate across the great ocean basins and pause briefly at their crests. Or it could be something as mundane as flotsam on the surface or a cloud in the sky that momentarily darkens the water at just the right time and rings the dinner bell of every stealthy creature that makes his living stalking and killing.

When it comes, the ocean implodes in a fury of tails and tentacles. The sea surface is showered from below by dark clouds of anchovy that flounce at the sky and occasionally into the beaks of ravenous seabirds. All the wild creatures from micro plankton to macro whales seem to be gathering into ever-tightening knots in a ritual of sacrifice and slaughter.

Even terrestrial bipeds in intricately fashioned sea pods venture out from land to join the pageantry by trailing nets and pretty lures behind their vessels. They are escorted by a herd of friendly sentinels, the dolphins, who create a field of white caps as they advance toward the boats. The dolphins are the frosting on the cake and only up-staged by their massive, leaping cousins, the humpbacked whales, or by a rare sperm whale or a surface-swimming whale shark.

But the main show is put on by the ocean itself which stokes the fire of life with fuel from its frigid depths and blossoms forth in shades of pink and brown on a field of royal blue and emerald.

For an encore with a largely different cast composed of squid and octopus and a thousand toothy critters of incredible design, we must wait until late summer in the middle of a special night when a bil-lion luminescent diatoms sparkle in response to nearby motions and thus, like a photographic negative, define the shape and motion of the action that rages near the surface.

Day or night, the flower fades within an hour or so. The tide rips dissipate and the ocean's surface resumes its uniform texture. Birds, boats and fish scatter in all directions to locate the remnants of the bloom, but they find only the tattered reminders of the glory that was there only moments ago and thus retreat sullenly to their workaday world as if rudely awoken from an exquisite dream.

But the thrill and the fear of the hunt and the hunted are recalled and eagerly anticipated in the bloom that's sure to come tomorrow or the next day when all the wild things meet.

THE BEST DAY

In the early seventies we fished for salmon out of Hole-in-the-Wall in Southeast Alaska and in the evenings when gnarly trees on rocky islets clawed out against copper skies and cast long shadows over marbled seas, we sought out the old-timers and assorted dockside eccentrics who with little urging spun out mossy yarns, about commercial troller boats that took refuge from a southeaster in a fully sheltered bay on Coronation Island only to be heeled over and swamped by hurricane force williwaws bearing down from towering peaks; or about three local boys from Craig who drowned when a sudden squall capsized their open halibut skiff; or the troller who, in an effort to raise his gear up over an upstart reef, cranked his engine up to a deafening roar but not loud enough to drown out the rifle shot sounds as his four steel wires—weighted down by 30 and 40 pound leads—snapped off one-by-one, nor did he ease up on the throttle to drag aboard what was left of his shredded gear or hoist the poles until he reached town whereupon he dropped anchor and rowed ashore to the Craig Inn; or my favorite, the old-timer who trolled out of Tenakee up in Chatham Straits back in the thirties, whose ambition—his obsession really—was to land a hundred-pound king salmon. Trolling herring bait behind a metal flasher, he had over the years caught his share of 60 and 70 pounders, but he could never hold on to the odd 100-pound colossus that came his way about once a year. The consensus was that Tenakee was a stopping-off point, a feeding ground for a particular run of Columbia River "royal chinook," hog-sized kings that today exist only in old sepia prints taken at the turn of the 19th century near the mouth of the Columbia where they were hauled ashore in reef nets by teams of big draft horses. That was before the big dams on the Columbia blocked them out forever.

Nailing a really big king salmon makes your mouth go dry. He jerks the line like a junkyard dog and bends a forty-foot pole like a casting rod. In the after end of the vessel, with your feet planted below the water line and thighs balanced against the side of the cockpit, you lean over the rail and wait for the big guy to surface. You never wrap the monofiliment leader around your hand if you want to avoid serious cuts. You hold it tightly between your thumb and forefinger where salt-water lubricant allows it to go out quickly and painlessly when the beasty makes his run. Sometimes you hunker down low in the pit so he doesn't lock eyes with you and panic. You tug and wait 'til he presents his head, a recalcitrant prisoner full of fear and loathing but more noble in his hatred than you in your greed. Then when he's alongside, you come up suddenly with your gaff, conk him soundly on the top of his head just behind his eyes, and quickly twist the gaff around and sink the steel point deep into the side of his head. Then aided by the combined roll of the boat and his death kick, you haul him over the rail. That's the way we did it and it worked best with the big kings who almost always died instantly and regally.

Once I pulled aboard a 58-pounder at Deer Harbor, Alaska. That was the Fourth of July, 1975. All the boats had gone in at noon and anchored or rafted out partying in the harbor. We were the only boat out trolling when a run of particularly big kings chanced by (big for those days anyway). I can still remember the weather: warm and sultry with a white-opaque cloud cover and no wind, a perfect day for fishing, with my wife and our son aboard and our little fish factory filling up with big slugs that in 10-15 fathoms of water came up thrashing like demons. I worked that fish for 20 minutes. It was my biggest salmon.

That day certainly would have qualified as the best day had not better days intervened. Like the time off Cape Muzon that my wife steered the boat in a little too close and dragged the leads over the reef, setting off all four bells at the tips of our poles, waking me out of a sound nap and causing me to jump up into the wheel house and rev the engines up to ¾ throttle in an attempt to lift the leads over the reef. I watched as the sounder fell off from 14 to 20 fathoms, deep enough for our 18 fathoms of gear to clear bottom; but the bells, inexplicably to my groggy brain, continued to ring. When it struck home, there was a mature king, silver, halibut, or lingcod on every of the some twenty-four hooks out there. Then after madly cleaning those fish we swung back over the reef for another slam-dunk, and then another, and again, until other boats that had ventured out around the Cape got suspicious and sauntered over our way. For the rest of the year it was the hot spot and for all I know still is. But for us, for one day, we owned it.

Then there was opening day off Washington and flat calm sea out on the "Prairie," some 30 miles offshore where we were dragging the top 30 of some 70 fathoms of water, with only one other boat in sight, tacking back and forth and picking silvers like ripe cherries, while my useless deckhand lay in the fo'c's'le sleeping off a hangover from a colossal shoreside drunk. Got over 220 silvers on that day's pull and cleaned and iced them on my own. I slept real good thinking about repeating it the next day, this time perhaps with some help. But in the morning the fleet fell upon us and it was slash and burn.

Better yet perhaps was the three thousand dollar day, complements of Danny, the red-headed Quilleute Indian who had been grinding away on a granddaddy-sized pack of kings for weeks during the Indian opening and had very generously let out the loran coordinates to a couple of his old buddies who like myself were non-treaty and had to wait until July 1 for the non-treaty opening. Of course it blew over 25 knots on the opener, so only a few of us lean hungry souls stayed on the spot, and while both nauseous and exhilarated by the six-foot seas running all day and my wife seasick below, I pulled over sixty large kings. It was pure avarice that carried that day and perhaps for that reason alone doesn't measure up to my best day standards.

Make no mistake: there were many, many days of the other kind, the mediocre and the downright horrid, days of no fish, foul weather, and breakdowns; but for now I choose to remember the standout days when the decks were awash with silver and the scuppers gurgling in red, when leaping dolphins led us to silky smooth seas where we fished among hump-backed whales or days in Cross Sound when we cruised through milk-green glacier waters that lent their colors to the fish, leading my wife to ruminate about "catching dream fish in dream waters."

But there was one day that stands out from the rest. It started when Archie lured us up to Whale Inlet early in the morning and introduced us to a yet another of his many little fishing holes. He showed me the lineups and how deep to set while we almost scraped the tips of our poles against sheer granite walls. He had probably a couple hundred of these spots all over Southeast Alaska and the word was he once led a young fishing couple on a prospecting tour that went twice around the whole of Southeast Alaskan waters and soaked up an entire summer season that ended short on fish but long on memories.

There had been the clash of wills between the avuncular Archie and the stolid, fish-savvy Jon. Jon with only four or five seasons behind him had already established himself as a legend around Craig as the first longhair hippie fisherman to learn how to pick fish at Little Roller when not even the highliners could catch. When he was on, all you could do was follow and painfully watch him pull two or three big slugs per pass. In my mind his success had less to do with the boat, gear, or technique—not that he didn't have all that down—but was fundamentally a mix of faith, karma, and something I would call fish-sense. It's something that most all of us got from time to time and when it struck we would more often than not fall prey to hubris and imagine that we had made fundamental connection with the sea and from then on the path to riches was layed out neatly before us. This was the delusion we all sailed under, but for some like Jon it must have tugged at him on a daily basis, so good was his "luck." Once as a prank, when his buddy Jim had been weeping all morning over the radio about his lack of fish, Jon and his partner tied an empty deck bucket to a fight line and tossed it overboard just as they were coming up on Jim's boat so that Jim could witness them "fighting" yet another big one. The joke back-fired when the drag proved so great that they couldn't get the bucket back and had to cut it loose to keep from pulling down the rigging.

But getting back to that day, before we had dragged one full tide, Archie got jumpy and slid off south about 11 a.m. to Snail Point on a vague tip from Mark or Jon. I'm not certain which, but they were both in the area. I was reluctant to leave this narrow channel that lay in the shadow of the legendary Coronation Island and an upcoming tide change held some promise. But the flood was not particularly productive and when about one or two in the afternoon Archie put in a quick call and slipped in a word about coffee—our code for "come quick"—I slammed the gear aboard and charged south not really expecting much, but unwilling to miss any opportunity. We probably didn't put the gear back in the water until four, but from then on, six miles straight out from Snail point, we started pulling kings real steady. The radio conversation was spotty and mostly vague, about dinner plans and what we were going to do next winter, that sort of talk. Certainly no mention of fish, in keeping with the de rigueur of silence in the presence of a hot bite.

There must have been at least eight boats working that bite, all from our little hippy fleet of "dock-sixers" as we called ourselves in those days in reference to the transient dock on Fishermen's Terminal, Seattle, where most of us had converged during the protest days of the late sixties. We had individually, as couples, and more or less as a group, bootstrapped our way from dockside dreamers into full-time entrepreneurs, cognizant of the bottom line, but still given over to the narrative. These were the years that if someone asked how your season had gone, you might talk about the beach barbecue at Launch Passage, ramble on about unpredictable breakdowns, storms, hot bites and all the other salty adventures of the summer, before getting around to summarizing the season in monetary terms. Not so later when one by one we either dropped away from fishing altogether or became committed little bankers and let Puff the Magic Dragon go his own way.

As the sun set spectacularly on that long summer eve, the bite tapered off and our little fleet turned silently towards shore for a final "beach tack." We ate salmon and baked potatoes. Our 2-year old played in his Johnny jump-ups that hung from the boom and watched wide-eyed as his mom and dad cleaned and lowered all those big fish down the hatch. What little breeze there had been, fell away and the golden sea undulated hypnotically under the setting sun. Someone played Judy Collin's lovely "Same Old Fishermen" over our semi-private FM frequency. The line, "the Japanese used to hunt for whales, now they hunt for snails," somehow stuck in my mind. There was a long pause at the end and Archie came back in a reverential tone, "That was real pretty."

We thought the bite was over. Then two, three more solid clangs from the cow-bells told us it wasn't. Slowly as if choreographed, our little fleet turned in unison and tacked once more offshore. In the fading light we watched the sultry kings surface in the twilight, swim partly ahead on taut leaders, and yield like lost sheep as we led them in hand over hand. No more words were spoken over the radio and few I suspect across the decks. We turned once again towards shore, pulled our gear and chugged in behind Snail Point to drop anchor and finish the day's icing on up close to midnight in total darkness.

It was the last time to my memory that our Alaska contingent of dock-sixers fished together as a cohesive group. Rifts would emerge or family concerns would prevail. We would go our separate ways, some staying longer than others, but all in time finding other grounds, other fleets, other adventures, none staying so long as the old-timer from Tenakee. He, as a last resort, had tied a dozen rubber snubbers in tandem, one end to the tip of the boom, the other fastened with a loop of braided wire. When the next 100-pound king got on, he managed to coax it to the surface, unsnap the leader from the trolling wire and quickly snap it onto the super-snubber. With the tubing stretched out at hair-width some twenty fathoms behind the boat, there was no way the fish could snap the leader. Somehow the old-timer, now in his late seventies, managed to drag it aboard and return to the dock at Tenakee with the fish hoisted up in his rigging. He sold the fish and the boat and never put a line in the water again.

How Grampa Lost His Luck

G. *Dann Irish*
for Pedro Villarde 1900-1976

Long time i fish and gamble
By Ketchikan, maybe 1925-26.
Ya, i row da godamm boat
All over.

One night i play card, make
Plenty money—bymby i drink
Littly-bit too much and walking
Down da float, slip—fall inna
Water. Somanabich!

Inna boat i lite da stove, lay
Out alla money, mosly $100 bill
Maybe 2000 dolla wort.

Now you see dis white rat lucky
Charm liv wit ol Pete onna boat
An i feed-um an evryting, he my
Fishin buddy.

Anyways i go some place bymby
Come back an hotdam! alla money
Gone! Shit i #*%^**!!!!!!Mad
Maybe i tink godamm rat take.
Den i cach um ring is neck an
Tro im over da side!

O me O my, bymby bymby i lookin
Fo somting an Holycow i fine alla
Money all wad up inna cubby-hole!

Eh you no what?

No more catch fish . . .
No more make gamble . . .
Quits drinkin too!

GRADES OF LIGHT
GRADES OF COLOR
GRADES OF FISH

After all there being
Nothing else to do
But get up
Say a prayer
On my way to coffee.

Get on my oilskins
Stand by the belt and
Pull fish:
Soki in this one
Dogs in that one
Humpys here
Silvers there
And Kings, well that's
Another thing.

I sort salmon while awake
And sort them in my dreams.

I wake up tired.

TRUE INDIAN MODERN STORY

George Silverstar

"All an Indian needs to fish the Columbia is a motor boat,
    fifteen-hundred feet of gillnet and a 30-30 to shoot back
    at the game wardens."—Uncle Henry

My father is a little drunk and it delays our departure.
We will drive a hundred late summer miles to Celilo Falls.
My brother and I are keeping our heads down in the back seat.
My mother is pregnant and sensible and the discussion is
    unpleasant up front.
I have the impression this is a long-shot.
We go anyway.

This is the last of Celilo's traditional fishing before the Dalles Dam
    project floods the grounds.
The falls are a natural drop in the Columbia River.
Forty-foot high waterfalls and rock curve sharply into the body of
    the river where the wall of the basin nearly parallels
    the shore and slopes
downward until the river is flat again.

Pole platforms are built along the face.
Indians with long-handled dip nets are catching salmon which fail
    to make the summit and fall back.
The salmon struggle—almost swimming in air; shaking off scales
    and river water—until, quiet in the weave, they are hauled
    into laps of many old gods.

Offer and good-bye, the Great Spirit has modern ideas.

There is smoke and flies and salmon drying on driftwood frames
    and innumerable Indian kids selling fish bigger
    than themselves.
We don't have the money to buy one.
Chief Tommy Thompson of the Yakima Nation makes his
    ceremonial appearance.
He is in a crowd of brown people who are all related.

He is in a beaded buckskin and full headdress.
He is old.
The Yakima Valley could be his daughter.

If my aunt were here we'd have a fish.
.She has money because she doesn't have children.
That's what my mom says.
Her current man works on the railroad.
He's white.
They live in California.
She brought me a baseball mitt and a Japanese Swiss Army knife.
None of my relatives lives in a teepee.

We go home and in the morning my dad the Indian goes to work
    in the mill.
We get a fish sometime after that.

Afterword to "True Indian Modern Story"

Celilo Falls was one of the most productive sites for the Native American Columbia salmon fishery, estimated to have yielded about 18 million tons a year. It was also a trade and cultural center for Pacific Northwest tribes for an estimated 10,000 years. Around the falls, which were carved out of basalt, salmon could be caught nine months of the year, with the heaviest runs in the spring and fall. Investigations undertaken before the falls were flooded out by the Dalles Dam in 1956 showed that dip net fishers at Celilo accounted for three-quarters of all salmon taken above Bonneville Dam. Fishing began at dawn and during times of full moon might run on into the night. From platforms constructed of planks and poles hung precariously over the pounding water, fishermen would use long-handled dip nets to wrestle 20- to 30-pound salmon from the river. Fishing stands on the rocks and islands, later expanded by blasting out channels and erecting cableways, were a family inheritance. When one man caught all his family could clean and prepare in one day, another took his place. In this way a dozen men might fish from one stand in a single day. When the Dalles Dam was about to inundate the ancient fishing site, the last of the "First Salmon Rites" was held at Celilo village. In the following Seattle Times *article, reporter Lynda Mapes describes a gathering of the tribes in March 2007 to commemorate the loss of the falls on the fiftieth anniversary of its flooding.*

—Editors

Tribes Mourn Loss of Falls

Lynda V. Mapes

CELILO VILLAGE—Fifty years of silence.

A loss so big, it took tribes from all over the Northwest to count its measure in a commemoration over the weekend of the death of Celilo Falls 50 years ago March 10.

They came from all over. By canoe, from Puyallup and Suquamish, Chinook and Wanapum. By plane and by car from around the Northwest. More than a thousand strong, tribal members gathered to help the people of Celilo remember the spectacular Columbia River falls and what was lost when they were flooded.

As the people of Celilo welcomed the canoes ashore, along with travelers from many other tribal nations and directions, they were gathering as their forefathers had by the thousands to fish, gamble, socialize and feast during the salmon runs.

The falls are considered to have been one of the world's most productive salmon fisheries.

It all came to an end in six hours March 10, 1957, when the U.S. Army Corps of Engineers closed the gates on The Dalles Dam, flooding out Celilo Village and washing away fishing scaffolds where Indians had caught the salmon that fed their families, and their souls, for thousands of years.

Today the river that once crashed and boiled through miles of basalt chutes, islands and rocks is a placid, 24-mile lake.

"My ancestry is right here, underwater," said Yakama tribal member James Kiona, as he worked at roasting some 700 pounds of chinook

213

salmon over alderwood fires to feed thousands of people gathered throughout the weekend to mourn the falls.

Born at Celilo in 1949, he still remembers the cool mist of the falls on his face. He remembers scooting over the falls in a cable car and getting soaked by the mist while the car swayed in the wind created by the crashing water. "It was so loud, I couldn't even hear myself scream."

He remembers watching his father fish, and being awestruck by the massive chinook hauled up in dip nets. "The fish were bigger than us [kids] in those days."

Head salmon cook at Celilo, Kiona comes back to the place he calls home for every ceremonial feast. About 20 cooks and 18 serv-ers rose at dawn to prepare lunch: salmon, taken from the river the season before; the meat of 13 deer, an elk and a buffalo; along with corn, salad, biscuits and pie.

Teenage girls in traditional wing dresses, head scarves, woven belts and moccasins brought the food to tables that ran the length of the earthen-floored longhouse.

The meal was late: Speeches ran on during the morning's com-memoration in the longhouse. The speakers were too emotional to think of the clock.

Col. Thomas E. O'Donovan, commander and district engineer for the Corps of Engineers' Portland District, holds the same job today as the man who closed the gates at The Dalles Dam in 1957. O'Donovan was aware of the burden of history his agency carries.

"I feel it very deeply," he said in an interview. "The corps is a con-tentious member of this community. There are many people who hate us deeply for what we did. But we can transcend it by behaving as nations do who are at peace, by talking things through about where we want to be today, and 50 years from now."

Part of that healing, tribal leaders noted, was properly commemo-rating the loss of Celilo Falls.

In ribbon shirts and in white buckskins, in eagle-feather war bonnets with ermine tassels and gleaming beaded regalia, tribal members turned out in their finest to mourn the falls, which they regard as an ancestor.

"Nothing is free," said Wilbur Slockish Jr., hereditary chief of the Klickitat people. "To the politicians and the ones who do all this massive construction, we are the invisible people. Wherever these massive construction projects go, someone has to pay. And there is another invisible people, the animals. No one asked them if they wanted to be flooded, or their feeding grounds taken.

"This is a sad time for us. We were a self-sufficient people. These are the things we have sacrificed. Fifty years of silence. Here. These are some of the things that need to be remembered."

His family would not let him watch the day the falls were flooded, Slockish remembered. "We were not supposed to be here," Slockish said. "It was like someone dying."

Nez Perce tribal member Allen Slickpoo Jr. thanked the U.S. government representatives who listened to the speeches stoically—the folks from the corps, the Bonneville Power Administration, the U.S. Bureau of Indian Affairs, members of Congress and others. "It's not your fault, what happened to us," Slickpoo said.

"Perhaps it's a spiritual spanking, though, for you forced our forefathers to agree to this Dalles Dam, and you told us we would not remove our sacred burial grounds or our petroglyphs. They are underwater now, like the falls."

To Rebecca Miles, chairwoman of the Nez Perce tribal executive committee, continued puzzlement about what the tribes want today, in return for the millions of acres ceded in the treaties, is disrespectful.

"What we want was spelled out in 1855," she said. "And that is a very small thing to ask in exchange for millions and millions of acres, to have fish for future generations and to be able to continue our way of life."

For all its massive power generation, if The Dalles Dam were proposed in its same location today, it would never be built, said Stanley Speaks, area director of the Northwest regional office of the U.S. Bureau of Indian Affairs.

"What a change in 50 years," Speaks said. "It took us so long to learn we could not make progress and destroy history and sacred sites and artifacts. For Celilo Falls, 50 years came a little too late."

Yet the river, and the salmon that even now are returning in the spring run, are still vital to the Columbia River tribes, said Yakama tribal member Debra Whitefoot, as she worked at a sink in the longhouse kitchen, thawing chinook for the feast.

"What's done can't be undone now, but we are trying to hold on to the memories of our ancestors," Whitefoot said. "That's not the way of our people to carry bitterness. That holds you down, it keeps you from enjoying the life you do have here. I still feel really connected here."

Her family still fishes nearly year round from a scaffold over the Columbia, she said. "It feels great to be by the river, it's calming. It's like a medicine to be down here, because my people's spirit is down here, and the spirit of the salmon."

ON THE YUKON

Judith Roche

Jessica could catch spawning salmon
in her hand net, set in river eddies.
We'd haul them, pulled up full,
to the fish camp she'd set up
and work all day cutting those
fine long strips of pink meat.
We did all the helping work—
no one could cut thin and sharp
like Jessica and her Finnish fish knife.
Dipped in sugar-salt brine and hung
on a line to dry, winter food they were.
We spent days shooing flies and whiskey jacks
off the parching fish. Ate the liver and roe
right away and kept on fishing
through hushed twilit night
while the sun circled the horizon
instead of going down.
Later on, when the dark came back,
we could see the Northern Lights.
The spirits are dancing,
interior Indians would say.

GRANDFATHER, HAULING IN THE NETS

Samuel Green

You can pray for as many fish in the floodlamps
as stars, but you better know the water.
I learned this bottom the hard
way, these rocks tearing the heart
out of my nets. Tides & currents
too, how they'll trick a man.
Everything I want trying to get away,
the love I wanted in my house,
what I couldn't set my nets for.
My sons, when they look at me
their eyes dull as these scales
drying on the deck.

I know this: a man wants something
he has to grab hold & pull hard.
My hands so hard
the jellyfish don't sting anymore.
How can a man be gentle with hands like these?

These Gulf winds, the storms here
rise out of whispers, from sounds soft as the love
a man might dream of. I dream
like a fish, dream deep & heavy, dream
something's after me. You think I like
the sound of fish flapping in the hold?
How they gape? How their goddamn gills
work & work until finally they just stop?

EXCERPTS FROM: TANKER NOTES

Gary Snyder

At Sea 29: VIII: 57

Picked up rucksack, saw hospital and immigration, & was took on launch to this ship, "Sappa Creek"—rusty and gray-covered with pipes and valves and shit, standing on fantail Mt. Fuji, the "new hip moon," Venus. In purple sunset. & below to the engine room to my work, Fireman. Tending seven red-eyed fires—roar and heat and sweat, jumble of pipes and valves. Up once for a break out of the noise and heat to cool air of fantail—Pleiades rising astern. Waves and machinery and music, bulkheads and drying overalls and underwears. Why all this oil? Ancient jungly heat of the sun.

Off Singapore 6:IX

Flying fish and a few bob-tailed shoreside-looking birds. Pulled a hot one today and sprayed hot oil around the fire-room. Now they say I'm a real fireman.

* * *

Caruso the Oiler was "living in jungles and on Salvation Army handouts" before he got this job. Now gone nuts over money and madly saving, spending nothing, because he wants to "leave an estate." His clothes are all beat up and he wanders about with a distracted little smile. Last night Singapore in a sudden cloudburst—nothing but a string of lights half-lost in rain. This morning the coast of Malaya—a low beach with low rugged hills behind it and tatters of cloud. Enter the Bay of Bengal.

—red wheel pipe-valves, silver-painted pipe elbows, pumps flows and checks. Red, black, aluminum. Water and oil. What curious forms love takes. Here in the belly of a whale.

Trincomalee Ceylon 12: IX

Woke early on my cot on the boatdeck & saw a bird flash in, soaring around the trees on shore—archaic planet epochs, bird-and-rock dawn, mountain and ocean feeling—curiously absent in Japan. Yesterday, coming into port, balancing burners and pressures and watching frantic wobbly gauges. British sailors with long blonde hair, in shorts.

Ashore up oil-&-pipe pier to drink Ceylon beer with Suquamish Indian Mason, & two beards Sandy & Jack. They on watch but drinking beer for coffee-time. Then walkt alone up hillside—scrubby dry sort of tough-leaved trees. Overlooking China Bay, oil tanks and rusty railroads, corrugated sheds and Tamil-speaking workmen. At a fresh-water storage place two monkeys jumped from way high and land WHAP on hard concrete, scampered off to the jungle, curly tails up high.

Midway 1: 1 X: 57

blue water breaking on the reef circle out there—white flat island with ironwood trees like feathery pine; fairy tern and long-tailed Tropic birds in the sky—and navy streets of gray buildings. Hawaiian Dredge Co. men with helmets & trucks, lift-trucks, steamrollers, dozers; yards of steel reinforcing, tar, building materials by the acre.

Drinking in the workers hall—dice games going—bearded Hawaiian-Chinese-Japanese mixtures in rubber zori and hacked-off trouser shorts. Sitting across from Caruso, wood table, cans of beer—the worst thing, he says, is greed. "Look at Me—greed ruined my life. Every time I see something I think I got to have it. But the more you grab the farther it gets away." Which advice in all humbleness I accept. & this morning, sense of presence as I stepped into the quonset Catholic chapel to scan the pamphlet rack; involuntary *gassho* and bow to the virgin.

White Terns—with delicate wing—and jetblack beak playing in the evening through boughs of ironwood. Shell of a dead tortoise. Body of a Frigate bird. Our own tracks seen again in the sand.

At Sea

talking with Perschke on the fantail. I ask him "What time do you go on lookout?"

—"When the sun sets. But I can't tell tonight, it's cloudy."

—"In Japan in the Buddhist temples they ring the evening bell when it gets so dark you can't see the lines in your hand while sitting in your room."

—"Full length or up close?"

—"Full length I guess."

—"Suppose you got a long arm. Maybe you're late. Are the windows open?"

—"Don't have any windows. The walls are open."

—"Always?"

—"Sometimes they're closed."

—"Can't always ring it at the right time, huh. What do they ring it for anyway."

—"Wake people up."

—"But that's in the evening."

—"They ring it in the morning too."

* * *

Reaching through hot pipes to turn nuts—the burned arm—squiggle lines and tiny surprise silver tube running off somewhere to tweet a gauge—box wrench 13/16; eye beam you beam, bulkhead sweat—flange leak and valve drip—old gasket pounder

—poke the big bolt through, seek nuts in pocket—whole ship twined about us, where do the pipes go? The engineer cursing and burning his unsteady hand—

* * *

At Sea 20: 111: 58

Cleaning, greasing, & labeling bearings. Hoover, New Departure, SKF, MRC, Federal. Shades of Bernhard Karlgren. A sunset of cloud-levels and alleys; hundred-miles-off cumulus peaks. The North Star sunk clean out of sight.

—madly singing and laughing, perched on pipes high on the shipside painting lower engine-room white—this is what I was born for—

Kwajalein 30:111

Americans are splendid while working—attentive, cooperative, with dignity and sureness—but the same ones seen later at home or bar are sloppy, bored and silly. Japanese almost the opposite—better at home than at work. (This when steering gear was out and we were all trying to figure why the hydraulic system wouldn't swing the rudder around. Air in the line.

Drinking with Joe: "If I'd 'v had education, I'd 'v been a MOTHERFUCKER.

15: IV: 58 approaching San Pedro

Five Laysan Albatrosses have followed us. The lights of San Pedro-seawater color changes, the air smell is different, the Albatrosses turn back, and the seagulls come to escort the tanker in.

AMMO SHIP

Clemens Starck

Mostly we hauled asphalt,
tens of thousands of drums of asphalt.
The master-plan
called for southeast Asia to be a parking lot.
If it wasn't asphalt, it was bombs.
The bombs were for the enemy.

One trip, four days out of southern California
in heavy seas, the cargo began to shift.
We climbed down into the hold with shoring timbers
    and wedges.
The bombs in their fragile wooden crates
tossed about like restless sleepers,
a nightmare screech of nails pulling and wood
splintering.
        The rest of the trip
morale was low. Not even
the cook's special blueberry pancakes
helped.

The people the bombs were for
scattered. Deer at the start of hunting season,
they knew we were coming
and they were scared too.

AT SEA

"Another Christmas shot to hell,"
the bosun says. Mid-ocean, last traces of Asia
five days astern.
Door to steel locker rattles softly.
Open porthole, cold air
sucked in.

"Nothing out here
but us!" the bosun says. Black lacquerware
sky, thin
sliver of the waning moon.

Course is zero-eight-zero. Following seas.

Bosun's name is McCaskey.
He's a high roller.
In the galley, over coffee and a cigarette, he discusses
women,
and the best way
of stopping off a mooring line.

THE PAN-OCEANIC FAITH

The night the Pan-Oceanic Faith went down
in a storm in the North Pacific,
we were a hundred miles south of her,
another freighter,
plowing through stormy seas.

As it turned out,
she was a sister ship—SIU, like us. Two of our crew
had boarded her in Seattle, months earlier.
But something about her
spooked them,
and they signed off before she sailed.

The sea that night was wild,
utterly unimaginable.
I had just been relieved at the wheel
when Sparks
stepped into the wheelhouse
to report to the mate that he'd picked up
an SOS . . .

When Conrad wrote, "The sea came at us
like a madman with an axe,"
he had it right.
Ten thousand tons of welded steel plate—buckled
and smashed, by water.

Three survivors, out of a crew of forty-two—
a messman,
the chief engineer, and one AB . . .

"Why those three?" we wondered
all the rest of the way in to Newport, Oregon,
and looked around
uneasily,
        weighing our chances,

sizing each other up.

First Trip

Richard Dankleff

He hated—hanging over the engine room
as the ship rolled—to soojy the grimed walls.
He had no stomach for riding the rope-slung
scaffold, dangling in fuel-oil fumes
and piston clang over the hot stokehole.
He loathed the 1st assistant, baked-red face
that spied from the gratings overhead
and yelled "Rub hard, wiper! Get it clean!"
Beneath the scaffold, leaning, twenty
thirty feet of space.

In soojy slush his hands turned slick as fish.
Hot steam lines curved like cats to nudge his legs.
Or oil got dripped on the sacred floorplates—
"Wiper!" By quitting time: too tired
to smoke. In dreams he swabbed
more grime, hot pistons clanged,
a scarlet 1st assistant finally
burst a vein, a mine field smashed
the bow, while he ignored "Abandon Ship!"
and stayed behind and scrubbed.

DEPARTURE

Down on the dock so many
gray-khaki police that (moments
before) they had overfilled
our wobbling gangway
dragged off to their truck
a still-well-dressed stowaway.
So many they could have carried him.
Instead had grabbed his ankles.
He was minus a shoe. His face dragged.

Cargo discharged,
we ride high in the water.
Off west, low sun daubs the clouds
blood red, break-glass-for-fireaxe red,
smudged-flag red like the logo
on the Panamanian freighter's stack
between us and the sunset.

From our bridge, a whistle,
broken English, the pilot
orders mooring lines cast off
and we slip away, eastward,
two kids stowed in our engine room
the uncle far
and farther behind us
with the gray police
and the ultraradical sky.

THE SPLASH

It makes me step quick to the rail:
dark ripples radiate like a watery echo
and drop behind in the night. Was that darker
something someone off the boatdeck?
Now's the time to shout an alarm
if I'm going to shout. Night, though,
wraps the place . . . . Maybe an ocean animal
rising, swashed, or was hit by the keel,
or an outsize wave slapped hard in the wake.
Nothing is left to see. Or hear,
except below, a monotonous clock,
the regular throb of the engines. Not reason
to shout Man Overboard, trigger lights
along three decks. No need to rush the mate
into the wheelhouse, push his hand
on the engine telegraph all the way over to Stop.
No need to make the helmsman bring her around
and steam slowly back through the thick dark
in a mile- or two-mile circle, while the stack blats
Boat Stations and a searchlight reaches ahead,
fluttering over the water, dimly,
too late. No real chance of tracing
the first track, wiped out, where a swimmer's cries,
weakening soon, already must be lost.
The swimmer, blind as myself, too tired now
even to care, his arms too liquid
to lift one more time, will yield
and flow away, like a grain of salt dissolving.
Beyond us both, the night sky misses nothing.

Without moving an arm
I also am sliding away, a spark
blown out of the stack overhead
and flaring to soot.

PACIFIC ROUTE

Between two layers of blue
that look as if they could absorb
whatever we are, as Asia through the years
takes care of its invaders, I steer
a course that matches a line
lightly penciled on the mate's chart.
Not clearly sky, not sea: commingled
blues. Through these we steam
as in some merely-rumored region
a level head might call unreal. To stray
off course or lose a grip
on what is roughly what
would be . . . easy.
Radar reports: nothing solid.
Low drifting cumulus
includes what was our bow
and forward hatch. On the port beam
the vague horizon, shifty, blue,
gone gray, comes in patches.
This yielding atmosphere could harbor
all our forwardness, combine
our thin identities with air—
or so, apparently, I'm willing
to believe. Like a slack-water bug
baffled by drift and tide,
we seem to get nowhere, even though
we trail a streak of black smoke
like an unraveling banner.

Working on Deck, Ten Years Later

Holly J. Hughes

Coil the line against the sun
    the old timers said,
clockwise on deck,
    and ten years later
my arms still breaststroke
    the familiar movement
loop upon loop
    rolling the line a quarter turn
so it won't kink,
    feeling the resistance give way in the hands,
    stiff fibers yielding:
the line knows how to lay
    if you let it.
Now all the old loops come back
    and my hands swim
down the line by heart
    and the line remembers
all its lives,
    the past carried firm
in its fibers,
    how they intertwine
coil upon coil
    circling emptiness
to make way for the next.

Point Colpoys, Alaska: Tendering

The shoreline sheathed in fog as we run east
    into dawn, we can't see a thing
  but the bow-wave carries the dawn
    and we follow, trusting.

6 a.m. and the radio's silent before the boats waken.
Coffee's on and we ease into the day at seven knots
      a speed I've learned is fast enough
         to go anywhere.

I re-read your letter now, telling of theater
in New York and I can't help but wonder
    what could be better than this,
     watching the fog curtain rise

as the gillnetters trail in, their long skirts flowing,
   shining holds empty and expectant,
     while the salmon wait, silent silver
      dreams in dark waters.

SEPTEMBER FROM ROCKY PASS

Marine radio calls for gusts up to 50,
rain thrums on the wheelhouse roof;
wind shrills in the rigging
as another squall rolls through.

On the back deck, five crabs scuttle
in a blue bucket, the scratches startling,
until I remember what makes them, think
how good they'll taste for dinner.

Yesterday I found a Steller's Jay:
breast picked clean, only tail feathers intact.
One creature dead, another about to be eaten,
the line crossed in a wingbeat.

Two days ago we ran aground,
had to wait for the rising tide to float us.
We could see the channel from where we were
but that didn't matter much.

I can't put that jay out of my mind. When Steller
saw him, he knew they'd reached Bolshaya Zemlya.
His servant shot the bird to bring home and
Steller drew the jay in all its blue-black beauty.

How young Steller was, how difficult the voyage:
Bering sick, crew weak from scurvy.
Still he wrote in his log the voyage was a success
though that winter, most of the men died.

In a few hours this storm, too, will pass.
We will eat crab for dinner,
crack and pick each red claw clean
and forget to think much about it.

Preparation Is Everything

You taught me to hang nets the old way:
I'd straddle your hanging bench,
my needle slowly learning to fly,
pick three, drop two, counting the meshes
like a mantra, leadline slowly dwindling

on the wooden spool. Then you'd
measure the hangings, your hands clawed
from years of fishing, accidents denied,
cold water curling them up like leaves.
You'd fill my needles so I couldn't stop,
tell of crossing the Gulf of Alaska
in 100-knot winds and 30-foot seas,
breaking ice from the rigging with baseball bats.

I love your needles made of whale bone,
though the plastic ones work better.
Best of all I like the needle that was clear green
like a pop bottle or an emerald.
I'd watch the pile of gillnet grow,
and imagine salmon swimming past
while I wove time with my green needle,
in a world where nets were not
entanglements, but tiny, open doors.

Now we climb the old wooden steps for dinner,
go to the kitchen, where you remind me
preparation is everything:

Cut the cabbage like this, little slices,
fine, bit by bit it becomes cole slaw
but you gotta have a sharp knife, you hear?
Just a little bit at a time. Like this.
Minnie makes the cole slaw, but I always cut it.
Fine, real fine.

Silver Sea

Michael Daley

We are going through the Ballard Locks. I don't know how to describe
the craving I feel when our boat slides down the walls and I stare at
the intense green of the algae. I am standing at the bow of the *Silver
Sea* after having tied us to a cleat on the port side, sea gulls haunting the air. To them we must become small when the water leaving
the locks, lowers us to the level of the sea—thalassa, the green algae,
muck on the water's surface, pleasure boats at their moorage in the
harbor, on our way to the sea lands, gull road, salmon-leaping path,
ship wake, ferry traffic.

After I've been out a while, and I am in my bunk reading, I hear a
little squeak, like music. I'm proud of myself, for recognizing the sound.
We must have tied up to a purse seiner, our fenders sing along their
gunwales. Damon and Sherman will hoist salmon from the seiner to
our boat. I will keep records and watch what they do, so I can take
over when the next boat comes in. They put on slickers, resolutely;
it is the middle of the night, and, sardonically grim, they seem to be
strapping on valor, chastened by what must be done. As they work,
even as they joke with the captain of the seiner, they seem to pass
precious cargo at times, and at others, brusque, they slap the fish
down on the deck, leaving a shine there. There are blood drops all
over, even on my sweater although I sit in the cabin with my pencil
recording the number and weights of brights and darks, chum and
king. Once, when I stepped out on the deck for a breather, a fish fell
into the water and escaped, darting away from us.

In the industrial, and romantic, glare of the seiner's light, some
of their crew are filleting fish, some are passing them, huge, ten- or

twenty-pound salmon, eyes wide and elegant. The seiner makes the sound of a factory at sea. The Greek word comes back again—thalassa—and reminds me, but mistakenly, of the old poem, not Homer but William Cullen Bryant's "Thanatopsis," death and earth its containment, as I now see death in the eyes of Coho.

On the *Paragon*, the seiner, fish have been kept alive in water in the ship's hold. Now, as they turn them over to us because we are the buyer's boat, we stand at the edges of the hold and hundreds, hundreds, of fish thrash, writhe, splash, and bang against one another to follow the water out of the drain. Then men go down there to throw them onto the deck, lifting gently—not to bruise them, sacramentally it seems—each fish into our arms. In the box where they are weighed for market, and counted, they still thrash, until they're dumped onto the ice where the spirit finally leaves. Having been kept alive for so long, they will make the freshest possible servings. Fish blood is on the scarlet surface of Shilshole Bay. A skiff slides across the blackened foam and scales; perhaps someone is going to the bar for last call. I watch the white wake of the *Alaska Blues*, another seiner, stripe the black water. November will be the month for chums, its skipper told me. He's been fishing Alaska, where they have had a good season. We have not had a good season, because of El Nino, they say. I close the door to the hold where the ice is. They flap to death. Eyes red open.

Under the sign of the "Cash Buyer," our competitor, the skipper of the *Myrna Rose*, has painted a shamrock on his wheelhouse wall. He comes over the VHF. His name is Bud Royal. "This is the *Myrna Rose*." And he says what he will pay for bright, not dark, red chums or dogs up to five thousand pounds. Then he says he'll only buy from gillnetters, who won't be in until early in the morning. He will fillet what he buys and send the fish by air to San Francisco, or at least that's what Damon has guessed. But when I ask Bud where he does send them, he says, "Texas!" Working for himself, and not for a company the way Damon does, he can pay whatever price he wants, but now that he has announced it so well in advance, he has raised the price that all buying boats must pay. Damon doesn't want to get on the VHF to confer with his boss, because of course he'd be announcing to everyone in the fleet that he has this problem. So we must row in to where there is a pay phone. He says most gillnetters won't come in before dawn, and anyone who shows up before midnight doesn't have shit.

We get into the dinghy like a pair of smugglers. I row, of course, and try to keep the oars as quiet as possible, which seems stupid since Damon laughing at his own jokes makes us as conspicuous as an outboard motor would. Sherman is content to stay on board with his dog, Higgins, who I am just as glad to be getting away from. This might be an elaborate excuse to head for the bar.

I don't remember how we got back on board. I must have rowed again, and I'm sure we were pretty noisy. I also know that we didn't leave the bar until closing time, and that Damon did get the word from his boss to raise his prices to just below Bud's. But at dawn I don't feel well, and the first gillnetters are tying up to us. They are as thick as flies: the *Ballerina, Twin Sisters, Astro*. On deck, a cup of Sherman's gritty coffee in hand, I am swimming in fish. They are sailing into the weight bucket. This morning, even dizzy I feel the romance of the salmon, so different now from last night with the lights of the purse seiners. As I unload, I remember my dream of seeing a big submarine go past us starboard. It was too small to have been a Trident. Another, a bigger one, went by further out at sea in the gray pre-dawn.

After the wave of gillnetters subsides, the Washington State Fisheries biologist comes aboard. He decides allotment: how many fish for Indians and how many for whites. How much time will it take for Indians to get their allotted percentage of the catch, how much for whites to catch up, and vice-versa. Each boat will have to sell all the fish; they can't keep any. The buyer can sell the fish back to the fisher. Because some fishermen keep their own fish to take home, although it is illegal, the biologist can't record all of the fish. With unrecorded fish it's impossible to estimate the total available and they can't make decisions on the number of fishing days for whites and Indians. Sports fishermen take the biggest percentage of unrecorded fish; they sell to restaurants, which is also illegal. Little private buyers like Bud Royal represent another big percentage because by the time the biologist comes along and tries to record, Bud's gone.

Two men stand on deck and discuss the deaths of friends. They are unsentimental, and sad, laughing. Damon tells me the story of the *Alki*, his own boat, which he sold to two "children" who were helped in buying it by an old man living in Anacortes. The man gave them whatever thousands of dollars they needed and took an IOU. He wanted to go to Alaska one last time with them. When the old man fell overboard and drowned, they got the boat and who the hell knows where they are now. Somewhere in Alaska— with or without his boat, he says, they got right with the Lord and who knows maybe they don't even owe the estate anything anymore. "Full fathom five thy father lies; . . . Those are pearls that were his eyes."

I am sitting on deck most of the time when we are in transit now. A small group of orca whales raced the *Silver Sea* yesterday, their black and white flashes cutting across the bow. But now, on the stern while Damon, Sherman and Higgins are in the wheelhouse, I imagine myself afloat on the wake. I can't grab anything. They can't hear me. I wave, they move way faster and I can't swim to them. My boots drag me down, my clothes are heavy, arms cold; the wake bubbles up into my mouth and tastes bad. I choke for twenty minutes before they are a speck.

The fisherman faces are haggard and hard, heroic like Odysseus. *Hercules*, the tug, pulls a barge long enough to be a floating skyscraper. The captain of the *Brenda Rose*, a young man with a face that's lived a century, heads down the Duwamish River. I wave to him as his boat passes us. Damon tells me to get back to cleaning the deck. I say I did that already. No, he says, there's a lot of minor blood-scrubbing left. Luckily, Higgins, who hasn't left the boat, hasn't pissed or shit in three days. I stay on deck because the wheelhouse smells of cigarettes, exhaust gasoline, and fish blood.

By the time I am really ready to walk on pavement and, as we've been saying to one another for days, "to get off the fucking boat," we get a call from the boss that there's to be another opening on Hood Canal, that is, another day or two for white commercial fishermen to haul in everything they can find. It means another ten thousand pounds of fish and maybe a hundred dollars for me. "Maybe five hundred, maybe a thousand," Damon says. So far I've made eighty-eight dollars. Greed competes with exhaustion; I tell myself I don't want the money that much. But it's no use.

The competition is incredible, the opening like a secret. Yet we have arrived too late, and the catch has already been sold. We beat them last week, Damon says, and they beat us this week. After we sit for hours waiting for gillnetters to sell us some fish, we decide to take what we have back to the fish buyer's pier. From Hood Canal off Whiskey Spit, we head for the Duwamish River, which is cluttered with shipbuilders. In among the moorages for the new craft is Booth fisheries, which buys not only salmon, but also apples, wheat, anything they're brought. I'm told that they own the Northwest. A guy at the bar one night told me, "Hang around with Damon Valera long enough and you'll see everything there is to see about how the Northwest works."

This is how it works: I shovel a ton and a half of ice and unload eight thousand pounds of salmon. Saturated by the bodies of the swimmers, I still remember how they pass without dignity into the huge bucket the buyer lowers into our hold and hoists up to fillet, to ice and to sell. Thousands of open eyes look at me in the ice hold; I grow a little panicky in the small tight place. I think about the totem of good harvest, and sit down on the remaining ton of slippery fish.

As soon as we unload we head for the Wharf Tavern and I begin spending the few dollars I draw against wages, which, in fact, will not amount to much. We drink to somebody's birthday; everyone hoists a drink bought with a hundred dollar bill. A man from Las Vegas is up on stage; we're certain he has never gone out on the water, as has his entire audience. He croons late Fifties tunes for us. He is wearing a sequined shirt, like fish scales, opened to the chest. It is one of the saddest stage routines I have ever seen.

THE SALMON OF THE HEART

Tom Jay

Speckled Dream
I went to the sea
for myself.
She fed me
health, new legs.
Perhaps a speckled dream
to wrestle in the night.

Years ago, working as a boat puller on a troller in southeast Alaska, something happened that is an image for the beginning and end of this essay. We were fishing the Fairweather grounds off Lituya. The skipper called me to bring the landing net to his side of the boat. He was working a big king on the kill line[1] and gave me instruction on how to approach the salmon with the net. It was the biggest king I had ever seen, perhaps a hundred-pounder and too big to gaff. As I brought the net behind and under him he began to swim away—not fast but steady like a draft animal pulling a heavy load. The moment had the inexorable quality of awakening: the salmon and I were in the same world as the kill line went taut and the hundred-pound test leader snapped and the fish flashed out of sight. I recall this story to remind me that salmon is free and that these musings are only lines and hooks that hold him momentarily.

As I turn 40 and enter the second half of life, it occurs to me how like the salmon is the life of the soul. Salmon is born in a rivulet, a

---

1. A rubber line to which the leader was attached while playing the fish.

creek, the headwaters of some greater river. He runs to the sea for a mysterious sojourn, his flesh reddens; mature, he awakens once again to his birthplace and returns there to spawn and die. Loving and dying in the home ground resounds in us. We all want a meaningful death in a familiar locale. Salmon embodies this for us, our own loving deaths—at home in the world. Salmon dwells in two places at once—in our hearts and in the world. He is essentially the same being, the sacred salmon, salmon of the heart.

The Leaper

The doctor was explaining how sperm moved, like salmon, and how the uterus gave them hold, created "current" so they knew which way to swim. I thought, "Jesus, salmon!" and knew I was one once. It was as real as this: I could remember the slow torture of rotting still alive in a graveled mountain stream. Humped up, masked in red and green, dressed for dancing, I was Death's own delight, her hands caressing me . . . and this is the part I can't remember: whether she laughed or wept as we rolled in love.

Introduction is a word that at root means being led into the circle. Here is one last introduction to salmon. Not long ago a friend and I were sitting by Admiralty Inlet, talking. I mentioned an idea to create a sculpted "rainbow" of salmon of all species. One end of the rainbow would rise out of Puget Sound, and it would end in a well in an alder grove on the shore. My friend responded to the idea by saying, "The salmon is the soul in the body of the world." Indeed the salmon is at least the soul of this biome, this green house. He is the tutelary spirit that swims in and around us, secret silver mystery, salmon of the heart, tree-born soul[2] of our world.

---

2. Trees provide detritus, organic energy forms, to feed caddis fly and other aquatic larvae that in turn feed salmon fry. In salmon spawning areas, the upper reaches of rivers, the major energy source is forest detritus. Trees also shade the home creeks, maintaining cool water temperatures vital to salmon. The forest is mother to the salmon.

This essay depends in part on the notion that, salmon-like, language bridges subject and object worlds, inner and outer. Language is the path, the game trail, the river, the reverie between them. It shimmers there, revealing and nourishing their interdependence. Each word *bears* and *locates* our meetings with the world. A word is a clipped breath, a bit of spirit (*inspire, expire*) wherein we hear the weather. Our "tongues" taste the world we eat. At root, language is sacramental. The study of etymology reveals that language is trying to contain, remember and express the religious event at the core of our mundane awareness.[3]

The heart of language is not merely communication but consecration, each word the skin of a myth. A telling example of this is our word *resource.*

In current usage, *resource* means raw material or potential energy. We have resource planning, resource development and resource allocation. In our day "resource" denotes an energized plastic something we practice our clumsy cleverness on. But beneath current usage lies a deeper, religious information. Etymology reveals that resource derives from *surge* and *re*. *Re* means back, as in return, refund. *Surge* is a Latin-rooted word whose cognates include regal, resurrection, right and rule, among others. *Surge* is a contraction of Latin *subregere*, to rule or direct from below. In its root sense, its heart sense, *resource* is a recurring directed energy sent by powers hidden from view. A *resource* surges back, sent by a hidden power. What the word knows in its heart is that *resources are sacred powers*, deities. A *resource* is the unseen river. The roots of the word tell us that they are attendable, venerable. *Resources* require our prayer and poise, not our machinations. The spear light above the numinous salmon, not estuarine fish factories where managed hatchery cannibal clones, hungry ghosts of

---

3. My bet is that very few modern "new" words will last, precisely because our age has lost the religious instinct. It is not "language" but human intelligence that has created most "new" words.

our cleverness, homeless seagoing spam, return for "processing." Part of this essay's intent is to re-awaken the religious sense nascent in language; to coax words and their objects back into the sacred realm where the *resource* is what we listen to and for; where our "tongues" are tasting sacramental food, and our speech is "soul food."

 Mircea Eliade said in his work, *The Sacred and the Profane*, "To settle territory is in the last analysis equivalent to consecrating it." We are nowhere near consecrating this place. We have destroyed the original human vision of this place, and now we are busy pillaging the *resources* that inspired it. Our culture here is prophylactic and profane, a kind of battle armor rather than careful turning and re-turning of the soil that the etymology of *culture* reveals. We see the world through the glass of a speeding machine whose servants we are. The locale, the *resource*, is just another road kill to quarrel over. This essay cannot stop the machine or consecrate the landscape; no one person can do that. But we can roll down a window, the *windeye*, and look into the local vision, let it see us, re-awaken our longing for connection, witness the vanity of our speed. I want to praise the sacred salmon, the salmon of the heart, shuttle of Gaia's loom, swift silver thread . . .

I once swam down the Duckabush River in a wetsuit and mask. It was during the dog salmon run, and there were a lot of fish in the river. The current ran both ways that day. I came to a deep pool where a river eddy had piled a perfect pyramid of golden alder leaves. Farther on, resting in the shallows by a large submerged snag, I mused on what I'd seen, when I noticed a shape move behind the snag. It was a large dog salmon, splotchy gray and yellow, vaguely striped, probably a male, spawned out but alive in his eyes. We were a foot apart. I looked into his eye. He saw me but did not move. I was just another river shadow, an aspect of his dying, an aspect of his marriage, another guest at the feast. He was the eye of the *resource*, the subterranean sometime King, fish-eyed inscrutable god, alder-born-elder, tutor.

248

The salmon of the heart is not *cuisine*; it is soul food. We are subsistence fishing in the craft of language. Everyone knows when they have a bite. Imagine what follows as hooks or cut herring, "hoochies" or knots in a net, eddies in the home stream; imagine the salmon in your heart, spawning, dying.

An Etymological Glossary of Salmon Terms[4]:

Salmon: from Latin *salmo,* from Gaullic *salmo,* "the leaping fish." Ultimately derived from Indo-European *sal* to leap; hence the cognates (words born of the same root): resiliant, exultant, exile, sally, and somersault.

Alevin: from Old French *alever,* to rear, from Latin *ad-levare,* to raise; literally: a reared one.

River: from Latin *ripa,* a river bank. Cognates are arrive, derive, rivalry. Deep in the root of this word is the Indo-European *ri,* flow, which is akin to Greek *rhein* (flow) whence Rhea, the mother of the gods. (Much of salmon's power derives from its connection to rivers, to the flow, mother of gods—silver shuttle in *Gaia's loom.*)

Anadromous: from Greek *ana,* up, and *dromos,* running. Salmon is the one who runs up. The Indo-European root is *der,* whence thread, treadle, trade, tramp, trap.

Redd: to put in order, to ready or arrange. Partridge, in *Origins,* has *redd* as salmon spawn from red, the color, in addition to *redd,* dialect English to tidy, arrange, as above. The two senses seem mixed in the salmon redd, the bed of gravel heaped over the fertile eggs. It's interesting to note that redd may be related to ride and road. (Redds like grave mounds, tumuli beneath the torrent, resurrection of the resource, cradle and the grave.)

---

4. A *term* is in its roots a terminus, a boundary, a moment looking at the other side, a *glossary* is a collection of glosses, terms hard to ken; *etymology* is the story of the truth in words.

Poach: from Middle French *pocher*, to thrust, hence to encroach upon, trespass. Probably akin to Middle Dutch *pocken*, to boast, talk, big talk, bluff. A cognate of poach is poker, the bluffing game. (A poacher pokes the resource; dangerous game.)

Spawn: from Old French *espandre*, to shed, from Latin *expandere*, to stretch, to spread out. Spawn is probably akin to *patere*, to lie open; cognates: petal and patent.

Milt: salmon sperm; Indo-European root *mel*, soft; with various derivatives referring to soft or softened materials, hence melt, mulch, bland, schmaltz, and smelt (metals). (Alchemical salmon, gold in the sea, mulching the soil, melting in the rivers . . .)

Roe: salmon ovum; "hard roe" are eggs, "soft roe" is sperm, milt.

Religion: from Latin *re*, back, and *ligare*, to bind. Religion binds us back. Religion is the tie that binds. Cognates include rely, ally, obligation, ligament, lien. Our connection to salmon is religious. He binds us to a sacred world, sews us into a sacred web.

Net: from Indo-European root *nedh*, to bind or knot. Cognates include node, nexus, denouement, and connection.

Troll: from Old French *troller*, to walk about, to wander. Probably akin to German *stroloh*, vagabond, and our *stroll*. The French had *trollerie*, aimless wandering of dogs. (Little boats bobbing on the great sea, hoboes.)

Fry: originates in the Indo-European word root *bhrei*, to cut, break, crumble. Hence friction, debris, fray and fry. Fry are the raveling ends of a mysterious rope.

Weir: from Old Frisian and Old Saxon, *wearian*, to defend, protect, hence to hinder others. The root sense is to warn. Cognates are guarantee, warrant, garret, and warn. (Indian weirs always had a hole to let salmon through. The weir warned both ways; the *resource's guarantee*.)

Parr: a young salmon. When runs decline, the parrs sometimes spawn early. Though the origin is unknown, I propose Latin *parere*,

to produce a child. Indo-European root is *per*, to procure
prepare. (*Oxford English Dictionary* suggests a Scottish orig

Smolt: a young salmon entering the sea. Akin to smelt. Ultimately
akin to Indo-European *mel*, soft.

Well: from Indo-European *wel*, to turn, roll, with derivatives referring to curved, enclosing objects. (The well rolls . . . the well wells.)

Tutelary: ultimate origin unknown but derived from Latin *tueri*, to
guard, to watch. Cognates are tutor, tuition, intuition. Salmon is a
tutelary spirit of this place. He teaches and guards our health.

"Scientists guess that Atlantic salmon migrated across the Arctic
Ocean during a warm period between ice ages, and then became isolated when renewed glaciation blocked the water passage above the
American or Asian land masses. Through specialization, these colo-
nizing salmonids separated into six species, taking advantage of some-
what different niches in the North Pacific environment. The Pacific
salmon developed one characteristic that separates them from the
Atlantic parent stock and adds greatly to their mystique—all six species return to the river only once, dying shortly after they spawn.

All salmonids prefer cold, oxygen-rich waters. They range between
about forty and seventy degrees north latitude. There is considerable
overlap in the individual species' ranges. Only the chum and pink
salmon inhabit the rivers of Siberia and northern Alaska that empty
into the Arctic Ocean, and only the chinook travel as far south as
Monterey Bay, but in the middle of their range all species are represented. The exception is the cherry or masu salmon, which is found
only on the Asian side of the Pacific, primarily in Japan."[5]

Nine years ago I read an essay by Freeman House entitled "Totem
Salmon." It changed my life then and is the inspiration for much
of this essay. His description of salmon's life cycle and behavior establishes a factual background to salmon's appeal to our imagina-

---

5. Philip Johnson, "Salmon Ranching" in *Oceans*, January-February 1982, page
42.

tions. I reprint a portion of it, subtitled "Salmon Mind," as a kind of "photo"-documentary of the resource-god's dance.

••

Salmon Mind

There are seven varieties of salmon which range and feed in the North Pacific. At the northern extreme of their range they frequent and feed in the Bering Sea, but at the southern extreme are rarely found south of forty-one degrees. These are their names:

Onchorynchus chavica: *called King, Chinook, Tyee, Spring, Quinnat*

Northern Hokkaido to the Sacramento River

O. kisutch: *called Coho, Silver*

Monterey Bay to the Kamchatka Peninsula

O. nerka: *called Sockeye, Red, Blueback, Nerka*

Fraser River to the Kurile Islands

O. gorbucha: *called Pink, Humpbacked, Humpie*

Klamath River to Korea

O. keta: *called Chum, Dog, Keta*

Puget Sound to Korea

O. masu: *called Cherry, Masu*

Amur River to the Pusan River of Korea

Salmo gairdneri: *called Steelhead Trout*

Klamath River to the Stikine in Alaska

Salmon eggs are deposited in more or less evenly graded gravel with enough cold water running over them to maintain an even temperature but not enough to disturb the eggs. The eggs are a brilliant translucent orange-red, about the size of buckshot. Sockeyes will spawn in lakes rather than streams. A single female will deposit up to a thousand eggs in a single "redd" or nest.

After a gestation period of 50 days to three months, the "alevins" hatch out with yolk sacs still attached. The babies nestle in the gravel for several weeks until the yolk sac is gone and they have gained an inch in size. At this point, they emerge from the gravel as"fry," quick and light-shy. It is at this stage of development that life is most perilous, the small fish being vulnerable to hungry larger salmon, other fish, water birds and snakes.

The fry feed at dawn and dusk and into the night on planktonic crustacea and nymphs, growing fastest in the summer when insects are most available. Most salmon remain in lakes and streams for two years, though pinks and dogs begin their journey to the sea in the first year, as fry.

The migration to salt water is an epic event involving millions of smolt (as the little salmon are called at this stage). On the Yukon River, the journey can be as long as 1,800 miles, on the Amur 700-800. The fish travel in schools, at night to avoid predators, following the guidance of a single larger smolt who seems to make decisions for schools at obstructions, rapids, etc. Out of two million eggs, perhaps 20,000 fish have survived to make the migration.

On the way downstream, the smolt can be killed by 1) natural predators; 2) irrigation ditches which confuse and trip the fish; 3) undissolved human sewage; 4) turbine intakes at dams which act as meat grinders; 5) nitrogen-rich water on the downstream side of darns; 6) wastes from pulp mills; 7) wastes from chemical plants; and 8) warm or oxygen-depleted water created by industrial flow-through.

Now the smolt will spend three to five months in estuaries and bays, gradually acclimating to salt water. They begin by feeding on zooplankton. As they grow larger and develop stronger teeth they will eat crustaceans such as shrimp (which some biologists believe colors their flesh), euphasids, amphipods, copepods, pteropods and squid.

It is at this point in the consideration of salmon that biologists begin to slide of into weary human-centered metaphors for the talents and strengths of the fish. We are talking about the great ocean migrations of the salmon, wherein they range and feed for thousands of miles in the North Pacific, grow to maturity and navigate unerringly back to the stream of their birth on a time schedule which can be predicted to within a few days.

In general, North American salmon make this circular journey in a counter-clockwise direction while Asian salmon move clockwise. Often the great schools' paths will mingle, sharing the search for food that has brought them halfway across the Pacific. Pinks make the circuit once and race home to spawn; sockeyes once each year for three or four years. The enormous schools travel at a general rate of ten miles per day until the spawning urge takes them and they increase their speed to thirty miles per day. The fish are nearly always found in the top ten meters of water during the migrations.

No one really understands the mechanisms that guide the fish through the trackless ocean and back to a specific spot at a specific time. Evidence would seem to indicate that the circuits are printed on the genes of the individual fish. It is probable that neither a consciousness common to a school nor memorized information guides them. There is, however, plenty of room for speculation. The evidence is in as of 1968:

• The migration is in a circular motion, rather than to and fro, eliminating the possibility of the fish backtracking on themselves.

• Salmon find their ways to the spawning grounds as individuals, not in schools.

• Arrival of the fish at the spawning grounds is less variable than the seasonal changes in the weather, making the use of temperature gradients as guidance cues unlikely.

• The nearly constant overcast in the far North Pacific makes celestial navigation unlikely (but not impossible).

• Migration routes tend to be across open water, even in areas where it would be easy to follow the coast, so that the use of physical landmarks is eliminated

• The fish swim actively downstream in and across the currents of the Pacific. The currents have subtle differences in salinity, but in order to use these differences as cues, the salmon would have to group up near the edges of the streams, which they do not do.

• Seawater is an electrical conductor moving through the planet's magnetic field, thus the ocean currents generate small amounts of electrical potential, Some fish are able to detect such small amounts of voltage and there is reasonable speculation on the part of Dr. William Royce et al. that salmon may have similar receptors and use the electricity as a navigational cue.

Salmon always find their way back to the stream or lake where they were born and spawn there again, generation after generation. As they approach fresh water, they have reached the peak of their physical and instinctual genius. Fat and shining and leaping, schools will swarm restlessly at the mouths of rivers and streams, waiting for optimal conditions of run-off. They feed voraciously now, generally on herring for they will not feed again once they enter fresh water. This is the time to take salmon for meat. The flavor and texture of the flesh is at its very best and, eaten fresh, the strength of the fish will stay with the eater.

It is likely that the salmon use their keen sense of smell to identify their home estuary and to choose the right forks as they push upstream. Biologists have run experiments on the fish at this stage of their journey, plugging the salmons' nostrils. Without a sense of smell the spawning run tends to move in a random manner and the fish get lost.

The trip upstream is an enormous effort. Even in the absence of human improvements on the rivers, cataracts, rapids and waterfalls must be overcome. In spite of obstacles, the fish travel between 39 and 90 miles a day until they have reached the spawning ground. The salmon now undergo striking physiological changes. Humpbacks will grow the hump for which they are named. Dogs grow long, sharp teeth and the upper mandible grows out and extends down over the lower. The body of the sockeye will turn fresh-blood red, its head an olive green. In general, the fish turn dark and bruised; the organism begins to consume itself, Drawing its last strength from ocean-gained fat, the flesh turns soft.

Now the salmon perform the breathtaking dance for which their entire lives have been in preparation. As they reach their spawning home, the fish pair off, male and female. A sort of courtship ensues, the male swimming back and forth over the female as she prepares the nest, rubbing and nudging her, then darting out to drive off other males. The female builds the nest with her tail, scooping out silt and smaller stones to a depth of several inches and in an area twice the length of the fish. Finally all that is left in the nest are larger stones. The crevasses and fissures between the stones will provide shelter for the eggs. The nest completed, the female assumes a rigid position over the center of it and the male approaches, curving his body up against hers. The eggs and clouds of milt are deposited simultaneously. The sperm, which stays alive in the water for seconds only, must enter the egg through a single tiny pore or micropyle, which itself closes over in a matter of minutes. In situations where the current is extremely fast, two males will sometimes serve a single female to ensure fertilization. The nest is covered and the process is repeated for a day or a week, until the eggs are all deposited. (Males fight each other for dominance, females fight each other for territory.)

A single female will deposit from 2,000 to 5,000 eggs, but only a small percentage of these are destined to hatch. The rest are eaten by fish or birds, attacked by fungi or washed downstream.

Now the fish, already decomposing, begin to die, and within days all have finished their migration. Their bodies are thrown up on the banks of streams and rivers providing feast for bear and eagle.[6]

••

---

6. "Totem Salmon" by Linn House, *Truck 18, Biogeography Workbook (1)*, Truck Press, Seattle, 1978.

The Atlantic salmon, a fish like our steelhead that does not ¡
after spawning but returns to the sea and may spawn again, was once
much more extensive with huge runs on all the major rivers of northern Europe. Runs extended as far south as Portugal and as far north
as subarctic Norway and Iceland. The fish were once so plentiful that
nobility would not eat them because they were a staple of their serfs'
diet. Today only Iceland, Scotland, Norway and Ireland have decent
salmon fisheries. England is trying to coax salmon back into its pol-
luted waterways with varied success. The fish is essentially extinct in
the rest of Europe except for a small one-river run in Normandy that
is being poached into extinction despite official efforts to save it.

Compared to its European cousin, the wild Pacific salmon is in relatively good shape. But it is by no means a healthy resource. Logging
has blocked streams, even whole rivers for a while. Soil failures, siltation and slope failures caused by clearcutting have destroyed spawning habitat. Over-fishing has depleted breeding stocks, and dams have
exterminated whole races of salmon. The most recent threat to the
wild Pacific salmon is genetic contamination and competition from
aquaculture clones which threaten to contaminate and/or starve out
a gene pool adapted to the essential climatic and geologic variables
of this locale. Clone salmon are genetically adapted to the economic
and technically determined environs of state and corporate aquaculture centers. Hatchery fish are virtually different beings from wild
fish. They are selected for their ability to survive the crowded, *single
feed* hatchery environment. (Wild salmon survive life in the ocean
at twice the rate of hatchery clones since they are better adapted
to natural conditions.) Aquaculturists brag of the differences. They
are breeding salmon to work for corporate interests, efficient production and high profit . . . in short, breeding salmon as anadromous Herefords. Soon there may be salmon with corporate names:
Ore-Aqua silvers, *Anadromous* kings, *Weyerhauser* dogs (all names of
aquaculture corporations).

Corporate fish biologists often use the buffalo-cattle analogy when discussing[7] wild and hatchery salmon. The plains were cleared of wild herbivores so the cattle industry could grow. Corporations interested in aquaculture argue that we needn't worry about habitat or spawning grounds, that they can do it all at the river mouths with technology and money. That means that watershed health is no longer essential to salmon livelihood and that watersheds may be indiscriminately developed. This may be part of the reason why timber companies are investing in salmon aquaculture. Perhaps they figure if they can keep salmon on the industrial consumer's dinner plate, the "consumers" won't yell so loudly when logging devastates wild salmon habitat.

An interesting aspect of the wild vs. hatchery salmon issue is the carrying capacity controversy. Some biologists have begun to argue that there is a limited carrying capacity for salmon in the ocean (common sense vs. the profiteer apologists again). They predict that heavy releases of clone salmon may further reduce the food of wild salmon. (Russia and Japan have extensive hatchery programs.) What the aquaculturists are creating is an "economy" that is exploitive, and hence unstable, in place of one that was/is highly productive, self-regulated and self-maintained. Wild salmon are a much more productive resource than phony resources like corporate aquaculture. Their drawback, from the corporate viewpoint, is that they cannot be manipulated and hence serve a market economy. Wild salmon have too many connections, too many harmonies. They are the thread of a story that is destroyed, taken out of context. Hatchery fish are comic book versions of epics . . . the Muzak version of a complex traditional tune. Of course, corporate and state aquaculturists pay lip service to wild salmon stocks as gene pool reserves

But the whole thrust of modern aquaculture is to "co-operate" with the industrial, not the ecological, economy. Consciously or uncon-

7. Much of what follows is from Philip Johnson's excellent article, "Salmon Ranching," in January/ February 1982 issue of *Oceans*.

sciously they are working to eliminate the wild salmon, the salmon of the heart. Fishermen of various disciplines—trollers, gillnetters, sportsmen—know the difference between wild and domesticated salmon. Their word for hatchery fish is "rag" (Washington State is beginning to pay attention to the importance of maintaining wild runs through habitat restoration and protection).

The decline of the wild Pacific salmon, especially the far-swimming chinook and the estuary-loving dogs, is tragic because it means the whole ecosystem is in decline. The salmon is the crown of the northwest forest biome, the *soul* of our ecosystem. It is, with cedar, the paradigmatic expression of this place. If the forests and their waters are healthy, if the sea is clear and uncrowded, then wild salmon thrive.

The salmon is a kind of current between forest and sea.[8] One study shows that salmon may accumulate rare trace minerals (boron?) that, passed on through the forest food chain, provide chemical materials for green plants that are unavailable to them through local geologic and hydrologic processes. In other words, the trees nurture salmon and salmon nurture trees (alchemical salmon turning sea into soil, salmon eyes in the treetops). The salmon is the archetypal resource—meaningful energy directed by unseen powers. It is the *incarnation* of the forest-sea connection, silver needles sewing the ties that bind, religious fish . . . The salmon travels in our hearts as well, swims in our blood, feeds and eats the dreaming tree of truth. The deep resonance between the salmon of the heart and the salmon of the world is the note of our dwelling here.

Well

An old Bavarian farmer told me
if I was unlucky

---

8. A Nisqually spokesman once made the Thurberesque remark that he saw salmon leaking out of all the light bulbs, probably because dams have destroyed so many runs

and could not take my water
from a stream,
I might keep a trout in my well
and the water would stay clean.

The salmon is a powerful symbol of the interdependence of the outer world but it is, as an image, also a manifestation of our inner health. Indeed the resolution of the two images, salmon of the forest and salmon of the heart, may be the inception of a healing myth. Jung associated *fish* with the nourishing influence of the unconscious (salmon comes from the sea to feed the *locale*). The alchemical stone, symbol of the immortal self, is said to appear like fish eyes. (The salmon knows the way home through the chaos of waters. Von Uexkell, a German ethologist, experimented with salmonids to determine their inner time and discovered they see twice as much per second as we do. Their world is hence much "slower" than ours.[9])

I once saw a rain cloak made of an enormous king salmon. The head was made into a kind of cap and the body draped over the shoulders. It was worn in the river drizzle while spearing salmon. I imagine it moving the wearer into salmon time, making the swift salmon walk. I imagine it decoding the rain. In Babylonian mythology there was a figure, Oannes, who came from the sea dressed as a fish to teach the people wisdom. Fish are symbols of wisdom throughout the world. What we fail to realize in our culture of alienated self-conscious rationalism is that fish, salmon in our case, are literal *embodiments* of the wisdom of the *locale*, the resource. The salmon are the wisdom of the northwest biome. They are the old souls, worshipful children of the land. *Psychology without ecology is lonely* and vice versa. The salmon is not merely a projection, a symbol of some inner process, it is rather the embodiment of the soul that nourishes us all.

---

9. Is salmon "time" a key to their uncanny navigational abilities?

We love salmon; it is the northwest *food*. But to the original peoples of the Pacific Northwest, salmon were not merely food. To them, salmon were people who lived in houses far away under the sea. Each year they undertook to visit the human people because the Indian peoples always treated them as honored guests. When the salmon people traveled, they donned their salmon disguises and these they left behind perhaps in the way we leave flowers or food when visiting friends. To the Indians the salmon were a resource in the deep sense, great generous beings whose gifts gave life. The salmon were energy: not "raw" energy, but intelligent perceptive energy. The Indians understood that salmon's gift involved them in an ethical system that resounded in every corner of their locale. The aboriginal landscape was a democracy of spirits where everyone listened, careful not to offend the *resource* they were a working part of.

The salmon was to the Indians what oil is to us. And while oil is a non-renewable resource, a "non-renourishable resource," and hence perhaps not a true *resource* at all, the salmon was a true *resource* and was paid great heed by aboriginal peoples. In Fraser River Salish mythology, the wife of Swanset, the creator spirit, was a sockeye salmon. In western terms we might say, "The organizing principle of the world was married to the salmon." Human life was bound to the salmon. Swanset lived at his wife's village and ate with them. In the evening when Swanset's wife and her brothers and sisters went to the river to bathe, his wife's mother could come up from the riverside, carrying a fish in her arms as if it were a child. She cooked it and, laying it on a layer of Indian consumption[10] plant, summoned Swanset and his wife to eat. Swanset's wife scrupulously washed her hands before she sat down and warned Swanset to do likewise. Her parents admonished him not to break the salmon bones but to lay them carefully on one side. When Swanset and his wife had eaten and washed their

---

10. So named because of its curative properties.

hands again, the mother-in-law gathered up all the bones and carried them to the riverside. When she returned from the river, a young boy followed, skipping and dancing gaily in circles around her. This happened at each meal. The salmon people loved to see the skipping boy; he was a joy to them.

Swanset was careless and lost a bone. The boy appeared that evening limping after the grandmother. This made the salmon people sad and after much effort the bone was found and returned to the water, whereupon the boy was made whole, and the people were glad again. This is the native understanding of the salmon. When the salmon *bones* are respected they experience life as a young boy dancing around an old woman. The wife of the human imagination (Swanset) was the salmon, their harmony symbolized in the young boy and old woman. Food tells a story—food has eyes, fish eyes. "Is this our body?"

One ritual common to all native American peoples who ate salmon was the first salmon welcoming ceremony. As mentioned above, Indian peoples believed that "salmon is a person living a life very similar to the people who catch him. The salmon has a chief who leads them up the streams during the run. In performing the ceremony for the one actually caught first, they believe that they are also honoring the chief of the salmon."[11]

In the Indian view salmon is endowed with a conscious spirit. It can present itself in abundance or not appear at all. This belief required special treatment for all living things and hence many taboos evolved to ensure safe relations with them. Below I list some northwest taboos and customs associated with salmon.[12]

1. The Klallam, like most tribes that use salmon extensively, have a certain veneration for the fish and mark its coming in the spring with a ceremony. The first fish is handled with great care. After be-

---

11. Erna Gunther, *Further Analysis of the First Salmon Ceremony* page 156.

12. Erna Gunther, *Klallam Folk Tales*.

ing cut along the two sides, the parts are laid together again and it is hung with the head up. The first fish is boiled into a soup and all the people of the village partake of it except the host. The cooking is done by the host's wife.

2. The Klallam of Beecher Bay share the British Columbian custom of performing this ceremony for the sockeye salmon which is considered the most important variety. When the first sockeye is caught the little children sprinkle their hair with down, paint their faces and put on white blankets. They go out to the canoe and carry the fish on their arms as though they were carrying an infant. A woman cuts it with a mussel shell knife, after which the fish is boiled and given only to the children to eat. The sockeye is just like a person, they say; that is why they must be careful. This ceremony is an example of acculturation, for the procedure is identical with that of the Vancouver Island people and not at all like that of the other Klallam.

3. When a salmon with a crooked mouth is caught it is regarded as an omen of a dreadful occurrence. To forestall this they boil the fish and let all the children of the village eat some of it. Then the backbone is taken to the end of the village and set up on a pole facing the water. The other bones are thrown into the water. Another informant speaking of the same occurrence limited special treatment to the dog salmon only. A dog salmon with a crooked lower jaw is called *suxqwxtaiyuk*. Such a fish is boiled, the backbone removed, and then it is roasted, being spread open with cross pieces of ironwood (oceanspray). It is eaten only by young people, who save every bone very carefully. When they are through eating they all go to the water with the salmon bones, dive under the water and release the bones. The fish is treated this way because it is considered the leader of the salmon and must therefore be shown respect so that the run will not cease.

4. When a boy catches his first salmon his grandmother, or in case she is dead, some other woman past her climacteric, cleans the

salmon, boils it and eats it. Only old people are permitted to eat of it. The bones are thrown into the water.

5. Children are always admonished not to play with salmon that are lying around before being cleaned. If they tamper with the eyes or make fun of the fish they will get sick and act like the salmon when it is dying. A girl of about ten was swimming in the Dungeness River and made fun of an old salmon. Soon after she became ill. Her eyes began to look like salmon eyes and her actions were just like the movements of the fish as they swim. Her people asked her if she had played with a salmon. She admitted that she had. The shaman could do nothing for her and she soon died.

6. It is the common belief that the old salmon come back to lead the young ones up the river. Some young men who had just been initiated into the secret society doubted this. They found a very old salmon, almost dead, on the bank of the river. The boys took off some of their ceremonial headdress and tied it to the fins and tail of the fish. Then they pushed him into the river, saying, "If you are the one who leads the young salmon back we will see you again next year." The next salmon season the young men went to the place where they had marked the salmon and found the old fish with strips of their head-dress. After they had seen this they became ill. The shaman could not help them. When they were dying they acted like dying salmon.

7. Each season new poles are made for drying salmon. It is believed the salmon play on these poles while they are drying and new poles make them happy. They are always treated as if they are alive.

8. Bones of salmon are burned or thrown into water.

9. Hearts of salmon are burned to keep them away from dogs.

10. Care is taken not to break bones.

11. Eyes are eaten.

12. People in close relation to death, puberty, birth are prevented from eating salmon.

13. Children are rubbed from throat to belly with the fat of first salmon.

14. It was believed that twins were salmon people and had power to call salmon and increase runs.

15. People of Twana Fjord (Hood Canal) prohibited garbage dumping and boat bailing during times when salmon were running.

To the original northwest people, salmon was a *resource* in the sense that the roots of our language perceive *resource*, that which is resurgent and regal. Salmon is an aspect of the ordering power of creation and must be respected. Salmon has a fateful connection to death, birth and puberty. It is a manifestation of the power of the other side. All biological systems are dependent on death, the detritus pathways, for health. We are nourished on death, supported by it, the way the dead heart of a tree holds it up in the light. Death is the sinew of the soul. There is a Nootkan tradition wherein the chief swims up-river towing skeletons of various fish to entice them back into the river. That salmon were eternal and moved between both worlds was a worldwide belief. Maybe salmon are a manifestation of the spirit world's migration through ours; radiant beings leaving us their warmth, their cloaks, the *blossom* of their souls. It is no wonder that northwest Indian peoples saw twins as "salmon born" and ascribed to them power to increase and predict runs. Twins are the literal expression of nature's ambivalence, the revelatory power of coincidence. Twins seem more "fated" than other children. People close to the power of the other side—children, widows, menstruating women, new fathers and mothers—had restricted relations with salmon. It was as if they were closer to and hence more vulnerable to the *resource*.

Researching this essay I discovered that the "flash" in our phrase "flash of inspiration" is etymologically grounded not in lightning but in the flash-splash of a fish. Ideas do not flash like lightning but rise like trout to caddis flies. Deep in our speech is the notion that fish are prescient witnesses to the cosmos. They are quick, as in quickened, quicksand, or that tender flesh beneath your fingernail. Each year the silver salmon return to the little creek that runs through the forest south of my home. I marvel at their speed and freshness and how they sense my presence long before I see them. My witness is always of them disappearing, flashing shadows. It is hard to imagine anyone hunting them with a spear. On the other side, the eternal salmon was a daily witness to the Indians' life. It played in the drying racks while gear was mended, berries gathered. We fail to realize how intimate the Indians, especially Indian women, were with the salmon. To dry salmon properly the women had to knead the flesh to break the fibers and allow air to enter. But the fish were "alive," *conscious* until eaten. The Indian world was so particularly animate that individual crows that Klallam women shooed away from the drying racks had names. Contrast our world-view in which resources are inanimate, soulless, "dead," because they are non-human, and the *native* (Indian, Ainu, Irish, Finn, etc.) view in which everything is alive; even the strips of meat in the alder smoke can play, know joy.[13] This is not sentimentality or naiveté on the natives' part. It is a deep recognition of a *resource*'s true nature. The bright light of our *objectivity* (ironic word) has eliminated the shadows, the shades. Even after contact with the whites gave them unlimited access to blade steel, the Indians continued to clean and dress the first salmon with the old mussel knife out of respect. It is as if we are overly enamored with the sharpness of our knives, in love with cutting. Our science, our knowing, lacks religion, reverence. We can cut the world apart but forget to call it home, and we are left alone with arid technical skills and their attendant bad dreams.

---

13. Can an industrially canned salmon dance?

The native peoples of the Northwest believed that orphans and others who have fared badly socially will get the best spirit guides because they will make the greatest effort to receive them. Our pride and greed have orphaned us from the earth inside and out. The tragedy is that we don't know it. We are proud of our isolation; we call it progress. The spirits are offended by our pride and avoid us, amplifying our loneliness until it becomes our *secret reason for self-destruction.*

The salmon was sacred to many peoples of the Pacific rim. The indigenous people of Japan, the Ainu, had a belief system similar to northwest coast people. In the Ainu world, everything is a *Kamui,* a spirit of natural phenomena. In their world the Kamui are Ainu, but when they come to this world they disguise themselves as salmon, bear, deer, etc. They bring this disguise as a gift to the Ainu. The Kamui are not ghosts but eternal spirits. Some researchers report that the Ainu believed that Ainu who lived well went to Kamui Land when they died. Because the Ainu experienced the Kamui as eternal *people* in the beings around them, the Ainu world is a humane place, and right human behavior—care, politeness, cleanliness—assured the Ainu that the Kamui would reside in Ainu locales and enliven their world. To the Ainu life depends on good relations with the *resource* world, not on owning it. The Ainu and northwest Indians knew that *resources* can't be owned any more than a Christian can own the Holy Ghost.

The Ainu believed that the house fire was an eye of the Kamui that watched and welcomed all game that entered through the hunting window. As game entered through the hunting window and the fire reported its treatment back to the appropriate Kamui community. Fire is the appropriate witness for the *resource,* flickering warm light rising from the broken limbs of trees. (The leaves of the cottonwood trees were the *food* of the salmon Kamui[14]) The mythic images circle

---

14. Intuitive knowledge of detritus pathways?

and knot together into a reality that is a story, a parable, where facts are legendary incidents, not data.

For the Ainu, river systems were families—major rivers, parents, and the tributaries, children. One could address the whole family by speaking to a member. You could address a whole watershed, its *being*, by invoking the main river-Kamui.

The Ainu cooked the first dog salmon and offered it to the fire spirit so it would report salmon's kind treatment. The bones were offered to the river spirit with other offerings so that all spirits involved in salmon's arrival were acknowledged. The Ainu also had a send-off ritual with which they bid the salmon spirits farewell as they journeyed in their boats back to Kamui Land. These rituals are described in more detail in Hitoshi Watanabe's *The Ainu Ecosystem*, which gives a thorough explication of their cosmology. It seems to me that modern ecologists have yet to *find* language that approaches the compact imagery of native peoples whose myths not only explain the workings of ecosystem ethics but *locate* the people in the story, *instruct* us.

River Song
I lay cold
and sleek
in that swift river.

The sun sang small
faint rainbows round
all there was to see.

I lay still like a fish
letting my body dream.

Waiting I lay watching
my quick dogs stalking
earnest on the shore.

I lay bright and dumb
as a stone
and while the river sang
I listened to my heart.
He sounded strong and far away.
He sounded like a man digging slowly
in a half-finished well.

As mentioned above, European peoples have a long association with salmon. In fact, if philologists are right, salmon have been with us from the beginning. Calvin Watkins, in a fascinating essay in the *American Heritage Dictionary*, "Indo-European and the Indo-Europeans," notes that we can tell much about the homeland of our linguistic ancestors from the roots of our language. In the Indo-European homeland there were, among others, wasp, bee, bear, wolf, mouse, eagle, thrush, sparrow, crane, eel and salmon. The Indo-European root word for salmon is *laks*, whence our word lox. (Our word salmon is from Latin *salire*, to leap.) Some interesting etymological coincidences constellate around *laks*; and while my thoughts are speculative, I offer them in hope that someone more skilled will comment on them. *Laks* is the root word for salmon. The root word for lake is *laku*. From this root word we have lagoon, lough, lacuna. It seems possible that *laks* and *laku* are related. Salmon could be "laks," the lake dweller. It is interesting that *laku* gives us Latin *lacuna*, originally a pool or cistern; Celtic myth has the salmon of wisdom living in a well. Last, there is the old English dialectic "to lake," to play or sport, from Old Norse *leig*, to leap or tremble. It is a thin line but salmon may be animating that word. (How sad that the animals are leaving our language as they leave our lives.) In any case the salmon was a sacred fish to our ancestors, who saw him in lakes, coming and going, a mysterious being. The sacrality survives in various ways—the aboriginal Finns found fire in the bowels of the salmon, the salmon's flesh being a form of fire. To the Norwegians, a happy person is a "glad Laks," a glad salmon. The Celtic peoples venerated the salmon as the fish of wisdom until Christian times, and numerous folk tales continue to bear witness to its sacrality.

> *Hunter's Song*
> Striking,
> stricken.
> An eagle with a fish too big to lift.
> I answer from my place.

In Celtic mythology there was a sacred well of inspiration and wisdom surrounded by hazels, whose blossoms or fruit fall into the well and are eaten by the sacred salmon, whose bellies turn purple from the color of the fruit. The salmon ate the fruit of the tree of wisdom and hence knew all. Remember the flash of inspiration is more like the splash of a fish than a bolt out of the blue.

The Welsh hero Mabon was once captured by a fiend. Gwryhr, his wife, asked the creatures to help her find him. She asked ouzel, who sent her to owl, who sent her to eagle, who, though he flew highest and saw farthest, could not find him. The eagle told Gwryhr this story: "I once tried to capture a large salmon but he drew me into the deep and I was barely able to escape.[15] I sent my kindred to attack him but he sent messengers and we made peace. I took fifty fish spears from his back. He will know where your husband is if anyone does." Eagle

---

15. Most salmon fishers have seen eagles swimming in the sea, unable to lift off with their catch.

took Gwryhr to salmon, who located her husband. In Celtic cosmology the salmon is the wisest of all the creatures.

The wife of Dagda, the good god in the ancient Irish cosmology, was driven by curiosity to approach the forbidden well of Boann, the well of wisdom with its hazels and salmon. All the creatures of the cosmos, even the gods, were forbidden access to this well. Only the salmon were permitted to eat of the well fruit. The Irish called them the salmon of knowledge. As Dagda's wife approached the well it rose up in anger and rolled away to the sea, freeing the salmon and creating the river Boyne. The gods may be powerful but they are not wise. Only salmon are privileged to wisdom.

Finn, the Irish hero, happened upon an old man fishing by a deep pool in the Boyne. This old man was Finn the Seer; he had been fishing seven years for the salmon of knowledge. It was prophesied that a man named Finn would obtain its wisdom. Finn the Seer caught the salmon the moment before young Finn's arrival. He gave the salmon to Finn to cook, warning him not to eat any of the fish but to only cook it and return it to the old man, who planned to eat it all and gain its wisdom. When Finn returned with the cooked salmon the seer asked him if he had eaten any part of the fish. Finn answered, "No, but while I was cooking it a blister rose on its skin. I put my thumb on it, but it burned me and I put my thumb in my mouth to cool." "It is enough," said Finn the Seer. "Eat the fish yourself. You must be the Finn of the prophecy." Thereafter Finn had only to put his thumb in his mouth to gain knowledge of the spot he was in at the moment. It seems that the salmon of knowledge is available to the innocent and lucky.

The Irish folk tale, "Country Under the Waves," is a charming story about a peasant family's fate, the well of wisdom and its tutelary animal, the salmon. (Charm is etymologically akin to *cirm*, Old English for clamor, cry, and to Latin *carmen*, song. Originally, charm meant a magic spell that was sung.) In the story a widow has three sons and a daughter. One of the sons is a dunce and the mother despairs of his future when she can no longer care for him. She consults a witch who advises her to visit the country under the waves where the hazel-ringed well of wisdom and the salmon are located. The witch instructs her to send her eldest son to obtain the hazel fruit on All Hallowed Eve when there is an "opening" in the world and he can pass into the country under the waves.[16] The eldest son undertakes his journey at the proper time and passes into the country under the waves where he meets the sea people who offer to help him. He accepts their hospitality but offends them with his bragging ways. The sea people evidently decide he is not worthy of the fruit of wisdom so they drug his food and he falls asleep at the well and turns to stone as the berries fall and the waters and salmon rise to eat them. A similar fate befalls the second brother, who goes the next year in search of the well and its fruit. He is lazy and selfish and so he is drugged and turns to stone waiting at the well. The widow's daughter pleads with her to let her make the quest for the well fruit. Her mother refuses on the grounds that she is her only whole child and she could not bear her loss. But on the next All Hallowed Eve the daughter steals away to the country under the waves. She too meets the sea people, whom she impresses with her ready wit and good manners. They guide her to the well where she catches the fruit before it falls to the rising salmon. Enlightened by the touch of the well fruit, she lifts the curse from her stoned brothers and returns home with them to cure their foolish brother. Evidently the wisdom of the salmon is *properly* won by a feminine spirit, the subtle path of right relations, rather than by bulling through or cutting through.

Following salmon is a winding path. The image is knotted in us like a nerve. But in our pose of modernity we do not know this. We waterski on the clear dark waters of Creation. But it is time to let

---

16. Another example of pagan cosmology: resourceful submerged, persistent beneath the Christian overlay.

salmon home again to our brook hearts, well hearts. "Old quartz nose," embodiment of wisdom, silver shadow, far-ranging flash of the sea, tree ghost, silver needle sewing our world together, mending the coat we wear, shuttle of dreams . . . sacred salmon, moon-bright tutor who teaches death is the door to love. If salmon disappear the splashing and flashing in the well will frighten us and we will become superstitious about the earth and our dreams. We need salmon to remind us; we are not alone.

Last, I want to offer an Estonian folksong, *The Wonder Maiden from Fish*. Estonians are a Finno-Ugric people who have lived in the same locale for perhaps 8,000 years. They have maintained their language and traditions despite crusading Germans, imperialistic Swedes and totalitarian Russians. It was the women in Estonia who kept the folklore alive. They were the singers; songs were passed from songstress to songstress—charms smoothed and polished like sacred stones. My mother-in-law, Silva Peek, a Finno-Ugric philologist who clarified a folklore text and German translation of that song, says it is probably part of an Estonian folksong tradition wherein a fish turns into a maiden. The song and its levels deserve longer treatment; still, it speaks for itself quite well. For me it is a kind of bell tone of the salmon of the heart, a shape to hold these disparate yet connected notes. It rings true.

Silva explained that this particular song is a kind of "nonsense" song wherein the original Estonian lines are joined by alliteration and rhyme rather than by any consciously chosen meaning, its shape and form worked by the unconscious wisdom of the people. This is precisely its *charm*. I hear the salmon singing through the wonder maiden, its wisdom and desire gliding bare beneath the surface of her song,[17] resurgent, the *resource* singing through human voice.

---

17. I have given Silva's translation nearly verbatim, changing only a few words for rhythmic reasons.

The Wonder Maiden from Fish

The spruce stands high in Kurland,
The alder, free and affable in Westernland,
The birch in Harrien beside the cow path:
Together their roots run,
Together the tops fall.
From below the roots a river flows,
Three kinds of fish therein:
One is whitefish, the blacksided one,
The other is pike, the graybacked,
The third is salmon, the wide blazed one.
I took the fish into my hand;
Carried the fish home myself.
I began cooking the fish
With the help of Father's well-stocked woodpile,
With the help of Mother's broad shavings.
The fish began to speak, saying:
"I wasn't brought up to be brutalized
Nor brought up to be roughed up.
Why, I was brought up to sing,
To sing to rhyme.
I sing, why wouldn't I?
I sing turf out of the sea,
     Tilth out of sea bottom,
     Fish from sea shores,
     Malt from sea sand.
I sing the meaning of some other tongue
Helper of teeth."

BIBLIOGRAPY

Clark, Ella Elizabeth. *Indian Legends of Canada*. Toronto: McClelland and Stewart Limited, 1960.

Elmendorf, Richard. *The Structure of Twana Culture*. Seattle: Washington State University, 1960.

Evans-Wentz, W. Y. *The Fairy Faith in Celtic Countries*. Princeton: Humanities Press, 1977.

Ford, Patrick. *The Mabinog; and Other Medieval Welsh Tales*. Los Angeles and Berkeley: University of California Press, 1977.

Gunther, Erna. *A Further Analysis of the First Salmon Ceremony*. Seattle: University of Washington Press, 1930.

_____, *Klallam Ethnography*. Seattle: University of Washington Press, 1927.

_____, *Klallam Folk Tales*. Seattle: University of Washington Press, 1925.

House, Linn. "Totem Salmon" in *Truck 18, Biogeography Workbook (1)*. St. Paul: Truck Press, 1978.

Jay, T. E. "The Leaper" and "Well" previously unpublished.

_____, "Speckled Dream," "River Song" and "Hunter's Song" from *River Dogs*. Port Townsend: Copper Canyon Press, 1976.

Johnson, Phillip. "Salmon Ranching" in *Oceans* (a publication of the Oceanic Society), 15:1 (1982).

Lockley, Ronald. *Animal Navigation*. New York: Hart Publishing Society, 1967.

Loorits, Oskar. *Basics in Estonian Folkbeliefs III*. Lund (Sweden): 1957.

McGerry, Mary. *Great Fairy Tales of Ireland*. New York: Avenel Books, 1976.

Partridge, Eric. *Origins: A Short Etymological Dictionary of Modern English*. New York: Greenwich House, 1983.

Squire, Charles. *Celtic Myth and Legend*. London: Newcastle Publishing Co., Inc., 1975.

Vannote, Robin, *The River Continuum: A Theoretical Construct for Analysis of River Systems.* Contribution #1 from N.S.F River Continuum Project, Stroud Water Research Center, Academy of Natural Sciences of Philadelphia, Mondale: 1984.

Watanabe, Hitoshi. *The Ainu Ecosystem.* Seattle: University of Washington Press, 1972.

Woodcock, George. *Peoples of the Coast: The Indians of the Pacific Northwest.* Edmonton (Canada): Jurtig Publications, 1977.

SALMON MOON

Robert Sund

Surf
of moonwave,
       mist of dawn by the sea.
Mist of long lovely night ending.

The moon steps through the night.
It goes out into the south and west.
Wind comes out of the south and west.

Between sparse old shoreland spruce
     the moon is a silver wing
          in the clouds.

All night
the clouds drift over.
All night salmon gather—
first of the run.

BELOW THE FALLS

Jerry Martien
for Wyn Tucker (1940–1997)

The pool is deep and like your sky
Lets you think you're seeing into it.

There's debris and silt of fall's first rains.
A green translucent wash of serpentine.

And where it meets the air you breathe
Where it reflects your life

A clear and supple skin
Ripples and shimmers and bends the light

Along the back of the fluent body
In which their many bodies swim below.

Current and upwelling as if a god
Deeper than any snag or rock down there.

Not the splash of small fry or jack—
A motion that takes its own good time.

Rises from the powerful roiling bodies
Waiting for the rains to bridge the falls.

Comes up slowly turning.
Comes up male and female.

New enough to be the salmon
You cooked last night for dinner.

Old enough to be the rock you're on
That once boiled up as mud.

He has lost his ocean shine.
She is partly river.

Partly the river bottom
Where soon she'll bury roe.

Each rises from the chalk green current
Slowly rolls and turns

To have its look
At heaven and earth and you

And in your spirit eye
And on your eyes of flesh

There on the slick worn rock
Below the falls

Leaves its river dragon's imprint—
Jaw and eye, gill and fin and tail—

To show your soul its way
And in that graceful easy turn

Sinks into the green depth where
Now your heart will swim forever.

—Grays Falls, Trinity River

Selections from Totem Salmon

Freeman House

Part One

The Mattole River runs through the westernmost watershed in California, cutting down through sea bottoms that have only recently, in geological terms, risen up out of the Pacific. It runs everywhere through deep valleys or gorges carved from the soft young sandstone.

Here, only a few miles from its headwaters, the river looks more like a large creek and is closely contained by steep banks. The fish are spooky during this culminating stage of their lives, which is why they run at night, and in murky water. Any light on the water, any boulder clumsily splashed into the stream, will turn a salmon skittering back toward the nearest hole or brushy overhang downstream. She may not try again until another night, or, in the worst case, will establish a spawning nest—a redd—downstream from the weir, in a place with too much current to allow her eggs to be effectively fertilized.

I inch down the bank crabwise in wet darkness, the gumboot heels of the waders digging furrows in the mud, the fingers and heels of my hands plowing the soaked wet duff.

On the bank of the river at the bottom of the ravine I hold my breath and let my ears readjust to the sounds of the water. I think I can hear through the cascades of sound a systematic plop, plop, plop, as if pieces of fruit are being dropped into the water. Sometimes this is the sound of a fish searching for the opening upstream; sometimes it is not. I breathe quietly and wait. I continue to hear the sound for a period of time for which I have no measure . . . and then it stops.

I wait and wait. I hold my breath but do not hear the sound again. There is a long piece of parachute cord tied to a slipknot that holds open the gate at the mouth of the weir. I yank on the cord and the gate falls closed, its crash muted as the rush of water pushes it the last few inches tight against the body of the weir.

And now that I am no longer trying to sort one sound from another in the sound of the water, it is as if the water has become silent. It is dark. If the world were a movie, this would be cut to black. When I hear the sound I am waiting for, it is unmistakable: the sound of a full-grown salmon leaping wholly out of the water and twisting back into it. My straining senses slow down the sound so that each of its parts can be heard separately. A hiss, barely perceptible, as the fish muscles itself right out of its living medium; a silence like a dozen monks pausing too long between the strophes of a chant as the creature arcs through the dangerous air; a crash as of a basketball going through a plate glass window as he or she returns to the velvet embrace of the water; and then a thousand tiny bells struck once only as the shards of water fall and the surface of the stream regains its viscous integrity.

I flick on my headlamp and the whole backwater pool seems to leap toward me. The silver streak that crosses the enclosure in an instant is a flash of lightning within my skull, one which heals the wound that has separated me from this moment—from any moment. The encounter is so perfectly complex, timeless, and reciprocal that it takes on an objective reality of its own. I am able to walk around it as if it were a block of carved stone. If my feelings could be reduced to a chemical formula, the experience would be a clear solution made up of equal parts of dumb wonder and clean exhilaration, colored through with a sense of abiding dread. I could write a book about it.

Part Two

Morning of the fifth day of the calendar year 1983.

We are at the place we call Arcanum, after the name of the business run by the two potters who own the land. They have given the same name to the little stream that runs though the shaded glade where our incubation and rearing setup has been built. Twice each day for the next two months, in whatever weather, John or Greg will leave their work in the potting shed to scramble down the steep quarter-mile path to the glade. They will backtrack up the little feeder creek to the two spring boxes that provide the water that keeps the eggs alive and developing. They will make sure nothing has clogged the line, will flush the filters built from fifty-gallon drums. They will note the temperature and flow, check for any fungi that might be growing among the eggs in the incubation trough. If they see anything alarming, they will get on the telephone to Gary, who will be on call for these two months,

For the first month, the eggs will sit in the trough, in baskets made from plastic mesh and clothes hanger wire, each basket containing the offspring of a single adult female. At this stage of development, the eggs are so fragile that a sharp blow to the plywood trough could damage them. John or Greg will raise and lower the padlocked lid as quietly and carefully as if they were art thieves in a museum at night. Once the fetus within each egg develops an eye large enough to be apparent through the translucent shell, the eggs will have toughened enough so that they can be moved to the nearby hatch box.

This morning a translucent layer of mist lies over the length of the receding river like thin white cream on the dirty coffee of the water just below. Occasional turbulence in the water sends a shredded column of mist floating up to the tops of the redwoods, where it hangs and swirls until it is dissipated by a bright, almost warm sun. The moisture in the air both softens and intensifies the light; the day envelops us like a great, moist, green bud unfolding.

Biologist Gary moves about, as briskly as any surgeon, mildly impatient with the random movements of the rest of us. Gary will have spent hours yesterday making lists and gathering gear for the job at hand. Now he is laying it out just so. The five-gallon white plastic buckets to receive the eggs sit in a row on the ground; the little bags of local anesthetic and the clever hatchery knives, razor-sharp little sickles attached to a plastic ring to fit around a finger, are laid out on a knocked-together bench beside rolls of paper towels and a length of surgical tubing. A fisherman's scale sits next to a yardstick borrowed from someone's sewing kit back home. Gary makes notes in a yellow Write-in-the-Rain notebook with one of the several mechanical pencils he has stuck in various pockets of his surveyor's vest: air temperature, high and low water temperatures as measured by the Minimax thermometer suspended in the river by a cord.

David moves restlessly among us with his usual slightly distracted courtliness, inquiring about our families, about news of the river and the weather and local gossip. His questions are full of kind concern, but his attention drifts if the answers are over-long. One moment Stevie is excitedly describing the adventures of the new year. Then he is pacing a little apart from the group, muttering to himself the drill of the work to come. I am fiddling with an ironwood killing club, a short length of wood so dense it will not float. It is ornately carved, a gift from an Alaska fishing partner years before. I only barely hear the conversation around me.

Each of us has performed this rite a number of times before, but it never ceases to be weighted with nearly intolerable significance, the irreducible requirement to do it right.

A small, galvanized stock-watering tank sits on the ground; we busy ourselves bucketing water up from the river to fill it. Everything is ready. Gary measures a few teaspoons of the anesthetic into the tank. We have been told the white powder resembles xylocaine, the same stuff the dentist swabs on your gums to numb them in preparation for the injection of Novocain. Stevie, nearly dancing with anticipation, runs to the holding tank once Gary tells him we are ready, lifts the New Year's female out of the water in her tube, and rushes her down to the drugged water in the stock tank. Once there, the staccato sound of her tail beating against the white tube slows to stillness. With no wasted movement, Gary pulls the cotter pin that holds the end of the tube closed, reaches in with one hand and lifts the great fish out of the water by her tail. Using two hands now, he holds her, head down, at arm's length away from himself.

I have handed the ironwood club to Stevie. By some unspoken calculation, it's his turn. Stevie holds the club over his shoulder with both hands. He is coiled tightly like a baseball batter at plate; he squints at the fish with his one good eye. It will be a mutual embarrassment if it takes him more than one blow to kill her. The club comes around at the same time as he is taking two quick steps toward Gary and the salmon, and it connects solidly at the back of her head, just behind her eyes. She shudders for a moment and is still. Stevie drops the club in the grass.

"Good," Gary murmurs, "good."

Then he slides one hand down the fish's sleek body to bring her head up almost parallel to the ground, careful to keep her tail elevated slightly with his other hand, so no eggs will spill onto the ground. He hands her to David, who waits while I scramble for one of the white buckets. Each of us is muttering cautionary instructions to the others, careful, careful, head down, head up, don't drop her now. No one hears. We have moved beyond our nervous ambivalence at the arrogance of our intention and are wholly occupied by the ritual. Gary is drying the fish now with paper towels—no water or slime can touch the eggs before they are mixed with the males' milt. Stevie is trotting up the slope once more to move the two males into the drug tank.

By the time the males have quieted down, Gary has finished his tender cleaning. He slides the spawning knife over his middle finger, with the little sickle blade pointed outward. Even after three years, it is rare for Gary the biologist to entrust this part of the ceremony to another of us. He inserts the tip of the curved blade an eighth of an inch into the opening called the vent, on the underside of the female salmon near her tail, taking care to cut nothing but the wall of the stomach muscle. He jerks the knife upward in firm inch-long strokes. We have fallen so silent now that we can hear the crunch of the knife slicing through muscle at each stroke. At the first cut, eggs begin to cascade into the bucket I am holding up beside the fish's tail, close beneath the vent. The eggs pour out, each short stroke of the knife releasing more.

The morning is bright but each translucent egg seems to glow brighter as if lit by a light from within. Gary ends his cut at the sternum of the fish, puts the knife aside, and reaches up into the open cavity to break loose any eggs still clinging within. He allows himself a small expression of pride at his judgment: "All ripe, every one of 'em ripe. I'll bet she's carrying more than four thousand."

The males are floating on their sides in the drugged water of the stock tank. David lifts one of them out belly up, the head of the fish cradled inside one elbow, its tail held tight in his hand. I support the fish's back while I wipe him clean with another length of paper towels. David massages the belly of the fish between fingers and thumb, with several firm strokes down toward the vent. A clear liquid jets from the vent onto the ground. As soon as the discharge turns milky, David holds the vent of the male over the bucket with the eggs while I hold the tail off to the side. An ounce or two of milt squirts into the bucket and the coelemic fluid surrounding the eggs turns cloudy. While Stevie returns the first male to clean water, we repeat the process with the second one. Afterward, I lower the fingers of one hand into the heart of creation and stir it once, twice. For a moment my mind is completely still. Am I holding my breath? I am held in the thrall of a larger sensuality that extends beyond the flesh.

286

By the time I have lifted my fingers out of the bucket, fertilization will have taken place or not. Clean water is now dribbled into the bucket through the surgical tubing. This will cause the single opening in each egg to close. Within an hour the eggs will have developed membranes strong enough to allow them to be moved gently to the incubation trough.

There is a flurry of busyness as Stevie watches to be sure the males revive in the fresh water. Gary weighs and measures the body of the female, makes notations, and returns her to the river where her carcass will contribute to the nutrient cycle that will in time nourish young fish. Then we sit quietly to wait for the eggs to harden. No one has much to say. Each of us sits or paces or smokes, each strays over to the white bucket now and then to stare into it. A little congratulatory hey! will come from one or the other of us: we have not done too badly today.

There is a hard knot of relationship in the act of killing a creature of another species. It is an act that dissolves the illusion of individuality, of separateness. Perhaps this explains the terror that attends each such occasion, the awe that has inspired rituals and regulations, ceremonies and prayers in all human cultures throughout the ages. We are reminded in the most immediate way of our own mortality, an idea with which we may or may not have come to terms.

Perhaps this explains the distracted nervousness of our particular group earlier, our quiet introspection now. Modernity has distanced us from wild reality so that when it comes to killing and dying, each of us must deal with the mystery of it alone and uneasy. But the meaning persists in experiences of killing and dying, beyond cultural interpretation. The lesson of interpenetration is always available to us, regardless of our cultural conditioning. It is also a lesson we humans seem to be increasingly happy to ignore as we allow distant and abstract economic institutions to disguise and conceal the relationship.

Could the food we buy in pretty shrink-wrapped packages ever have been alive as we are alive?

I am thinking now, on this morning, of a moment in my life ten years past, a moment that I have never fully comprehended. It was my second or third day out of Ketchikan, Alaska, as crew on a salmon purse seiner.

In the Pacific Northwest, the purse seine has its origins in prehistory, in long, shallow nets made from twine woven painstakingly from the fiber of wild iris leaves, from cedar bark, from wild hemp, from willow bark. These nets, with a smaller mesh than others used to entangle the gills of fish, might be sixty to a hundred and fifty feet long, six to twenty feet deep. Making such a net was a communal endeavor that must have taken weeks, months: fibers no longer than the length of a forearm were twisted into long loops of cord, which were then woven and tied into large nets with an exactly measured mesh. (The knot used to tie the mesh five thousand years ago is the same one used today, the ubiquitous sheetbend.) One end of the net was anchored to shore in deep but quiet waters. The other end was towed out by a canoe, then towed back to shore to form a circle. The net was weighted with rocks to hold down its bottom while wooden floats kept its top edge on the surface of the water. As the ends of the net were pulled ashore the circle became ever more constricted and the fish crowded within it were delivered to fishers with dip nets or spears. Versions of this sort of beach seine are still used by subsistence fishers in the inland waterways of British Columbia and Alaska.

With the arrival of the Euro-American commercial fishery in northwest North America, the old technology was adapted to deeper water, and eventually to diesel-powered boats. The nets, constructed now by clever machines, have grown to a quarter of a mile long and fifty feet deep. Polystyrene floats and lead-weighted lines have replaced wood and stone. Brass rings were added to the bottom of the net, through which a line is passed. The net is towed into its pretty circle by a skiff only slightly less powerful than the mother ship. Then, when the line running through the rings at the bottom of the net is winched on board, it closes off the whole expanse of water inside the net, along with all the life within it—like the drawstrings on a pouch, the purse seine.

For many years, the large nets were then drawn on board the mother boats by men straining with all their strength against the weight and pull of the water. (To the deckhands, it can't have seemed much of an improvement over the older native practices, which in my mind I see as leisurely and festive events.) In the days before sonar fish-finders and carefully coded radio transmissions, finding the schools of salmon that triggered the setting of the net depended on the hard-earned skills of the skipper, skills based on experience and observation. It was a calling to which the best of them devoted a life. Experience taught them a sense of timing that combined the day of the year with water temperatures and local weather patterns. Anomalies in the way sea mammals and birds were acting were a language they learned to understand; a boil of herring or a congregation of birds spoke to them more clearly than did their wives on the too-rare occasions when they returned home.

The perfect set enclosed a few thousand acre-feet of water swarming with schools of salmon—innumerable small pink salmon, their numbers compensating for the low price dictated by their eventual processing into canned food for pets and poor people; Chinooks, less abundant but huge, and Cohos, sleek and firm, which brought a better price and were headed for regional dinner tables. The great prize was the beautiful red-fleshed sockeye, prime food delivered fresh or frozen to expensive restaurants in distant capitals.

By 1973, an innovation had been added to purse-seine technology that increased its efficiency enormously—the power gurdy. A gurdy is a stationary pulley hung on a davit. On salmon trollers, which catch fish by hook and line, the davit holds the pulley out over the water away from the boat, to provide smooth passage for the fishing lines when they are being pulled in or let out by hand, or by hydraulically powered winches. On a purse seiner, the power gurdy is a large, hydraulically powered hard rubber reel, hung by steel beams twelve feet above the stern of the boat, large and powerful enough to haul in both ends of the purse seine and drop them onto the net platform below.

Now the net, weighing several tons, could be pulled on board mechanically, the large winch started and stopped by a remote push-button. The time it took to play out the net and pull it in was reduced to half an hour, increasing the number of sets that one crew could make in a day by a factor of four or more. The work of the crew changed from two hours of long, slow pulling to ten minutes of frenzy for a stern crew of three whose job it was to stack the incoming net under our feet at the same time as it was descending on our heads. We worked in full raingear with our sleeves and pants legs taped shut against the stinging jellyfish and the enormous amounts of water. The occasional smaller gill-entangled fish was ignored.

The independent skippers of these fishing boats had embraced the new machinery as the promise of their own survival in the fiercely competitive race to catch enough fish each year to make payments on the expensive new gear, to make mortgage payments on the house on shore, to keep food on the table for the kids. The new gear allowed them to catch more fish; the expense of the new gear required them to catch more fish. They were like caged squirrels on an exercise wheel.

For the crewman, the first challenge of the new machinery was simply to survive it. We were driven by the speed at which the power gurdy poured the bulk of the net down upon us. We worked in short bursts of incredible effort. It was the four-hundred-yard dash of fishing. We couldn't have moved any faster than the inexorable turn of the gurdy pushed us, and had the net been fifty feet longer it would have been an effort beyond our endurance. I was thirty-five years old, the oldest green member of the crew by a good ten years. The younger men on either side of me were of the type that rises full-hearted to challenges to their strength and stamina. Like athletes, they turned the challenge into art, a wild muscular dance. For my part, I thought only of trying to keep up with the younger men. The crew on the stern gave all their concentration and strength to meeting the demands of the machine. Sticks and twigs must be removed so as not to foul the net when racing to make the next set; if the power gurdy had to be stopped to remove debris, the skipper might fly into a rage. Keeping pace with the speed at which the seine came on board would for ten or fifteen minutes occupy every corner of consciousness, every fiber of muscle.

The moment of truth at the end of each set comes when the pocket at the bottom of the purse has been drawn in close to the boat, the remainder of the net stacked on board. If the men on the stern, the web-men, have performed well, this will be the first time the power gurdy has paused in its relentless turning. Now the whole crew—all seven of us—rushes to the side to see the size of the catch. Each one of us hopes to see the frenzied boil in the water that will tell us the catch is a big one, the payload that will make our day or our week. With the whine of the power winch stilled, the idling engine of the boat and the raucous scream of gulls are background noises that frame a moment frozen in time. The bunched floats bob and drift in the swell. Someone will break the curious stillness with a shout of "Payload!" if the net's pocket is full, or "Water haul" if, as happens more frequently, it is empty. Most often, twenty to a hundred salmon of various sizes circle languidly within the enclosure. One or another of them will be charging the seine, searching for a way out of the strange obstacle that has interrupted its migration. The net is full of motion and life; it is a cell isolated suddenly from the living plasm of the sea.

Two or three of the crew hold the top edges of the seine up out of the water with long boat hooks, an occasionally successful attempt to keep the jumpers inside. Two more gather the seine at the level of the rail and tie it tight with a line that is attached to a separate winch that will lift the bottom of the net with its captured fish on board. The power winch whines again, and the writhing cell of web and fish is hauled over the deck, pouring a ton of sea water as it comes up and is muscled on board.

A trip-line opens the purse, and the load of fish falls to the deck. They flop and writhe noisily, their tails pounding against the wooden deck. They are ignored or kicked aside as preparations for the next set are made. (Only after the net is ready to be deployed into the water once more will a large hatch in the center of the stern deck be lifted so the fish can be put into the hold. They take a long time to die down there. Often, while we are hosing down the deck to clear it of seaweed and jellyfish, and the bolder seagulls are making runs at the flotsam, we can hear the fish drumming themselves to death below our feet, the sound amplified by the echo in the mostly empty space.)

In retrospect, I can see that we were a perfect microcosm of an extractive industrial economy. The cannery owned and maintained the boat, which was leased to the skipper. The skipper owned the huge web of net, which had to be repaired daily and replaced entirely every two years or so at a cost of several thousand dollars. Boat, net, skipper, and crew each were recompensed by a share of the profits from the catch after fuel and food expenses had been taken off the top. Our livelihoods depended entirely on the size of the season's catch, and it was not impossible to work for four months of intermittent twenty-hour days and find oneself broke at the end of the fishing year. Each one of us was unthinkingly married to the goal of taking all the fish we could in the shortest time possible, and the pace and practice of our work was determined by the machinery we used.

Under such conditions, the nature of what we were doing—taking life in order to feed ourselves—became obscure, if not lost altogether. We could not afford to see the creatures dying slowly on the deck and in the fish hold as manifestations of creation equal in complexity and vitality to ourselves. We could only allow ourselves to see the salmon as objects, as product, a product that we hoped would allow us to pay the rent at home for a little longer than the duration of the fishing season.

This conditioning was reinforced by a collective psychology in the social pressure cooker of seven men isolated on a fifty-foot boat. It was a taboo all the stronger for remaining unspoken that the death of the fish was not to be discussed. Perhaps taboo is the wrong word, coming to us as an anglicized version of a Tongan word which can be translated as sacred. But the economic objectification of what we were doing was, in fact, violating something in us that does lie in the realm of the sacred: individuality disappears except as it can be defined in relation to the whole. By denying ourselves the perception of our relation to the creatures dying on deck we were in some essential way denying ourselves a wholeness of being. And that knowledge lay large and dark and unarticulated just below the limited range of expression our condition allowed.

For non-Indian Americans too new to the land and waters of the Pacific Northwest to have developed ceremonies of place, the messages that salmon bring us are the same messages they have always brought, but they are not heard by most of us. Now—here—the message of the wild is fairly screaming at us in the midst of a deckload of slowly dying fish, but the message is carried at a different frequency than the one pulsing between the twin poles of our modern cultural icons of property and individualism. All of us on the boat speak English, and among us there is a smattering, too, of Norwegian, of Czech, of German—all languages which have been twisted over time into compliance with the dictates of economics and the physical sciences. None of us knows a word of Tlingit or Haida or Salish, languages that still resonate with the lives of salmon. Nevertheless, each of us retains some genetic memory—a memory imbedded in our flesh—of the wild relationships out of which we have evolved. The demands of the power gurdy rob us of all but a dim and paradoxical remnant of direct engagement with the processes of life, with the genteel ethic of the clean kill the expression of respect and compassion that recognizes the relationship between eater and eaten.

On the day I am thinking of, the lines have been carefully coiled and the stacked web checked to make sure it will flow out smoothly during the next set; the skiff is snubbed up close to the mother ship. The diesels roar at full bore as we take a position among the other purse seine boats to wait for the next set. Only now are the fish on deck given attention, Most of them are still vigorously alive, struggling and flopping against the alien media of full light and air. The crew react variously to the prospect of turning flesh into product. Some have leaped forward in their minds and are already calculating pounds and translating them into dollars; they do their work gleefully, shouting happily. Others sweep the fish into the hold tight-jawed and silent. One, a college boy/naturalist, had signed on to get close to ocean life forms. Although no one has told him so, he knows as well as anyone that he dare not take the time to dispatch the fish respectfully and individually, He seems to go crazy, kicking the fish and shouting curses at them. I notice that he seems to be aiming the kicks of his steel-toed rubber boots at that spot behind the head of each fish that will kill it quickly.

I have no memory of having arrived where I did by any logical thought process; I don't remember telling myself that this is what I should do. But I found myself alone in a dark corner of the fish hold squatting with a ten- or twelve-pound sockeye salmon still alive across my knees. With a knife opened up its chest cavity just enough to find the heart and tear it out with two fingers and a thumb. It came with a ripping and squirting sound. I popped the heart into my mouth and bit down once, hard, through the gristly thing. One bite brought a flavor like all of Icy Straights and enough saliva to float ten salmon hearts, enough to swallow it whole. As I swallowed, all MY floating terrors gained a name and swept through me with the intensity of a hurricane. Fear of fish flesh and cold blood, fear of slime on the flesh of fish and its absence on the skin of snakes, fear of the strangeness of other species, fear of a world barren of human thought, fear of death: my own and all of it.

I was back on the deck minutes later; no one seemed to have noticed my absence. I resumed the drill of preparing for the next set with an unusual clarity of vision and emptiness of mind. The shards of light reflecting from the surrounding sea, the crazy screams of the gulls and terns, the fading colors of the dying fish, all took on the aspect of a single thought that may or may not have been my own.

Some years afterward I found this passage, written by David Abram:

"Naturally then, the mountains, the creatures, the entire nonhuman world is struggling to make contact with us. The plants we eat or smoke are trying to ask us what we are up to; the animals are signaling to us in our dreams or in forests; the whole Earth is rumbling and straining to let us remember that we are of it, that this planet, this macrocosm is our flesh, that the grasses are our hair, the trees our hands, the rivers our blood, that the Earth is our real body and that it is alive."

I stayed on to finish the season and went home to Puget Sound with four thousand dollars in my pocket, more than I had ever made in an equivalent time before. I had managed—hundreds of times—to keep my feet out of the vicious coils of rope that could have pulled me into the killingly cold brine as they raced out with the net. I had also learned the ropes of the industrial hierarchy: it wasn't long before I had lobbied my way into the cook's job, which no one else wanted much anyway, so I no longer had to perform that mad dance stacking web on the stern. (During a set, the cook was the person who held the push-button box that stopped and started the power gurdy.) I had

managed to not quite drink myself to death at the bars in Ketchikan
and Hoonah and Petersburg during the intervals between four-day
openings. At the end of the season I knew I wouldn't return; I ended
my industrial fishing career muttering comparisons to the last of the
buffalo hunters. From that point on I would do my killing for food
one creature at a time.

I had gone west to make my fortune, like many others had before
me. But I had found a great deal more than the wad of money that
would keep me in the months to come. If the purse seine boat was a
model of a commodity economy, salmon had shown me that it was
floating in a sea of natural provision, the boundless generosity of the
Earth. Salmon was but one of the more dramatic expressions of the
gift of food, the gift of life. That revelation was itself a gift that would
keep me forever if I could learn to translate the obligation it placed
upon me. Lewis Hyde, in his priceless book *The Gift: Imagination
and the Erotic Life of Property*, has this to say about that obligation:
"The gift that cannot be given away ceases to be a gift. The spirit of
the gift is kept alive by its constant donation." The gift that does not
continue to move, dies.

In part, I have come to be by the river on this winter morning in
1983, ten years after my season on the purse seiner, in a half-conscious
attempt to keep the gift moving. And, as Hyde also says, "the giving
of gifts tends to establish a relationship between the parties involved."
In the hour of heightened perception after the salmon eggs have been
fertilized, the little group in attendance is experiencing a new range
of relationships. We are bound to each other through our tentative
and cautious engagement with the very processes of creation. We are
related through direct engagement with a race of salmon; the fertilized eggs have been tenderly placed in the nursery built with our own
hands; the blood of the mother fish is still seeping into the ground
nearby. We are bound to the people, our watershed neighbors, who
will tend the eggs and their emergent fry, and to the children who will

296

return them to the wild in a few months. Most importantly, we have begun our engagement with a place, a place defined by the waters of the river we work in, a place where we may yet come to be at home.

From A Road Runs Through It

More than Numbers: Twelve or Thirteen Ways of Looking at a Watershed

——Freeman House

(with apologies to Wallace Stevens)[1]

1.

> *It was evening all afternoon.*
> *It was snowing.*
> *And it was going to snow.*
> *The blackbird sat*
> *In the cedar-limbs.*

It's December again and curdled aluminum cloud cover extends all the way to where it kisses the iron of the ocean horizon. At its mouth, the river runs narrow and clear. If you've lived through many winters here, the sight is anomalous; normal December flows are more likely bank to bank, and muddy as corporate virtue. A storm had delivered enough wetness around the time of Hallowe'en to blast open the sand berm that separates the river from the sea all summer and fall. The salmon had been waiting and they came into the river then.

All through November and December the jet stream has been toying with us, diverting Pacific storms either to the north or south. The fish have been trapped in pools downstream, waiting for more rain to provide enough flow to move them up fifty or sixty miles to their preferred spawning habitat. By now many of the gravid hens

---

1. The epigraphs at the beginnings of some sections of this essay are from Wallace Stevens' poem, "Thirteen Ways of Looking at a Blackbird."

will have been moved by the pressure of time and fecundity to build their egg nests, called redds, in the gravels in the lower ten miles of the river. Come true winter storms, too much water is likely to move too much cobble and mud through these reaches for the fertile eggs to survive. They'll be either buried under deep drifts of gravel or washed away entirely.

I have committed the restorationist's cardinal sin. I have allowed myself a preferred expectation of the way two or more systems will interact. For the last two winters, steady pulses of rain have created flows that were good for the migrating salmon, carrying them all the way upstream before Solstice, but a desultory number of fish had entered the river those years. This year, from all reports, the ocean is full of salmon, more than have been seen in twenty years. So I have allowed myself the fantasy of a terrific return combined with excellent flows.

I know better than to hope for conditions that fit my notion of what's good. Perhaps as a reaction to my wishful thinking and its certain spirit-dampening consequences, I am suffering from a certain diminution of ardor.

2.

I am suffering from diminished ardor. As I look out the window on the hour-long drive to Cougar Gap[2], I'm seeing the glass half empty. As my eyes wander the rolling landscape, they seek out the raw landslides rather than indulging my usual glass-half-full habit of comparing what I'm seeing with my memory of last year's patterns of new growth on the lands cut over forty years ago.

It's one of the skills you gain in twenty years of watershed restoration work—to see the patterns in the landscape and be able to compare them with a fairly accurate memory of what was there last year. I've come to believe that I have restored in myself a pre-Enlightenment

---

2. Names of persons and places have been changed.

neural network that interprets what the eyes see, what the ears hear, what the skin feels in terms of patterns and relationships rather than as isolated phenomena numeralized so that they can be graphed. It's a skill given little credibility in the world of modern science, but it's deeply satisfying nonetheless.

Among the raw scars on the landscape to which my eye is drawn today, some are the result of human activities and some are the natural processes of a rain-whipped, earthquake-prone, sandstone geology. Their patterns don't change that much from year to year; the soil that would allow them to recover rapidly has been washed off the steep slopes and into the river. It'll take hundreds if not thousands of years for that soil to rebuild itself. It'll take generations for the mud in the river to be flushed out to sea.

These are patterns with cycles longer than the individual human life. It's satisfying and useful to be cognizant of them, too. Such knowledge tempers our human tendency to want to fix—read tamper with—everything in sight.

I'm beginning to feel better. Thinking about numbers has made me realize that it's numbers that have been getting me down.

3.

A man and a woman
Are one.
A man and a woman and a blackbird
Are one.

Numbers have been getting me down. Twenty years of this work. The numbers of returning salmon decreasing each of the first ten of those years. The numbers creeping upward during the second decade so that they stand now at close to the point where we began. The rational insistence of the agencies and foundations who pay for our projects that we quantify our work—numbers of fish, miles of road and streambank treated, numbers of trees planted, the percentages that have survived. Our numbers have looked good enough so that our little community-based watershed restoration organization is anticipating a half-million dollar budget in the next fiscal year. Abandoned roads will be decommissioned; managed roads "storm-proofed" to make them less constant conduits of mud into the waterways; trees grown from locally gathered seed will be planted; with luck, more wild salmon will be captured, their eggs fertilized and incubated, and schoolchildren will release the juvenile fish back into the wild. A number of local jobs will be generated. Similar budgets have provided me with an office job for the last two years. High on my job description is the mandate to keep that cash flow coming. I have been successful enough, and I'm really a little old to be planting trees or hefting rock, but after a while there comes to be something demeaning about pursuing public funds for a living.

While there is an increasing number of fifty to seventy-five dollar per hour professional scientists and consultants involved in watershed and ecosystem restoration, any work that involves moving heavy things around or getting wet and dirty is still done by volunteers or locals working for ten to twenty percent of those amounts.

Some of the amateurs go on to become professionals, make a career of it, but most of the practitioners are satisfied with the rewards of an ever-deepening relationship to the places where they live; by the sense that they are returning some small part of the enormous gift of Creation; by a growing knowledge that humans are capable of reunion with the life systems that support them. At its best, the work is an act of love, of communion, and as such delivers its own rewards. "Work is work," writes Jim Dodge, "but it's a pleasure to sing for one's supper when the song itself provides sustenance."

4.

For most of the twenty-plus years that Rochelle has lived in her country neighborhood, the most logical expectation has been that the industrial timberland owners who owned the remaining old growth forests nearby would liquidate their inventory. The most efficient and cost-effective way to turn those trees into timber is by clearcutting, a practice that leaves the steep lands barren under the driving rains of winter. Often, topsoil needed for the recovery of vegetation will end up in the streams, choking salmon habitat.

Rochelle had experienced the prospect as a piercing sadness. It had become clear to her that if corporations couldn't be held responsible for damage they inflicted on the lands they managed, then it was the responsibility of the resident landowners to resist that damage, and in the event that the resistance failed, to plan and implement a strategy for the recovery of the land and waters. The land means everything to Rochelle, and she quietly assumed that her neighbors, surrounded by the same beauty, would eventually come to the same conclusions. It may or may not be possible to stop the corporate practices, she reasoned. One certainly is compelled to try. But if you take the long view, the land itself can become the context and rationale for cooperative management strategies assumed by people who <u>live</u> on the land. Cooperative because natural succession proceeds at the level of the landscape and ecosystem rather than within the boundaries of property. When people live on damaged land, they can learn to act like watershed paramedics. As the land recovers, their management can begin to resemble preventative medicine. Some of the people she talked to were interested in small-scale sustainable timber production; others could not imagine a chainsaw in their hands biting into a living tree.

Rochelle had been talking to the crankiest bunch of individualists I can imagine, and it has taken a lot of persistence and patience. But now, with the recent purchase by conservation buyers of most of

302

the industrial timber lands in the area, including several thousand acres of old-growth forest, her slow work is consolidating like ripening cheese. There are enough landowners talking cooperative conservation-based land management that, together, they might quilt a mosaic of wild and well-managed lands.

The road on which I'll be been traveling once I turn off the paved county road is one of the log-haul roads pushed in on the cheap forty or more years ago. Like most logging and haul roads cut in that frenzied boom time, it had been designed, if that is not too grand a word, for one-time use only and then abandoned. In aerial photos, you can see a spaghetti-like tangle adding up to more than 2,500 miles of such roads in this three-hundred-square-mile watershed.

Later, in the 1970s, when large ranches were being subdivided, developers "improved" the roads, adding as few culverts as county codes would allow them, and called them access roads to the parcels that were being snapped up by back-to-the-landers. The improvements proved to be less than adequate in terms of the large amounts of sediment they bleed into the waterways each winter. The far larger numbers of still-abandoned roads periodically hemorrhaged landslides and stream-crossing washouts during the wettest years. At a rate frighteningly rapid in terms of geological time, but harder to see in the brief span of human lifetimes, the watershed is slowly bleeding to death.

In 1988, the local watershed restoration group had inventoried catastrophic earth slides in the basin and found that eighty-seven percent of them were related to roads. Some ten years later, state and federal funding agencies had begun to think in terms of watershed economics. Wouldn't it be more cost-effective in the long run to stem the chronic flow of sediment into waterways than it would be to apply band-aids after the bleeding had begun?

Everyone involved —the state, the feds, the community groups, the professional consultants—knew that cost-effective didn't necessarily mean cheap; there probably wasn't enough money in the world to put to bed or upgrade all the roads that had been carelessly built in the American west in the last half-century. But the local groups had been waiting for such an opportunity for a long time and jumped into the scramble for limited funds with a grand ten-year plan to inventory all the roads in the basin, prioritize the largest bleeders, and launch projects, tributary by tributary, to storm-proof the active access roads and remove the stream crossings that hadn't yet blown out on abandoned ones.

It is one of Rochelle's day-jobs to enlist the cooperation of neighboring landowners in such projects in the three basins surrounding her place. With the threat of clear-cut logging reduced, it seems to her like a win-win-win opportunity. Not only will landowners get otherwise unaffordable work done on their properties, but they will in the process become well educated about road maintenance. Soil, and water, and all the myriad creatures including humans, will benefit. Both terrestrial and aquatic habitats would become more productive and the very need for restoration projects might gradually dwindle.

5.
Among twenty snowy mountains
The only moving thing
Was the eye of the blackbird.

As usual, I get lost on the way to Rochelle's place. Where the county pavement ends there begins a maze of muddy roads, one of those hastily built thirty or more years ago. It's easy to get confused unless you thread this maze every day.

When a few ranches were subdivided in the early seventies, a little land rush was inadvertently created. There were at that time in American history the extraordinary number of young people who had come all willy-nilly to resist the institutionalization of primary experiences like birth and death, and providing one's own food and shelter. I have no idea why so many people seemed spontaneously to develop the same actualization of this resistance. But like lemmings, tens of thousands of urban people moved "back to the land" to test a faith unsupported by any evidence or personal experience that they could provide for themselves and each other and thus reclaim their confidence as humans.

Rochelle is one of the survivors of the hegira, as am I. She's been singing the song that provides its own sustenance for a good part of her time here. After the clearcuts and fires of the early eighties, she and her community planted tens of thousands of streambank trees, trees that have grown high enough now to cool the water again.

A gorgeous fireplace and chimney, hand built from rocks of many shapes and colors, stands eerily alone in her yard. A few yards away, the newer house sits unfinished. It's the third house Rochelle has built in this country. The first, on another property a mile or two away was burned to the ground in a fire that was supposed to be controlled. The insurance money moved her on to this place, a little larger at ten acres. The house that surrounded the beautiful fireplace fell down in an earthquake in 1991. Her husband Thomas is always busy. Whenever I visit he has little time for small talk. Often I'll just catch an occasional glimpse of him moving from task to task. This year, the third house will be expanded to include the pretty fireplace that was the heart of the second.

Up until a year ago, industrial timber lands surrounded Rochelle's 10-acre parcel. A good part of those had been cut over carelessly in the eighties, but large parts of it were still untouched. The piece directly upstream of her, the parcel that protects the steep headwaters of the creek that runs near her place had worried her. Back when the timber market was steady and before the feds had reduced the cut in the national forests, Rochelle had approached the local corporation that owned the headwaters of her stream, and for a small fee had obtained a piece of paper that gave her last bid should the parcel come up for sale. At the time, neither Rochelle nor the timber company imagined that it would ever come to anything.

6.

At the sight of blackbirds
Flying in a green light,
Even the bawds of euphony[3]
Would cry out sharply.

We get out of the truck and step into drizzle, after another five miles of rough road into a wilder terrain. I want to see a certain view. Rochelle wants to look at a certain road. We are at one of the higher elevations near the eastern ridge of the watershed. Despite the drizzle, we can see nearly a hundred miles to the south, and twenty miles to

---

3. A bawd is a procuress of prostitute. Euphony is "the quality, esp. in the spoken word of having a pleasant sound" (OED). Wallace is speaking of sweet-talking hustlers here, or perhaps of poets in general. He then separates himself from the crowd with the non-euphonious (to my ear) phrase that follows, "to cry out sharply." I hear the cry of the Western raven, a very black bird.

Language will always fall short of describing the beauty of nature, no matter how skillful the speaker. We are attempting to describe Creation form within Creation, one of the binding paradoxes of the human condition. By extension, to call our rehabilitation efforts "ecological restoration" is to hubristically claim a power equal to that of evolution itself. There is no such thing as ecological restoration, except in controlled experiments carefully kept free of random human cultural effects, which more properly describes the science of restoration ecology. The rest of us amateurs (*practitioners of love according to Stephanie Mills) living deep within the variables of diverse human ambitions can only hope to put ourselves into the picture in a way that we hope to be coevolutionary. Dennis Martinez uses the phrase "eco-cultural restoration" to describe his work among first peoples, recognizing that the renewal of indigenous cultural practices must be accompanied by the rehabilitation of the indigenous landscape. We newcomers are practicing something else. In my better moments, I like to think that we may finally be discovering a culture appropriately based on the constraints and opportunities of the diverse places in North America.

the west (though it seems much further), where the horizon is the ridge that rises straight up out of the Pacific on the other side of it. I bathe myself in the prospect before me, thinking of Gary Snyder's "mountains and rivers without end." Close in, the landscape breaks itself into the mosaic of prairie and forest that characterizes the region. Further into the distance, the mosaic fades into a wash of forest greens and upland prairie browns, differentiated by the deep green of Douglas-fir and the celadon green of tanoak.

Although we can't see the ocean, we can get a sense of the weather system coming from it, which is changing its nature before our eyes. Under the overcast, the colors are faded, but where there are breaks in the cloud slurry, sunlight pours down to make blazing splashes amidst the gloom. Where the light cuts through columns of mist, it breaks into discreetly defined rays, like signals from the gods.

You can look at the view spread out below us and imagine that it is uninhabited, or inhabited only by a community with bear and cougar at the top of the food chain. I know better. Parts of the land <u>are</u> uninhabited by humans, and those parts are managed either by state and federal agencies or by industrial timber corporations. The inhabited part, more than four-fifths of the land laid out before me, is privately owned by ranchers or back-to-the-landers or outlaws or some combination of the above: new indians, new cowboys, dope-growers, new scientists, old pioneer families, traditional rednecks, environmentalists, new rednecks, vegetarians, treeplanters, and check here for other. Because I have been down many of the roads in this part of the watershed and have talked to the people at the ends of them, I know that the region closest to us is mostly populated with second- and third-generation ranchers and more recently arrived agricultural outlaws. Both groups call themselves environmentalists while being practitioners of the most conservative sort of private property rights, each group for different reasons. I tend to be slightly more sympathetic to the ranchers, who are more honest about their espousal of John Locke's eighteenth century philosophy of property and pride.

7.

Economies develop or devolve according to their own rules. Conservation buyers have purchased most of the private industrial timber lands in Rochelle's neighborhood in the last two years to be preserved for public management. The previous owner was a local corporation with a mill too large to be adequately supplied by its own too-small land base. When, due to protection of the Northern spotted owl, cheap timber from the national forests had become less readily available, the local corporation found itself competing for logs on the open market with larger corporations that could afford to underbid them.

At the same time, a local environmental group was successfully challenging in court each one of the local corporation's logging plans. The company saw the long window of time opening up to swallow it. The corporation—mills, lands, and all—was put up for sale. Other organizations, some of which included Rochelle, started raising money in an attempt to outbid the same larger corporation that had helped run the smaller one out of business.

The effort attracted the attention of an international forest pres-ervation organization that was looking for a project that would es-tablish its presence in North America. These several thousand acres of old-growth Douglas fir, scattered between a state park on the east and a national conservation area on the west, looked like a winner. The international org developed its strategies around the philoso-phy of the Wildlands Project, which recognizes that even if every unexploited area in the developed world were put out of bounds to economic development immediately, there still wouldn't be a large enough land base to do more than slightly slow down the rate of the extinction of species. The Wildlands Project has demonstrated the need for "corridors" between the pristine "core areas," places where human activity is limited in favor of their uses by other species. The theory is scientifically sound in the abstract, and presents a conservation strategy simplified enough to have gained a significant number of adherents in centralized government land management agencies. The purchases were going to require a great deal of money, a large part of it public funds.

Combine the word "corridor" with public funds and the result may or may not make for viable wildlife habitat, but it will certainly create the expectation of public access to places where the human presence had heretofore been minimal. Public funds had been used for the acquisitions, generating a vague expectation on the part of the state that at some time in the future, some kind of trail would exist through the reserves. On the part of the locals who lived on parcels separating the newly acquired forests, a well-defined paranoid expectation bloomed: many hikers in expensive REI gear, closely followed by uniformed rangers on the lookout for illegal activities of all kinds.

Up until the point at which the purchase was secure, the international forest preservation organization had acted in a fashion in keeping with the techniques and strategies of most centralized and urban-based organizations working from high-minded and abstract principles. The climate of political expediency can intensify in direct proportion to the numbers of acres, or dollars, at stake. Soon, the end of preserving big parcels of undisturbed habitat was justifying the means of describing the landscape as if it had no human residents. The needs and concerns of the locals had been treated as an irritation. The situation had been described to funders in such a way as to make it legible and attractive to them, ignoring the potential social problems locally.

To its enormous credit, however, the international forest preservation organization did not stop with the acquisition and leave someone else to deal with the social fallout. Following Rochelle's lead, the fundraisers not only recognized the potential of local interest in reinhabitation, but also developed a program that begins to address two of the outstanding flaws in the Wildlands Project strategy.

Once beyond the grandeur of the Wildlands Project vision, it becomes apparent that the challenge is much more complex than arrogant lines drawn on a map. Each biome—each microclimate, in fact—presents a complex knot of relationships that requires exact knowledge of two functions or features of locale where a "corridor" might be located. What are the requirements of each plant, animal, or community native to that particular fold of the planet? Based on that knowledge (which can best be gathered over time by resident humans with help from professional ecologists), what kinds of economic activities are harmonious with those needs? Until the second question is answered, one doesn't have much to say to the people who inhabit the "corridors" one might be proposing.

The international forest preservation organization researched other sources of money and mounted a stewardship initiative in the area of the newly public wild lands. The skills of half a dozen local organizations, whose local expertise had been gained by systematic immersion in this unique biome, were put at the service of the people who lived in the area, providing information and experience needed for a co-operative effort in conservation-based land management. The group that had worked on salmon restoration for twenty years would train people to gather credible data on water quality and aquatic habitat. The sustainable forestry outfit would teach people to think about timber production in the long term and conduct workshops in fuel load reduction in the brushy forest effulgence that follows clearcutting. A local land trust would teach conservation easement potentials to those who had no interest in commercial production. The watershed council that had worked for fifteen years to reduce sediment flow into the waterways would systematically inventory poorly constructed and abandoned roads and seek public funds to help landowners repair or decommission them. Another local organization that concerns itself with the needs of terrestrial creatures would teach people how to track and identify their animal neighbors. The twenty square miles of sub-drainages and its human inhabitants began to be understood as a reciprocally functional unit.

The road Rochelle shows us is like a highway compared to the rutted roads we've traveled today. The State Parks Department, one of the public agencies involved in managing the newly protected areas, built the road in the last dry season. It is two lanes wide and well graveled and it connects the assumedly private roads behind us with land recently acquired by conservation buyers, assumedly for the protection of wildlife. "Parks," as the state agency is known, has a clear mandate to provide recreation for work-weary Californians. A draft land-use plan being circulated by Parks shows blue circles designating proposed campsite developments right on top of the largest population of northern spotted owls yet identified in the protected area. "Looks like we'll have to protect the land from the protectors," says Rochelle. She's received no clear answers to her inquiries about the Park's intentions, but she has managed to get a spur road closed for the winter with yellow plastic signs to protect against the spread of sudden oak death syndrome.

8.

He rode over Connecticut
In a glass coach.
Once a fear pierced him,
In that he mistook
The shadow of his equipage
For blackbirds.

Sudden oak death syndrome is a plague that has appeared to the south of us and is spreading. It is a fungus, *Phytophthora,* currently believed to be water-borne, that rapidly kills tanoak, black oak, and coastal live oak. Three counties to the south, whole mountainsides present the grim panorama of standing dead trees, kindling for some catastrophic future fire. It has also been discovered to infect huckleberry bushes, another vector for the spread of the disease. It's been identified in nursery rhododendrons in Germany and the Netherlands and central California. Students of algae tell us *Phylophthera* is related to the fungus that caused the Irish potato blight of the last century. Journalists remind us of the chestnut blight of the last century, which along with opportunistic cutting, eliminated that species from eastern woodlands. Two unconfirmed sightings of the disease have been made in the park to the east of where we are standing.

Some climatologists, using computer models, have projected that an increase of two degrees Fahrenheit in the global temperature will destroy the redwood forests nearby.

Four thousand or so years ago, during a warming cycle, salmon colonized rivers further and further to the south as the glaciers receded. Our little river is close to the southern extreme of that range. Salmon have a rather narrow temperature range in which they can flourish. As air temperatures rise on the planet, the ocean will heat up, and so will rivers. The range of the salmon will retreat back to the north where the waters are cooler. Russian scientists call the likely effects of climate change "ecosystem reorganization," unpredictable, chaotic. Watershed restoration? What can the words mean in a time of plagues? How shall we go on? What shall we restore?

These are not new questions. How could we have avoided asking them as we devoted ourselves to our tiny watershed during the same time as the larger world gave us Chernobyl, Bhopal, AIDS. Global warming had hit the news around the same time we had begun work to enhance the spawning successes of our precious wild salmon. *We have never for a moment known if we would succeed.* But we have known that for any success to be enduring, changes would not be measured in numbers of wild creatures so much as in human attitudes toward the wild.

Plagues are a symptom of the human economies being institutionalized by treaties like NAFTA and GATT, which create supra-national institutions that move us closer to what Wendell Berry calls the total economy. In the total economy there is no value but in personal wealth, no form of measurement but in numbers. In a total economy, a marriage contract would be framed in deliverable ergs of sexual energy, hours of homemaking; profit and loss statements would take the form of tangible property including children. What's clean water worth? A salmon run?

9.

The blackbird whirled in the autumn winds.
It was a small part of the pantomime.

Protection and preservation of "pristine" lands is no more than half a strategy. If the lands between the preserves are understood as economic sacrifice zones (which they will be until they are described otherwise), whose army will defend the preserves fifty years from now? The accommodation of wildness in the inhabited lands between the preserves is essential to the viability of the preserves themselves. Once a community of humans begins to understand itself as a functional part of the landscape, and learns how to act that way, then the protected lands can be understood as sacred. Watersheds are more than museums with wild lands hanging on the walls.

10.

After another short haul in the truck, we can see a column of smoke. As we get closer, Rochelle grows positively gleeful. We pull into an opening in the doghair forest with an old homestead cabin in the middle of it. Two burn piles smoke and occasionally blaze up nearby. At least two chainsaws snarl away out of sight on the hill-sides rising up steeply around the homestead. From a distance, the work site looks like an anthill. A steady stream of people is pulling sections of wet green slash larger than themselves down out of the woods and onto the smoky fire.

I recognize one of the brush-pullers. I know her by her forest name, Velocity. The name fits. Velocity rarely stops moving and if there is another human nearby, she's likely to be talking enthusiastically. "Isn't this great?" she cries. "We'll have two acres fireproofed by the end of the day."

Velocity is a forest defender, one of twenty or so who have set up an encampment some fifteen miles to the north in order to resist the liquidation of the largest stand of undisturbed old-growth Douglas fir in the watershed and in the state. A rotating crew of twenty or so maintains the encampment, a trespass its residents call a free state. Legal ploys to stop the cut have failed and the young people will try to hold off the contract loggers while another group of residents looks for the money to purchase the forest.

Velocity had arrived in the watershed a couple of years earlier, when itinerant practitioners of non-violent civil disobedience were defending the same forest. That time, the courts had agreed with the protestors. Both during the earlier defense and the current one, the occupation had been augmented by legal blockades on public roads by residents of the valley. After that success, other activists moved on to other crises, but Velocity and two comrades had settled in the valley, recognizing the power of neighborly protest. They had found a place to live, grown gardens, performed odd jobs, and waited for the next move on the forest.

This time around the blockades are larger and the free state has a different demographic. Some of its residents are young people who have grown up within twenty miles of the threatened forest. As residents, they have been encouraged over the years to become watershed paramedics, and they have independently intuited the cautionary words of the brilliant restoration ecologist Daniel Janzen: "An increasingly competent medical profession should not promote participation in potentially lethal acts."

Formulists of watershed restoration have a slogan: preserve the best and restore the rest. The formulas were developed on public land where decisions about "saving the best" could be part of administrative policy. I'm not sure the scientists who invented the catchy mnemonic phrase would recognize this local iteration of their excellent strategy. Preservation may be only half a strategy, but it's the first half.

Because the law requires the loggers to stay off the dirt roads for two days following a rain, the free state can be maintained by a skeleton crew. Today some forest defenders are taking advantage of the respite to earn a few bucks working on a fuel load reduction project.

This forest was cut over thirty years ago. Because it was cut before the law required replanting, and because of the aspect and microclimate of the slope, the site has grown back in a thick tangle of tanoak and coyote brush. The straw bosses are the guys with the chainsaws. One of them is Rochelle's husband Thomas who is smiling broadly. He describes the work of the day: to remove the highly flammable brush in the understory of the second-growth forest. Thin some of the spindly oaks to encourage the better trees to grow faster and straighter and to allow more sunlight into the grove so that the dominant Doug firs can grow again. Cut the limbs up as high as the saws will reach, and burn them. When the next wild fire burns through here, there'll be a better chance that it will burn slow and cool and won't be able to leap to the crown. Salvage a little firewood while you're at it.

The other sawyer is an old friend. Drawn to the valley for its opportunities in restoration fifteen years ago, Dave has become a new age gyppo logger, pouring months of work into resurrecting a self-loading log truck that had been abandoned in the fifties. He works at small logging and thinning jobs, promoting the promising new market in sustainably harvested California hardwoods. He has built a home out of lumber he has milled himself on a homestead carved out of a rehabilitated logging site. He is inventing a life and raising a family in what he hopes is a system of coherence, with the lands and waters surrounding as the binding medium.

11.

I was of three minds
Like a tree
In which there are three blackbirds.

Jack Turner writes in *The Abstract Wild* that he believes ecological restoration to be a passing fancy. I think it more likely that it will turn out to be something else, incorrectly called ecological restoration, and resembling more the restoration of our relationship to the places where we live.

Ecological restoration is a natural process occurring wherever there has been ecological perturbation. When a clearcut is allowed to recover according to the dictates of local natural succession, it is ecological restoration. In a Doug-fir forest, the system sometimes recovers to the point that timber can be taken from it again in sixty to eighty years. It will take four times that long for the forest to recover its mature complex of flora, fauna, and habitat. When human inhabitants gain adequate knowledge (preferably through immersion) of the eccentricities of local natural succession, they may begin to take actions that hasten it toward more diverse and mature stages of development.

The truest value of this work called watershed restoration is measured in relationships that are difficult if not impossible to turn into numbers. Like new and ever-deepening relationships with portions of the landscape, or another species. Like the coagulation of relationships with neighbors, which as they thicken begin to resemble the chaotic stew of community. What is restored is some aspect of watershed and ecosystem *function*. More importantly, we're rediscovering our own human species function as a natural part of life systems. This definition of ecological restoration cannot realize its potential except as it is practiced in community vernacular life. It should not be confused with the science of restoration ecology, which will likely endure as what William Jordan has called "experimental ecology," carefully controlled and isolated from human economic activity. We will continue to need the insights and methodologies of science, but if we allow the *practice* of restoration to become the exclusive domain of professional consultants and centralized government agencies, we will have lost its greatest promise, which is nothing less than a redefinition of human culture. It is equally possible for a fully professionalized concept of ecological restoration to become part of the price of doing extractive business as usual, a form of systematized mitigation that is one more cipher in a total economy.

12.

I do not know which to prefer.

...

The blackbird whistling
Or just after.

Sometime in the mid-eighties, I was occasionally offered the shelter of a retreat cabin at a Cistercian monastery near a remote watershed restoration work site. I enjoyed these respites, both for the calming simplicity of the cabin, and for the opportunity to chat with the abbess, a wise and elderly Belgian woman. Once, when one of those plague signals had just erupted on the world—Bhopal, perhaps, or Chernobyl—I found myself in a state of despair. What was the sense, I asked her, of pursuing this difficult work in the face of a social order disintegrating so rapidly that it may well mean the end of the world?

"What does it matter?" she answered. Her Flemish consonants sound like a stream working its way around an obstacle.

" Say you know the end of the world is coming tomorrow morning. How do you want to face it? With a clear mind and an open heart, yes? Now, say the world isn't going to end. How do you want to wake up in the morning and approach your work?" She pauses for effect, but not long enough for me to answer. " "With a clear mind and an open heart!" She beams. "End of the world or not, same answer. Go on with your work."

WHILE YOU WERE SLEEPING

Erin Fristad

"*To witness mindfully is to grieve for what has been lost.*"
—Freeman House

By August 15th, everyone knows the fish
aren't coming. Your skipper buys
a pickup truck, starts drinking
and driving. The crew joins him.
You wear large hats, put the dogs in between you,
drive to the neighboring fishing village. You make up
some silly reason for this ritual, perhaps luck,
but you all know it's better
than staring at an empty ocean.
At the first mile marker, you snap
your bottle caps out the window,
raise your beers in a symbolic toast
and look straight ahead.
You know it's the end, the first end.
You joke about working at McDonalds
but lay awake at night staring at the fo'c's'le
hatch thinking of who you might call
for a construction job over the winter
or maybe another fishery. You calculate
how much money you'd make in three months of trawling,
then imagine leaving Seattle the day after Christmas,
New Year's Eve puking out the wheelhouse window

somewhere in the Gulf of Alaska encased
in darkness. You think about crossing
icy decks and balancing on your knees to bleed fish.
This image makes you sick to your stomach
turning on your side you think:
maybe the fish will hit tomorrow.
Trying to fall asleep you imagine
telling this story five years from now.
A late run of Sockeye, a jump in the price
of Chums, your end of the season dinner
filled with good wine and laughter.
Your optimism swells enough
to let you sleep. What you can't imagine
is five years from now
you'll be painting yachts and sailboats
in a dusty boatyard in the lower forty-eight.
You don't know this yet, you're still sleeping
to the sound of a refrigeration system chilling water
for fish you won't catch. What you don't know
is that the fish will come back next season,
but no one will want them. You still believe
a low return will bring up the price
next year, like in high school economics—
it will all balance out in the end.
But you can't imagine the end.
An eight hour work day, a paycheck every two weeks,
shorts, flip-flops, sitting in traffic watching the heat
rise from blacktop. You'll be standing
around a barbeque, someone will joke
about a town full of fishing refugees. You'll notice
the man next to you leaning slightly forward,
his feet too far apart, braced for the swell.

You can't imagine sitting at a desk
in August, reading books about salmon,
trying to learn the scientific terms
for what they do. You'll catch yourself
studying the pictures, trying to name the river,
trying to find a rock you once rested on.
You'll stare so long you'll start to smell
the rotting carcasses. But for now,
I watch you sleeping.
In another hour, you'll wake
and pull anchor.

Advice to Female Deckhands

Erin Fristad

You will be the cook.
In addition to wheel watches, working
on deck, unloading fish, fueling up,
filling fresh water, mending nets,
grocery shopping whenever you come to town,
you also will prepare three meals a day
and two hearty snacks to go with coffee.
You must keep the kettle on the stove full
and the juice jug and two gallons of milk in the fridge.

You will learn to slice vegetables, prepare a marinade,
cook pasta and fillet a salmon
in twenty minute intervals
while the net is out. You will learn
to ignore the other crew members sitting
at the galley table reading. You must know
how to create a corral in rough weather,
so pots of soup don't end up dripping
down the firewall behind the stove. You will need
bungie cords to keep the cast iron skillet from sliding.
These cords melt if they touch the stove top.
Keep a squeeze container of Aloe Vera gel
under the galley sink for the burns
on your hands and forearms.

The stove will blow out on windy days
when you're exhausted,
your skin stinging with jelly fish.
The crew will say they're not hungry on these days
but when you slide behind the Cape, it will be flat
calm and all of you will be starving. Before relighting the
    stove
determine how much diesel has built up.
If it's more than an inch deep,
turn off the fuel source
by flipping a breaker in the engine room.
You don't have time for ear protection. Get down there
and back before someone hollers for you on deck.
Passing the engine, watch the straps on your raingear,
your ponytail, where you put your hands.

When cooking, remember all odors from the galley
drift directly into the wheelhouse. Fish sauce
smells like dirty tennis shoes. Once she smells this,
your skipper's daughter will refuse to eat anything
she suspects has fish sauce. As a woman and cook
you will be expected to have a special bond with the
    skipper's daughter
and you will. Have art supplies in a shore box in the galley,
a drawing tablet under a cushion, collect starfish,
Decorator crab, and Spiny Lump Suckers in a deck bucket.
Teach her what you know can kill her. When she cries
put your arm around her, kiss her
on the top of the head and let her cry.
Allow her to use your cell phone to call friends
in exchange for making salads, pots of coffee,
washing lunch dishes, carrying groceries to the boat.

Develop sign language for communicating
when she stands in the galley door
peering out at you on deck.

This isn't what I intended.
I set out to give you advice for taking care
of yourself, now it's about taking care of a girl
you're related to by circumstance.
This is exactly what will happen.
You'll notice a hum
more penetrating than the engine.

Lost & Found

Mike Connelly

My great-grandfather, Neils Bjerre, was known as "Gussy Boy." He was a poet—the only one in the family that anyone knows about. When he was an old man he did something he had wanted to do for a very long time. He took a boat back to Denmark, the place where he was born. He hadn't been there in forty-five years.

During his trip he kept a journal, which he sent back to my great-grandmother in weekly installments. She had decided not to go. Perhaps she understood that this was something he was going to have to do alone. After all, it was his past that was absent. She was born right where she still lived, on the northern coast of California.

Somehow, after years wandering around, I have ended up in Oregon, east of the Cascades, just north of the California border. We farm near the headwaters of the Klamath river, and as I watch the water pass I think of the place where it meets the sea, down near the home my great-grandparents shared. This water went there before we were here, and I imagine a clear day with Gussy Boy and Memo sitting on the bank where the fresh meets the salt, dipping their bare feet into the cold, pushing their toes down into the mud. It's autumn, and there are others around, gathered to watch the salmon pass.

Not long ago mother retired, and joined us here in Oregon. She was going through the last few boxes when she found Gussy's journal. She set it aside, and brought it over later that day. She told me she thought it was something I ought to see. She told me again, "Gussy was a poet." I don't think she knew just what that meant. I think that was the point she was trying to make.

May 16, 1951 (Tues)

Well, we are on our way. The landing bridge was cast off at 12:10, and the ship shook itself and started moving at 12:12 pm. The Statue of Liberty waved us Good-Bye, as we passed out of the East River and the American Continent is now fading in the west. We've had lunch—and a very good one too—and the passengers are stretched out in their deck chairs on the sunny afterdeck. The ship is filled to capacity, mostly with Danes, going home to visit the Fatherland. I have with me in my cabin two Danes and one Swede, all elderly and apparently respectable citizens. The trip looks promising.

I was very busy when Mother came by with the journal. I had a meeting to go to, and the phone kept ringing. I may have been short with her, and I regret that I just laid the journal down on top of a stack of bills. I knew I had to eat before I left, and I asked her if she wanted something, but she said no and left.

I cleared a spot on the table and sat down to eat. I picked the journal up off the stack and started reading it. I finished my lunch at about page five, but I didn't stop reading until the end, fifty pages later. I never made it to my meeting, and when the phone rang I just let it.

May 19 (Fri)

Last night I ran into a man from Hurup in Thyland, Denmark. Close by that place is a large estate, where once back in 1898 I was invited to a very jolly harvest celebration. The man knew the place and the people well. Another man I met this afternoon turned out to hail from Holstebro and knew several of my many relatives in that neighborhood. This world is getting too small to hide in. Lucky I don't have to.

But the world is not small. It's as big as it's always been—bigger in a lot of ways. Gussy runs into people who know his family on a boat in the middle of the Atlantic Ocean. After twenty years of roaming Gussy settles down near the mouth of the Klamath River, and fifty years later his great-grandson settles near the headwaters of the same river. Can anyone tell me why this means the world is small?

The world is enormous, and we oughtn't to think of it otherwise. Our claim that the world has grown smaller stems from our reluctance to acknowledge that we humans—each and every one of us—have just grown much bigger. We have built machines, and by touching these machines we extend our presence—our sensory dominion—quite literally to the ends of the earth. We can float and drive and fly where once we could only walk. We plug our senses in, and we see, hear, taste, smell and touch things and places we could only imagine before. Each of us is a tiny, silent, fleshy nucleus, with mechanical tentacles stretching out as far as we choose. We have made ourselves so large that the earth itself seems to have shrunk, shrunk to the point that most of us feel like the earth itself is something we can wrap our thoughts around, something we can "get a handle on." We tend to act like it's our job to comprehend it, to manage it, to consume it. We have grown so large that its very salvation is something we feel we're in charge of.

We've forgotten that our plugs can be pulled, our gears jammed, our lines cut, our industrial tentacles amputated, leaving us fragile, mute and alone, the hungry monkeys we have always been, wandering around our tiny homes, forced to learn, once again, how to live within them.

May 25 (Thu)

I sometimes wish I had kept up the diary I started 44 years ago, when I began my journey eastward, a journey which now, at last, completes my "trip around the world." Such a diary, while of little interest to others, would nevertheless now afford me a good opportunity to see myself in retrospect, to note my trials and errors, my growth and deterioration, all of which would be useful in giving advice to my grandchildren. On the other hand, it might be said one should not waste time looking back;

world progress is built by men who look ahead, not stopping to lament over past mistakes. So maybe I, too, better keep looking ahead; if I can't build an empire, a world of peace or a society of contentment, perhaps I can build a henhouse for the Madam when I get back home.

The Klamath River is a salmon river, but there are no salmon in the Upper Klamath now. Long ago they were fished into a precarious fix, and we long ago changed the way their habitats work. Those that still return to the river hit a couple of concrete walls just south of the border.

We often hear that the salmon problem is vastly complicated, and that the solution will have to be equally complicated. Others feel that the solution is simple: Take the dams out, stop cutting trees, and shut the water off to the farms. Eliminate the influence of humans on the river. And there are still others who say the solution is even simpler than that, because it's a solution to a problem that doesn't exist.

What seems simple to me is that there are a lot fewer fish than there used to be. It also seems unlikely that this decline is unrelated to the arrival of Europeans in this region. What seems complicated to me is the relationship between this decline and this arrival—not because the impacts of industrial development are so thorough and far-reaching, not because very powerful people have a direct interest in maintaining and expanding those developments, and not because there are so many innocents whose very lives, as it stands now, are dependent upon these developments.

The relationship is complicated, or at least seems complicated, because it is big, or at least it seems big. The systems and forces that exceed the productive capacity of the watersheds are big, and what's making matters worse is that our attempts to confront the forces or alter the systems are just as big, and getting bigger all the time. Occasionally someone says out loud that the bigness itself might be the problem, and that all the issues identified in our EIS reports and lawsuits and legislation and strategic plans are just by-products of this bigness. And occasionally this idea catches on with powerful people, who then get together to form a national non-profit, with major foundation funding and headquarters in a big city, with membership in the hundreds of thousands, dedicated to promoting the idea that "small is beautiful." The hugeness is justified as "temporary," as "just a tool," as a necessary expedient to bring about the necessary change, like some kind of dictatorship of the environmental proletariat.

May 25 (Thu)

This ship seems filled with old, tired men. They may have won the struggle for riches, but they look battered and bruised and not particularly happy about it. They are returning to the shores of the past for one last look, fearful of what they might find. Disappointments will be many and cruel, and when once more they return to their adopted country, they will have seen the Fatherland, but their dreams have died. Which is best: a beautiful dream of home, as we remember it or as we have built it in our imagination, or to go back to that home and see with cruel clarity what Time and Fate have done to it?

Someone claimed recently that "after all our efforts to save the salmon, we may come to see that it is the salmon who are saving us." The life cycle of the salmon is dramatic, mythic; it's metaphorical in a way that fits fairly neatly into the stories we have been telling about ourselves for the last several decades. Their scarcity works like a warning.

But perhaps more critical is the fact that salmon fit into most of our much older stories, as well. Born into the brightness and rush upstream, they stay awhile and then head on out toward the deep. They never really know their mothers, their fathers, although their very lives depend on the death and decay of the generation before. They reach the sea, and wander long and far, but always with the mute knowledge that by striking out they are headed home, that by fattening up they are feeding what's coming after.

What they do then has been called "unimaginable." And it's important, meaningful, that we have called it that. From out in the ocean they find their way back. Among thousands of river mouths they find the right one. Faced with fork after fork, they almost always go the right way. They turn into monsters, red and hooked and humped and fanged, scraping and lunging their way up. They rub their faces raw, digging their nests in the cobble. The water mucks up with flesh and clouds of fertile white. So much of it futility, and yet there is no other way.

It is innocence, exploration, endurance and luck, selfishness and sacrifice—limitlessness, and the gravity of home. These are themes we cling to. We've talked of them for fifty thousand years. The history of this region, the life cycle of our own species, is exactly as dramatic, exactly as heroic, exactly as tragic as that of the salmon. Our instinct for home is as mysterious and irrefutable, and the consequences of losing our way just as bloody, final and, perhaps, necessary.

Our story is their story and theirs is ours, and yet we call it "unimaginable." We are like the boy who couldn't recognize his identical twin. Our problem is not that a fish's life is so alien that "imagining" it is impossible, it's that we've lost the habit of doing that kind of thinking. That faculty is so atrophied, as busy as we are with other things, that we're no longer up to the task.

This is not, as so many seem to think, a permanent flaw in our genetic make-up. It's a basic requirement of the conditions of our lives. Our inability to identify with the natural systems that surround us and sustain us, our reluctance to celebrate or even recognize the mutually creative, mutually destructive bonds between people and nature, is simply the result of having our attention directed elsewhere. Nowadays, trying to keep these things in mind is like trying to read a book on a merry-go-round. Everything's big and bright and loud. The pull is centrifugal, away, outwards. No matter how badly we need it, the gravity just won't hold.

May 27 (Sat)

I found myself on a pier, surrounded by hundreds and hundreds of strangers. Then suddenly, while scanning this sea of faces for traces of "my family," I heard a feminine voice cry out; a pair of soft arms encircled my neck and a determined kiss was planted on my cheek. It was shock, although not, I admit, an altogether unpleasant one. I discovered that my assailant was a very beautiful young lady, who now proceeded to claim, and prove, legitimate relationship to me, to wit: Her father is a nephew of mine. Nor was she alone. A full dozen of relatives had come to bid me welcome home. I didn't know them. Only one of them had I ever seen before.

A while back my uncle, Gussy's grandson, mailed us an announcement for a family reunion, to be held on the north coast of California. There was a long guest list attached, letting us know who would be there. Out of about a hundred names I knew maybe five, people I hadn't seen since childhood, mostly. The tone of the announcement was festive and familiar. There would be food and drink, and family in the area had opened up their homes for people who would need a place to stay. They called it a "once in a lifetime opportunity." I read the announcement, and then slid it across the table to my wife, She read it, slid it back to me and said, "That's neat." I picked it up and looked again and said, "I don't know any of these people." We never even talked about going.

My mother gave me Gussy's journal about a year after that, and as I read it I kept wondering why it had never even occurred to me to go to the reunion, why the fact that I didn't know my family was a reason not to go, instead of a reason to go. My uncle went, and he told us that people had come from all over the country. There were even people from Denmark, who had planned their American vacation so they wouldn't miss it. Why hadn't I wanted to go? I've never been able to figure it out. But maybe I'm asking the wrong kind of question. A better one might be: Why, after reading the journal, do I now wish I had?

The greeting Gussy received at the docks in Denmark is hard for me to explain away. If I think about encountering a distant relative, one that I haven't seen for a half-century, or that I have never seen, I can only imagine a sort of awkward cordiality. Perhaps we would sit and talk a while, if there was time, about the people we have both known, about places we've both been. When our time was up we'd shake hands, wish each other well, and suggest that we stay in touch, knowing full well how unlikely that is. Maybe it's only preconceptions like these that would make such an encounter turn out that way. Maybe it would turn out differently if only I wanted it to, if only I imagined it would.

Maybe. But everywhere Gussy went in Denmark he was met by boisterous crowds of overjoyed strangers, some of whom traveled far to see him, most of whom wept openly when it was time for him to leave again. These encounters feel "alien" to me, and I suspect I'm not alone in this. Like Gussy, I would no doubt feel "shocked" and "moved" to be treated this way, after so many years, by a bunch of strangers whose only connection is a word, a name, and the place they all called "home."

But maybe that's enough. Maybe Family and Home, if we think about them right, if we put them in the privileged place they deserve, are enough to make folks act this way. What power there must be in these two things: over all that time, across all that space, a young girl shouts and waves, wraps her arms around, and kisses the face of an old man, an old man she has never seen before.

June 8 (Thu)

For two days I have been the guest of my brother Hans and his wife Kirstine, in their idyllic home in the heart of the forest. In daytime I wandered about under the majestic beeches with his little 5-year-old grand-

*daughter, picking wildflowers, and in the evening I sat listening to the tales
my host had to tell about my father and mother's last years. Kirstine was
in bed—still weak after the shock of her daughter-in-law's recent sudden
death. Only a few weeks ago, in a state of complete nervous collapse, she
took her own life. Her husband, Neils, has a fine and well-appointed house,
bought only a few months ago, in the hope that his wife's sick nerves might
be benefited by the larger place and the better surroundings.*

During his stay in Denmark, Gussy visited at least one grave a day.
They were not at all sure that Kirstine would go on living. She was
unable to go when her son and husband brought Gussy to the place
where his parents were buried.

June 14th (Wed)

*I placed an armful of flowers from Kongensgaard's garden at the foot
of the stone, as a last greeting from their wandering boy. I cannot think of
a more restful spot for mother and father to sleep. The plot is good-sized
and brother Jacob and his wife are also buried there. The always faithful
Hans sees to it that the place is well taken care of.*

When a species of fish gets in trouble, there has, for the last few
decades, been a fairly standard approach to getting them out. Data is
collected and compiled, and a petition is made to classify this single
species as "endangered" under national law. If the petition is successful, then it becomes illegal to harm either the species or its habitat.
Federal agencies begin the process of determining the biological needs
of the species, designating critical habitat, and developing a recovery
plan. Any other agency that seeks to carry out an action that may
affect the species is required to complete an "impact statement" to
determine whether or not the action is legal.

Advocates for environmental protection begin filing lawsuits al-
leging negative impacts, and federal agencies decide whether or not
they're right. Corporate development interests hire their own lawyers, and develop risk management plans, which often allow them to

continue doing things that even they know they shouldn't be doing. Millions of dollars are spent on litigation. Even more is spent on studies, assessments, action plans and monitoring. This work is done by "professionals," who occasionally keep the rest of us informed about what they have done and what they intend to do. Occasionally they will even ask us for our "input," which is recorded, reproduced, and included as an appendix to their final report.

In almost every case, this approach has not led to species recovery. Every year the list of endangered species gets longer, and every year the fiscal and human resources of the recovery agencies are spread thinner. Advocates hold up the growing list at press conferences, warning the world how desperate the situation has become, and yet nothing much seems to change. In fact, if the advocates are right, it just keeps getting worse, despite all the time and money we've spent.

Everyone seems to have someone to blame for this. Advocates blame industrial earthrapers and their shoeshiners in the federal agencies. Corporations and industry groups blame the pinko treehuggers and their lapdogs in the federal agencies. Federal agencies blame Congress for not giving them enough money, and lament the inability or unwillingness of The Public to fathom the sacred mysteries of agency technical expertise. Meanwhile, the overwhelming majority consider the health of nature to be somebody else's business, and even those who profess concern over environmental issues generally limit their involvement to sending a check now and then, or consulting the voter's guide at election time.

This approach hasn't worked for the forty years we've been taking it, and I can't think of any good reasons why we should expect it to work in the future. In fact, most everyone, at one time or another, has come to pretty much the same conclusion, recognizing that in order to bring about any enduring improvement there will have to be a more diffuse transformation in the hearts and minds of everyday citizens, of people who really do have more pressing concerns than "maintaining biodiversity" or keeping the polar ice caps frozen. These people are trying to keep the house warm, trying to keep the kids in school, trying to keep the fridge full, the car running, the rent paid, the family together. And they are looking for something like love—a sense of belonging that doesn't feel like submission, a sense of certainty that doesn't feel like stagnation.

As any seasoned advocate knows, it is difficult to take people's minds off these things. Many advocates come to the point where about all they expect is a check now and then, or a petition signed, or a vote this way or that. It often seems like some such advocates develop a sort of contempt for "the masses," and approach the general public like a giant, mindless herd that needs to be hazed into heading the right direction. The health of the earth is what matters most, and the health of the earth is something separate from, even opposed to, the trivial concerns of all these human hordes. All those greedy, unenlightened people are, at best, an inconvenience, an unfortunate impediment to overcoming our environmental crisis. More often, they are seen as the reason for the crisis.

But there have always been a few for whom this just didn't feel right, who figured there had to be a better way, who noticed early on that what we like to think of as our greatest successes—publicly-owned lands—weren't doing much better than anywhere else, and in some cases were doing much worse. We had successfully persuaded the public to "appreciate" these natural spectacles, to see them as a source of joy, of escape, re-creation. Some even began to value these places as a source of life, as repositories of "ecosystem services," as the loving arms of our Mother Earth.

But still things were going to hell. The most sensitive and critical ecosystems had been overrun with humans long before Teddy Roosevelt and Aldo Leopold came along, and even those systems we had managed to set aside were being appreciated into oblivion by the same folks who sought their protection in the first place. In desperation, we started calling for "wilderness," for nature "untram-meled by man," and even that hasn't stopped us hurtling headlong toward ecological ruin.

But there have always been a few who knew this would happen, who understood that recreation and entertainment were soft stones, a flimsy foundation upon which to build an enduring respect for the natural world. Joy, escape, and even love of life itself—these would not be enough. There were some who looked deeper into nature, and saw suffering, decay, death, and an appreciation—a commitment—that wasn't ultimately contingent on one's ability to hop back in the SUV and head back to town for some burgers.

We all want the world to be "sacred." But many are noticing that nothing sacred ever avoids the darker, more difficult aspects of our earthly tenure. The "successes" of our environmental advocacy are, in large part, dependent on suppressing, devaluing or ignoring such things, as dependent as the national mythology that started us gob-bling and stomping our way across this continent so long ago, as dependent as the advertising campaign that got us to buy that SUV in the first place. This is the one thing we haven't changed, and it's looking more and more like it's the only thing that ever really needed changing.

It's beginning to occur to people that it's not enough to think of nature as therapy, as spectacular, as a nurturing mother and source of all life. If our common goal is to "see to it that the place is well taken care of," then we should take a tip from Gussy's brother Hans. Always faithful, we need to see nature as a grave.

June 24 (Sat)

No sunshine yet but it's mild and there is no rain. Hans and I went to church in Lemvig this morning and nostalgic memories came back to me, as I sat in the old church, where I had come with my parents as a boy. The preacher had chosen for his text the story of the Prodigal Son, and

I couldn't help feeling there was a message in it for me. I've come a long way from the beliefs of my childhood, many of the dogmas have gone by the board, but the well-known hymns brought back to me the old feeling of restful peace and reverence. I am glad I went.

On the northern coast of California, between where Gussy lived and where the Klamath meets the sea, there is a small salmon river called the Mattole. We crossed the Mattole once, on our way to the black sand beach of Bear Harbor, where we drank wine from the bottle and woke to find a bull elk standing alone at the edge of the meadow. As we left we heard the helicopters, and when we got back home we read about the troops that had landed, armed to the teeth, looking for pot farmers. Like the rest of the west, it's sometimes hard to tell who this land belongs to, and who belongs to it.

About ten years before then, a rather strange thing started happening in the Mattole river watershed. It started with the fish, and a few people who didn't think they could live without them:

A state fisheries biologist told us that this race of native king salmon is done for. . . . "The state Department of Fish and Game is spread thin. They can't afford to expend their scarce resources on a river that has next to no hope of continuing to produce marketable salmon for a diminishing fishing fleet. But a small number of residents of this remote little valley have not been able to bring themselves to stand by and watch while one more race of salmon disappears, especially the one in the river that runs through their lives. They have begun with little idea of what can be done. They have to talk to other people like themselves, and also to ranchers, loggers, academic biologists, and commercial fishers. They have read books and sent away for obscure technical papers. They've developed a scheme that they hope will enhance the success of the spawning of the wild fish. Through stubborn persistence they've convinced the state to let them have a go at it."

This passage is from *Totem Salmon*, a book written by Freeman House, who was one of the instigators of this effort. The "scheme" they developed was to capture live wild salmon, females and males, on their way up to the spawning beds. One of the main causes of salmon declines in the northwest has been the degradation or loss of spawning habitat, and this has also been the case on the Mattole. So a group of local residents set out to build and operate home-made, small-scale fish hatcheries at various points along the river. Although they received guidance from agency biologists, this help was almost cancelled out by the resistance they got from the agency bureaucracies. At times it seemed like the powers in charge of species recovery would let the fish go extinct, rather than let locals try and stop it.

As a matter of necessity, this was a do-it-yourself affair, which is why, to my mind, the Mattole effort is so much more important than all the "official" efforts in progress throughout the northwest. They had to beg and borrow everything they needed, be it hardware, technical expertise, human labor or moral support. They couldn't afford to be picky, to alienate citizens who could lend a hand or private landowners who managed so much of the salmon's historical habitat. They reached out to everyone—hippies, ranchers, logging companies, fishermen, and anyone else—with respect and humility. They formed the Mattole River Salmon Group, and later the Mattole Restoration Council, to serve as a forum for hashing out difficult and divisive issues. Twenty years later, the effort is still going strong.

In *Totem Salmon*, Freemen House never actually comes out and says whether they have done what they set out to do: improve the wild salmon runs. And this, to me, is what makes the book so fresh, so courageous. Some have pointed this out as a fault. More confrontational advocates have taken it as proof of their righteousness in pursuing more litigious, coercive approaches to restoration. I take it as just the opposite.

The first step to finding effective, enduring solutions is the accurate characterization of the problem you're trying to solve, and if you insist that our problem is merely declining salmon runs, this is like trying to cure cancer with a box of Kleenex. The residents of the Mattole watershed realized early on that declining salmon runs were just a symptom of a much deeper malady. They realized that treating the fish problem by itself—without dealing with the relationship between fish and people—would produce, at best, a temporary fix.

Freeman House speaks frankly about the difficulties of trying to make respect for nature a more central aspect of the shared values in a given community, of reconfiguring a community around notions of stewardship and reverence. He also documents how, even among the region's original inhabitants, thriving fish runs have not automatically meant peace and security within and between human communities. House describes the "war and feuds, intolerance and enslavement, starvation and displacement" that must have been part of the settlement of this place by the Yurok, the Karuk and the Hoopa peoples. But he wants to believe that "over and over again, salmon kept drawing people back from the cusp of failure to try again to establish peaceful coexistence."

Or so I like to imagine. It is important to me. I am drawn back to this kind of dreaming whenever I reach a point of despair about our difficulties in communicating with our neighbors about land management practices. I don't believe we have a thousand years. Neither do we have any choice but to take the time it takes to do it right.

The residents of the Mattole were a little ahead of the curve, but since they began their efforts in the late seventies, the idea that salmon should thrive has taken hold throughout the northwest. It is a massive effort, in which the vast majority of time and money are spent on paperwork and process. There is much frustration and discouragement at the pace of progress and the level of conflict. But it still feels to me like we're going to pull it off. It feels this way not because of the financial and institutional power behind the effort, but in spite of it. It feels this way because people in places like the Mattole are demonstrating a willingness to have patience and faith without sacrificing passion, a willingness to allow a fresh set of stories to emerge from encounters between all different kinds of people, to allow their minds to be changed, even while they're trying to change the minds of others.

This is not "consensus." This is not "compromise" or "collaboration." This is culture, living, breathing and growing—a ceaseless cycle of splitting apart and fusing together, not everywhere at once but here and there, now and then. It is a sort of trial and error, by which we fine tune our communities until they fit neatly into the landscapes where they've come to rest.

But this is not all there is to it. Obviously, not all conflict ends with a peaceful, productive resolution; and obviously even peaceful, productive resolutions do not always help us on our way toward enduring, indigenous communities. But there's something different this time around. There is something in the way people are talking about salmon that marks a departure from conventional advocacy. There is something about the way others are talking that marks a departure from conventional "extractive' development. There is a gathering together, coming in close around something that can only be found where we live, that only shows itself to those who have stayed long enough to let their senses adjust. It is not new. In fact it is very old, although what we bring to it is new. Our encounters with it will produce something that is not new and not old, because those are names we give to things, and this is not a thing but a growing—something that is "taking place." It's an iteration, ongoing and everchanging, a conversation between a people and a place which are both, themselves, ongoing and everchanging.

Because you see, Freeman House was a fisherman. He killed salmon for money and for food. This experience underlies his struggle to figure out how he should relate to these fish. As when he points out that the Yurok word for salmon means "That which is eaten," and that the Ainu word means "the real thing that we eat." Throughout the northwest, alliances have been formed between commercial fishermen, native American tribes, and conventional, urban, Euro-American environmental advocates. These alliances have had a distinct effect on the standard rhetoric of species preservation efforts, particularly within the ranks of conventional advocates. The reason for this is simple: the salmon, while they satisfy the same criteria—beauty, drama, marketability—that made the bald eagle and the spotted owl so useful to advocates, are the first endangered species that most of us love to kill and eat.

Not long ago I met a commercial fisherman, whose boat had been idled since the early nineties. I asked him about his relationship with urban environmental advocates. I suggested that while irrigators like myself may impact salmon indirectly, and accidentally, through degradation of habitat, he kills them outright, on purpose, for money. I asked him what made him think these people wouldn't come down on him once they were done with us, after the fishermen were no longer useful to them. He said some guys worry about that a lot. Then he said, "But listen to what [the environmentalists] are saying. They're telling hardluck stories about hardworking families that have been run out of business. They're talking about keeping small towns on the map and keeping their economies going. You would've never heard that kind of talk back when it was the owl. Hell, they sound like a bunch of damn wise-users. I don't think they realize it, but this salmon thing is messing with their heads."

And they are not the only ones. Landowners and private land managers throughout the region are making increasingly undeniable progress toward incorporating the notion of sound stewardship into their business philosophies. In Oregon, Governor John Kitzhaber took the unprecedented step of persuading federal fisheries managers to not put salmon on the endangered species list, even though they qualify under federal law. Instead of relying on federal regulations, the governor brought together an astonishing variety of interests within the state. Together they developed what is known as "The Oregon Plan for Salmon and Watersheds." It is an imperfect document, but the cornerstone of the plan is a reliance on "local, voluntary" efforts focused on education, outreach, and each community's pride of place. The state government's main involvement is through the Oregon Watershed Enhancement Board, which is, as far as I know, the only agency of its kind. Its mission is to restore the watersheds of the state, but it has no regulatory power whatsoever. Its sole function is to provide technical, administrative and financial assistance to community groups interested in taking better care of their watersheds. They don't tell people what to do, and they won't do it for them, but if people want to do it themselves, OWEB is there to make sure the bills get paid and the forms get filled out.

The Oregon Plan has, unlike any other attempt before it, been dramatically successful in getting landowners and everyday citizens involved in restoration efforts. And it has changed the way people in resource-dependent communities think and talk about the natural systems that sustain their livelihoods. One Oregon rancher, when told about the need for age-class diversity in streamside vegetation, said, "We might just be able to work something out here. You say you want old willows, middle-age willows, teenage willows and baby willows, and all we want is old ranchers, middle-age ranchers, teenage ranchers and baby ranchers." There's also the running joke about how ranchers used to meet at fenceline and talk who's got the highest weaning weights, and now they talk about who's got the best willow stands. Whether intended or not, they are making connections, inventing new metaphors.

Small farmers and ranchers have always had the direct, daily experience of the deeply complex, morally ambiguous workings of natural systems—the dependence of life upon death, the inextricable marriage of growth and decay. These have always been part of the everyday lives of rural people. The problem has been that they haven't had any real good way of talking about it, of turning that experience into something that draws the people and the land together, that reminds them daily that their two fates are really only one. Urban people, on the other hand, have come up with some very clever ways of talking about people and nature, but they have had to do it without the benefit of daily engagement, without the daily affirmation that our lives are made possible by the death of what we love.

Salmon are giving us a way to fill in each other's gaps, and they happen to be ideally suited to making us do it in a very particular way—the only way that is both deep and durable enough to outlast all the corporate and bureaucratic hugeness that has thus far kept us from coming together. Mr. House, again, helps us out:

"There is a hard knot of relationship in the act of killing a creature of another species. It is an act that dissolves the illusion of individuality, of separateness. . . . We are reminded in the most immediate way of our own mortality, an idea with which we may or may not have come to terms. Modernity has distanced us from wild reality, so that when it comes to killing and dying, each of us must deal with the mystery of it alone and uneasy. But the meaning persists in experiences of killing and dying. The lesson of interpenetration is always available to us, regardless of our cultural conditioning. It is also a lesson we humans seem increasingly happy to ignore as we allow distant and abstract economic institutions to disguise and conceal the relationship."

Salmon not only force us to confront, accept, even celebrate the role of death in our lives, our own roles as killer and killed, they also force us to do it in particular places, within finite landscapes and communities, at scales compatible with the standard equipment of the human organism. Some have said that returning salmon can smell the long-gone flesh of their mothers and fathers, smell it in what they eat, in what was fed by the spent carcasses of the ones who gave them life. Salmon have sorted themselves out into hundreds, maybe thousands of uniquely adapted populations, hard-wired for the specifics of this or that little crease in the earth. If they survive, if we are going to help ensure their survival, we will have to do almost exactly the same thing.

July 5th (Wed)

My brother Hans and I went for a stroll around town, and once more to the cemetery, this time to see my sister Sidsel's grave. Then toward evening a car came from Kongensgaard to take me elsewhere on a farewell visit. It was now time to say good-bye to Hans. This was not easy. He is 77 years old and not too well. We both realized this was our last meeting, and our eyes were wet when we shook hands.

My wife and I hadn't had a vacation for seven years, so we headed for the coast. We took the road that ran along the Klamath, all the way to the sea. We drove through the homes of the Karuk, the Hoopa and the Yurok. On the Hoopa reservation we saw a child pushing his bike. Both tires were flat. Someone said we should give him a ride, and I said, "Yeah, we should," and kept on driving. The boy never even looked our way. He wasn't looking to us for help.

On the coast I walked the docks alone, counting "For Sale" signs on all the small boats, remembering the same signs on the farms where I live. In rows on each boat there were colorful license stickers with pictures of salmon leaping—'89, '90, '91, '92—and then they would stop. There were taverns nearby, loud with wrinkled, reddened faces—angry just like we are.

We were headed down where Gussy had lived. I was going to see his grave. Gussy had made it back safe and sound, and then not long after, he died. Just before he left the docks in Denmark he wrote, "It was wonderful to make this pilgrimage to the Homeland, but it'll be nice to get back home." He put more than one home in that sentence, but it doesn't sound like he noticed. I think a lot of us are like that.

He is in the ground on the north coast of California, and down with him he brought a heartful of stories about that place and the people he loved. He also had stories of a place on the other side of the world. He had people in the ground there—and in the trees and the air and the streams. That knowledge made him go back, and it helped him find his way.

My people are buried all over this world. There is no single place I can go to and find them. I have no family in the little graveyard at home, where the waters of the Klamath first hit the ground. But I know the stonecarved names there. I sit and talk and eat with people who have those names now. Last year, hat on my chest, I stood with neighbors and watched a man lowered into the ground. A man I had known, a man I had worked with, a man who had helped me. Someone once told him he'd better watch out, that "someday they'll run us out of this country." He just looked back to his work and said, quietly, "I'm not going anywhere."

I like to think this is how it starts. That talk, this work, this shared place—they have made a part of his life a part of my own, and there is nothing anyone can do about that. I have stories to tell about this man, and the stories he told, we will tell again. He is planted in the land here, and because of that these stories are rooted here, too. And because of that so are the storytellers. There is nothing anyone can do about that.

My mother and father will be buried here. I will have stories to tell about them, and those stories will hold me to the ground where they rest, and I will see to it that "the place is well taken care of." These stories are the part of our dead that lives on, and our dead are down in this ground, coming apart, coming back up, alive and green and reaching for the sun. This green will feed the river, and the river will keep our children fed. Our children, grown, with children of their own, sitting around the table, telling stories about us.

CODA

"Are You an Environmentalist or Do You Work for a Living?": Work and Nature

Richard White

In Forks, Washington, a logging town badly crippled by both over-cutting and the spotted owl controversy, you can buy a bumper sticker that reads "Are You an Environmentalist or Do You Work for a Living?"[1] It is an interesting insult, and one that poses some equally interesting questions. How is it that environmentalism seems opposed to work? And how is it that work has come to play such a small role in American environmentalism?

Modern environmentalists often take one of two equally problematic positions toward work. Most equate productive work in nature with destruction. They ignore the ways that work itself is a means of knowing nature while celebrating the virtues of play and recreation in nature. A smaller group takes a second position: certain kinds of archaic work, most typically the farming of peasants, provides a way of knowing nature. Whereas mainstream environmentalism creates a popular imagery that often harshly condemns all work in nature, this second group is apt to sentimentalize certain kinds of farming and argue that work on the land creates a connection to place that will protect nature itself. Arguments that physical labor on the land establishes an attachment that protects the earth from harm have, however, a great deal of history against them.

There are, of course, numerous thoughtful environmentalists who recognize fruitful connections between modern work and nature, but

---

1. "Timber Drama Hits Home in Town of Forks," *Seattle Times*, Aug. 5, 1994, A 14.

they operate within a larger culture that encourages a divorce between the two. Too often the environmental movement mobilizes words and images that widen the gulf. We need to reexamine the connections between work and nature.

They form perhaps the most critical elements in our current environmental crisis. The attitudes of most Americans toward work indicate fundamental problems with how we conceive of the natural world and our place in it. By failing to examine and claim work within nature, environmentalists have ceded to the so-called wise-use movement valuable cultural terrain. The loss of natural terrain can only follow. The wise-use movement confuses real work with invented property rights. It perverts the legitimate concerns of rural people with maintaining ways of life and getting decent returns on their labor into the special "right" of large property holders and corporations to hold the natural world and the public good hostage to their economic gain. As long as environmentalism refuses to engage questions of modern work and labor, wise use will prosper, and our children, in the end, will suffer.

There is no avoiding questions of work and nature. Most people spend their lives in work, and long centuries of human labor have left indelible marks on the natural world. From pole to pole, herders, farmers, hunters, and industrial workers have deeply influenced the natural world, so virtually no place is without evidence of its alteration by human labor. Work that has changed nature has simultaneously produced much of our knowledge of nature. Humans have known nature by digging in the earth, planting seeds, and harvesting plants. They have known nature by feeling heat and cold, sweating as they went up hills, sinking into mud. They have known nature by shaping wood and stone, by living with animals, nurturing them, and killing them. Humans have matched their energy against the energy of flowing water and wind. They have known distance as more than an abstraction because of the physical energy they expended moving through space. They have tugged, pulled, carried, and walked, or they have harnessed the energy of animals, water, and wind to do these things for them. They have achieved a bodily knowledge of the natural world.

Modern environmentalism lacks an adequate, consideration of this work. Most environmentalists disdain and distrust those who most obviously work in nature. Environmentalists have come to associate work—particularly heavy bodily labor, blue-collar work—with environmental degradation. This is true whether the work is in the woods, on the sea, in a refinery, in a chemical plant, in a pulp mill, or in a farmer's field or a rancher's pasture. Environmentalists usually imagine that when people who make things finish their day's work, nature is the poorer for it. Nature seems safest when shielded from human labor.

This distrust of work, particularly of hard physical labor, contributes to a larger tendency to define humans as being outside of nature and to frame environmental issues so that the choice seems to be between humans and nature. "World War III," Andy Kerr of the Oregon Natural Resources Council likes to say, "is the war against the environment. The bad news is, the humans are winning."[2] The human weapon in Kerr's war is work. It is logging, ranching, and fishing; it is mining and industry. Environmentalists, of course, also work, but they usually do not do hard physical labor, and they often fail to think very deeply about their own work and its relation to nature.

Like Kerr, most Americans celebrate nature as the world of original things. And nature may indeed be the world we have not made—the world of plants, animals, trees, and mountains—but the boundaries between this world of nature and the world of artifice, the world of things we have made, are no longer very clear. Are the cows and crops we breed, the fields we cultivate, the genes we splice natural

---

2. William Dietrich, *The Final Forest: The Battle for the Last Great Trees of the Pacific Northwest* (New York: Simon and Schuster, 1992), 209.

or unnatural? Are they nature or artifice? We seek the purity of our absence, but everywhere we find our own fingerprints. It is ultimately our own bodies and our labor that blur the boundaries between the artificial and the natural. Even now we tamper with the genetic stuff of our own and other creatures' bodies, altering the design of species. We cannot come to terms with nature without coming to terms with our own work, our own bodies, our own bodily labor.

But in current formulations of human relations with nature there is little room for such reconciliation. Nature has become an arena for human play and leisure. Saving an old-growth forest or creating a wilderness area is certainly a victory for some of the creatures that live in these places, but it is just as certainly a victory for backpackers and a defeat for loggers. It is a victory for leisure and a defeat for work.

Work and play are linked, but the differences matter. Both our work and our play, as Elaine Scarry has written, involve an extension of our sentient bodies out into the external world. Our tools, the products of our work, become extensions of ourselves. Our clothes extend our skins; our hammers extend our hands. Extending our bodies into the world in this manner changes the world, but the changes are far more obvious in our work than in our play. A logger's tools extend his body into trees so that he knows how the texture of their wood and bark differs and varies, how they smell and fall. The price of his knowledge is the death of a tree.[3]

Environmentalists so often seem self-righteous, privileged, and arrogant because they so readily consent to identifying nature with play and making it by definition a place where leisured humans come only to visit and not to work, stay, or live. Thus environmentalists have much to say about nature and play and little to say about humans and work. And if the world were actually so cleanly divided between the domains of work and play, humans and nature, there would be

---

3. For loggers and knowledge, see ibid., 39.

no problem. Then environmentalists could patrol the borders and keep the categories clear. But the dualisms fail to hold; the boundaries are not so clear. And so environmentalists can seem an ecological Immigration and Naturalization Service, border agents in a socially dubious, morally ambiguous, and ultimately hopeless cause.

I have phrased this issue so harshly not because I oppose environmentalism (indeed, I consider myself an environmentalist), but precisely because I think environmentalism must be a basic element in any coherent attempt to address the social, economic, and political problems that confront Americans today. Environmentalists must come to terms with work because its effects are so widespread and because work itself offers both a fundamental way of knowing nature and perhaps our deepest connection with the natural world. If the issue of work is left to the enemies of environmentalism, to movements such as wise use, with its single-minded devotion to propertied interests, then work will simply be reified into property and property rights. If environmentalists segregate work from nature, if they create a set of dualisms where work can only mean the absence of nature and nature can only mean human leisure, then both humans and nonhumans will ultimately be the poorer. For without an ability to recognize the connections between work and nature, environmentalists will eventually reach a point where they seem trivial and extraneous and their issues politically expendable.

Given the tendency of environmentalists to exaggerate boundaries, to make humans and nature opposing sides in a bitter struggle, any attempt to stress the importance of work needs to begin by blurring the boundaries and stressing human connections with nature. Work once bore the burden of connecting us with nature. In shifting much of this burden onto the various forms of play that take us back into nature, Americans have shifted the burden to leisure. And play cannot bear the weight. Work entails an embodiment, an interaction with the world, that is far more intense than play. We work to live. We cannot stop. But play, which can be as sensuous as work, does not so fully submerge us in the world. At play we can stop and start.[4] A game unfinished ultimately means nothing. There is nothing essential lost when recreation is broken off or forgone. Work left unfinished has consequences.

It is no accident, then, that the play we feel brings us closest to nature is play that mimics work. Our play in nature is often itself a masked form of bodily labor. Environmentalists like myself are most aware of nature when we backpack, climb, and ski. Then we are acutely aware of our bodies. The labor of our bodies tells us the texture of snow and rock and dirt. We feel the grade of the incline. We know and care about weather. We are acutely conscious of our surroundings; we need to read the landscape to find water and shelter. We know where the ground is soft or hard. We (some of us better than others) know the habits of fish because we seek to kill and eat them. The most intense moments of our play in nature come when it seems to matter as much as work: when the handhold in the rock matters; when we are four days from the trailhead and short on food; when whitewater could wreck a craft. It is no wonder that the risks we take in nature become more extreme. We try to make play matter as if it were work, as if our lives depended on it. We try to know through play what workers in the woods, fields, and waters know through work.

This confusion of work and play, the segregation of nature from real work, and the denigration of modern labor are complicated phenomena. Among the sources of confusion are two widespread convictions shared by many Americans. The first is that the original human relation with nature was one of leisure and that the first white men in North America glimpsed and briefly shared that relation. The second (not wholly reconcilable with the first) is that the snake in

4. Elaine Scarry, *The Body in Pain: The Making and Unmaking of the World* (New York: Oxford Univ. Press, 1985), 82.

the garden was the machine. It tempted humans away from whatever benign possibilities work in nature once held. These two assumptions need critical examination.

We supposedly still get a hint of an earlier and proper relation between humans and nature embedded in the first conviction, which connects nature and leisure during our own excursions into the backcountry. In buttressing this belief in a connection with nature through play, we tend to mask the ways humans have known the natural world through work.

To make the case for an original relation with nature in North America that predates work, modern environmental writers—and, I suspect, many environmentalists—tell stories that make it seem as if play provided a primal and pristine contact with nature that work ruined. In effect, popular environmental writing tells an old Judeo-Christian story. Work is a fall from grace. In the beginning no one labored. In the beginning there was harmony and no human mark on the landscape. This is also the story told in the backcountry. This, we say, is how it must have appeared to the first white man: the mythical first white man whose arrival marks not just specific changes but the beginning of change itself. We identify our acts in the backcountry with the acts of historic figures emblematically connected with nature, and we make their work seem the equivalent of our play.

The first white man is, I think, a critical figure in our confusion about work and nature. We are pious toward Indian peoples, but we don't take them seriously; we don't credit them with the capacity to make changes. Whites readily grant certain nonwhites a "spiritual" or "traditional" knowledge that is timeless. It is not something gained through work or labor; it is not contingent knowledge in a contingent world. In North America, whites are the bearers of environmental original sin, because whites alone are recognized as laboring. But whites are thus also, by the same token, the only real bearers of history. This is why our flattery (for it is usually intended to be such) of "simpler" peoples is an act of such immense condescension. For in a modern world defined by change, whites are portrayed as the only beings who make a difference.

In telling stories about the first white man, environmentalist writers aren't just narrating a history. These accounts pretend to be history, but they are really Just-So Stories about the paradise before labor. Over the last two decades academic historians have produced a respectable body of work on humans and the environment in North America that concentrates on how Indian peoples shaped the natural world they lived in.[5] But, by and large, this literature either has not penetrated popular treatments of nature or has been dismissed. The first white man always enters an untouched paradise. The first white man must also always be a white man. French metis trappers and traders penetrated and lived in the West long before more-famous first white men came along, but they tend to drop from the accounts. Working people of mixed race entering a region of modified nature can't carry the story line of the wonder of a world before work.

The most popular first white men remain Lewis and Clark and Daniel Boone. Daniel Boone is Wendell Berry's first white man.[6] Bill McKibben uses Lewis and Clark, and so does Philip Shabecoff, a good and intelligent environmental journalist. In A Fierce Green Fire, his recent history of the environmental movement, Shabecoff follows his first white men through lands "unchanged by humans."[7] The last

---

5. For a summary of this literature, see Richard White and William Cronon, "Ecological Change and Indian-White Relations," in *History of Indian-White Relations*, ed. Wilcomb Washburn, vol. 4 of *Handbook of North American Indians*, ed. William Sturtevant (Washington, D.C.: Smithsonian Institution, 1988), 417-29. For a bibliographical essay, see Richard White, "Native Americans and the Environment," in W. R. Swagerty, ed., *Scholars and the Indian Experience: Critical Reviews of Recent Writing in the Social Sciences* (Bloomington: Indiana Univ. Press, 1984), 179-204.

6. Wendell Berry, "The Journey's End," in *Recollected Essays, 1965-1980* (New York: North Point Press, 1993), 259-62.

7. Philip Shabecoff, *A Fierce Green Fire: The American Environmental Movement* (New York: Hill and Wang, 1993), 23.

of the first white men was Bob Marshall, who, consciously imitating Lewis and Clark, often gets credit for walking through the last areas in North America unseen by human beings. But the Central Brooks Range of Alaska, where Marshall hiked, had been inhabited by the Nunamiut in the nineteenth century, and they had returned in the 1940s. It is very unlikely that the areas Marshall traveled had been unvisited.[8]

These first white men are fascinating and sympathetic historical figures in their own right, but my concern with them is as cultural figures constructed by environmentalism. They are made into viewers of a natural world "as," according to McKibben, "it existed outside human history."[9] But it is not nature that exists outside human history; it is the first white men who do so. For environmentalist writers depict not how these travelers actually saw the natural world but instead how we would have seen it in their place. In this construction, the first white men travel through nature untouched by human labor and are awed by it. Shabecoff's brief account in A Fierce Green Fire is typical. He quotes a journal entry by William Clark praising the scenery "in a country far removed from the civilized world." Shabecoff admits some "slight impact" on the environment from European introductions such as horses and guns, but he stresses how much of the continent was "unchanged by humans." Lewis and Clark serve both to reveal the untouched continent and to set its destruction in motion.[10]

This is not, however, the most likely or persuasive reading of what Lewis and Clark saw and did. They were, first of all, quite aware that they were moving through landscapes where human work had altered

---

8. For Marshall as first human in the area, see Bill McKibben, The End of Nature (New York: Anchor Books, 1989), 53. For Nunamiut, see Ted Catton, "Inhabited Wilderness: The Making of Alaska's National Parks" (Ph.D. diss., Univ. of Washington, 1994), 174-212.

9. McKibben, End of Nature, 52.

10. Shabecoff, Fierce Green Fire, 22-24.

e. Lewis and Clark described Indians farming, hunting, fishing, grazing their animals. Their journey west was punctuated by fires set by Indians to shape the landscape, influence the movement of animals, or signal each other.[11] They described a landscape that we know, partly through their accounts, was already in the midst of wrenching change as a result of human labor.[12]

Nor did Lewis and Clark spend much time being staggered by the beauty and the sublimity of what they saw. They are not blind to the beauty of the world, but they are matter-of-fact: "the country still continues level fertile and beautifull," Lewis noted in a typical entry.[13] Even when touched, as in the Missouri Breaks, by "Seens of Visionary enchantment," what engages far more of Lewis's and Clark's attention is the laborious work of moving upstream.[14] Their labor gives them their most intimate knowledge of the country. In describing work, their writing becomes expansive and detailed. They are not just seeing the country. They are feeling it; they are literally enmeshed in it. Here are Clark and Lewis describing their struggle to pass through the Missouri Breaks. First Clark: "we Set out, and proceeded on with great labour & the banks were So muddey & Slippery that the men could Scercely walk The land near the river, the land they struggle through, is 'much hard rock; & rich earth, the Small portion of rain

11.   Gary E. Moulton, ed., *The Journals of the Lewis & Clark Expedition*, vols. 2-4 (Lincoln: Univ. of Nebraska Press, 1986-87), entries of July 23, 1804, 2: 415; Aug. 15, 1804, 2: 483; Sept. 17, 1804, 3: 80; Sept. 23, 1804, 3: 104; Oct. 29, 1804, 3: 210; March 6, 1805, 3: 309; May 28, 1805, 4: 237; July 20, 1805, 4: 407; July 25, 1805, 4: 428.

12.   One of the best examples is recent literature on the decline of the bison. Dan Flores, "Bison Ecology and Bison Diplomacy: The Southern Plains from 1800 to 1850," *Journal of American History* 78 (1991): 465-85. 1 have also looked at the Indian role in shaping the environment in Richard White, *The Roots of Dependency: Subsistence, Environment, and Social Change among the Choctaws, Pawnees, and Navajos* (Lincoln: Univ. of Nebraska Press, 1983).

13.   Entry of May 6, 1805, in Moulton, *Journals*, 4: 117

14.   Entry of May 31, 1805, ibid., 223-25

which has fallen causes the rich earth as deep as is wet to Slip into the river or bottoms."

Now Lewis:

> the men are compelled to be (much) in the water even to their armpits, and the water is yet very could, and so frequent are those [sic] point that they are one fourth of their time in the water, added to this the banks and bluffs along which they are obliged to pass are so slippery and the mud so tenacious that they are unable to wear their mockersons, and in that situation draging the heavy burthen of a canoe and walking ocasionally for several hundred yards over the sharp fragments of rocks which tumble from the clifts and garnish the borders of the river; in short their labour is incredibly painfull. . . . [15]

What most deeply engaged these first white men with nature, what they wrote about most vividly, was work: backbreaking, enervating, heavy work. The labor of the body revealed that nature was cold, muddy, sharp, tenacious, slippery. Many more of their adjectives also described immediate, tangible contact between the body and the nonhuman world. Environmental writers have edited this out; they have replaced it with a story of first white men at strenuous play or in respectful observation.

We have masked the work of first white men. We have equated their work with our play. We have implicitly presumed that the journey of first white men must have been one long backpack across the West. But they did not gain knowledge of nature through play; they knew and connected with the world through work. And we unwittingly admit as much when we make our own play mimic their work.

---

15. Entries of May 30 and 31, 1805, ibid., 223-25.

This masking of knowledge gained through work is typical of one environmentalist approach to labor, but the actual role of labor is easily unmasked. Examples of human knowledge of nature gained through labor are readily apparent if we look. For millennia humans have known animals largely through work. Work gave the people who trained and worked with animals a particular knowledge of them. "There is something about a horse that isn't an engine, you know," Albert Drinkwater, a British Columbia horse logger, explained; "A horse won't work for everybody the same. He'll work for one man and he'll pretend to pull for the other one." "The horses themselves became . . . part of the man that drove them."[16] Today the animals we know most intimately are pets; they share our leisure, not our work. We find working partnerships only in a few odd places. One of them is the circus. There the joint labor of humans and animals survives as entertainment.

Circuses where humans and animals connect for a common task are today often marked as unnatural or even cruel. Animals that work are pitied and presumed abused. But such pity is misplaced in the circus world that Diana Cooper describes in her recent book, *Night after Night*. To work intimately with a trained animal is, she says, to know something nonhuman, vividly and deeply. She writes of trainers as being "deep in their work, focused on the animals and their human partners and what they are all creating together."[17] It is the trainer "who, through knowing Toto, has taught him what he needs to know."[18] And what trainers learn about elephants and horses is not only something about elephants and horses in general but also a

---

16. Quoted in Richard Rajala, "The Forest as Factory: Technological Change and Worker Control in the West Coast Logging Industry, 1880-1930," *Labourl/Le Travail* 32 (Fall 1993): 84.

17. Diane Star Cooper, *Night after Night* (Washington, D.C.: Island Press, 1994), 129.

18. Ibid., 135 (italics added).

deeply particular knowledge of individual elephants and horses. This is knowledge we possess because we have bodies with which to work. Embodied, we encounter not ideas of the world but other bodies. We confront the intransigent materiality of the world itself. To know an elephant or a horse through work is to know that for all the general knowledge of horses or elephants you may have, what also matters is a knowledge of this particular elephant at this particular time. It is precisely this recognition of how work provides a knowledge of, and a connection to, nature that separates a minority of environmentalists, particularly those sympathetic to Wendell Berry, from the dominant environmentalist denigration of work. But this second, minority position limits such good work to labor done without modern machines. It relies, to varying degrees, on the second conviction of modern environmentalism regarding the work in nature under examination here. In doing such work, people supposedly once had a truer, more benign relation with the natural world, one that technology has severed. It is supposedly modern work, not work itself, that has made us into dangerous monsters. Consequently, both our salvation and the land's can be found by harking back to a time before modern technology, to a time, in Shabecoff's telling, before the "new machines" degraded the landscape.[19]

The demonization of modern machines and the sentimentalization of archaic forms of labor allows a bifurcation of work into the relatively benign and even instructive, and the modern and destructive. Nowhere does this bifurcation show up more than in agriculture. Some, but again hardly all, environmentalists romanticize peasants, non-Western farmers, and even some premodern American farmers, granting them an earth knowledge derived from their work. But in an age of vast, mechanized agribusinesses, in a land where farmers have given way to growers and where the very category "farmer" has

19. Shabecoff, *Fierce Green Fire*, 29.

now disappeared from the census, environmentalists grant no such knowledge to most modern farmers.

John Berger doesn't write from such motives, but his essays on peasants and peasantry, *Pig Earth*, can stand as examples of peasant knowledge.[20] In these communities "working is a way of preserving knowledge."[21] There are no peasants in the United States, but there are farmers who embody some of the peasants' working knowledge of the land. Farmers in the mountains of New Mexico, for example, once shared the life Berger describes.

Jacobo Romero was a New Mexican farmer in the Sangre de Cristo Mountains of New Mexico. Along with the Rio de las Trampas, a small river that is really little more than stream, he is the central figure in William deBuys and Alex Harris's haunting *River of Traps*. Romero knew nature through work. Like Berger's peasants, "inexhaustibly committed to wresting life from the earth," he was so wedded to a particular place that to move him would have been to change who and what he was. He worked his land along the river, and his work yielded knowledge that could be passed on. Working—how one works, how one wields a spade, how one handles a horse—imparts a bodily knowledge and a social knowledge, part of what Pierre Bourdieu calls habitus. Such knowledge is connected with physical experience, but it is not derived solely or often even directly from physical experience. Working communicates a history of past work; this history is turned into a bodily practice until it seems but second nature. This habitus, this bodily knowledge, is unconsciously observed, imitated,

20. John Berger, *Pig Earth* (New York: Pantheon, 1979), 1-12, 195-213.

21. Ibid., 75.

adopted, and passed on in a given community. Our work in nature both reinforces and modifies it.[22]

Luckily, in *River of Traps* Bill deBuys and Alex Harris were outsiders, too old and slow to learn in the usual way. Jacobo Romero had to articulate and explain what would otherwise be second nature at their age. His first and most telling injunction was "never to give holiday to the water," but instead "to put every drop to work."[23] To deBuys and Harris, watching Romero fulfill this injunction is to watch his shovel become a "tool of art." He tuned the water, "watching and listening to it like a technician attending his instruments, amplifying the flow here, muting it there, adjusting, repairing and rearranging."[24] He knew his ditches and fields intimately and precisely; he knew them because he worked them. He knew how to work water, because, from years of working with water he knew that "you got to let the water show you. You take your time, and sooner or later the water will show you."[25]

Wendell Berry is the environmental writer who has most thoughtfully tried to come to terms with labor like that of Romero or Berger's peasants. He is not only one of the few environmental writers who takes work seriously; he also has the impressive consistency of actually laboring in his own fields. But Berry quite purposefully and pointedly makes his own labor archaic and unusual; he relies on animal power and urges others to do this same. It is advice best taken by literary farmers. It is only Wendell Berry's writing, after all, that enables him to farm with horses. Such work resembles gardening, a favored model

---

22. Pierre Bourdieu, *Outline of a Theory of Practice* (Cambridge: Cambridge Univ. Press, 1977), 78-79; idem, *The Logic of Practice*, trans. Richard Nice (Stanford: Stanford Univ. Press, 1990), 66-79. Bourdieu, however, has relatively little to say about how habitus intersects with actual work in the natural world.

23. Berger, *Pig Earth*, 198; William deBuys and Alex Harris, *River of Traps: A Village Life* (Albuquerque: Univ. of New Mexico Press, 1990), 11.

24. DeBuys and Harris, *River of Traps*, 23.

25. Ibid., 24.

these days for a reconciliation with nature.[26] It is admirable; it yields lessons and insights, but it does not yield a living. It is not really our work in the world. Environmentalists still withhold from modern workers—those who work with machines that depend on more than muscle or wind for their power, those who gain their livelihood from work—the possibility of connections to and knowledge of nature.

The inroads that Wendell Berry, or Jacobo Romero, or Berger's peasants make into the general environmentalist disdain for work in nature are ultimately dead ends. For such work is always either vanishing or unable to yield a living. Wendell Berry and Jacobo Romero serve only as additional critiques of modern farming, logging, fishing, ranching, and industry. They don't change the basic message that modern work is the enemy of nature.

How modern work came to be alienated from nature has become the subject of another Just-So Story. This story, ironically, is often told by workers themselves. It is not racialized, like the story of the first white men, but it is just as gendered: it treats work and machines as if they were male or female. Once, this story says, there was real manly work that took skill and strength and was rooted in the natural world. This was the work of Berger's peasants or Jacobo Romero. But this good work has now been contaminated by machines.

This story, like the story of the first white man, uses history without being a history. There certainly is a very real sense in which machinery did both deskill workers and alienate them from nature. As work became less physically demanding, as it required less bodily knowledge, workers who once possessed the skills now made irrelevant by machines felt robbed of something valuable. Old loggers in Coos Bay, Oregon, for example, denigrate modern logging. Their own work among the big trees demanded judgment, strength, and hours of strenuous labor on a single tree, all of which might be lost

---

26. Michael Pollan, *Second Nature: A Gardener's Education* (New York: Delta Trade Paperbacks, 1991), esp. 209-38.

if the tree fell wrong and broke. But modern loggers harvest "pecker poles." The old loggers knew big timber, but loggers are cutting "dog hair these days."[27] This is, of course, hardly the view of modern loggers, although they, too, prefer the harvest of old growth.[28]

In the nineteenth and early twentieth centuries, blue-collar workers regarded physical work as a mark of manhood. They often saw the machines that broke their connection with nature as emasculating them; they associated these machines with women. Charley Russell was a working cowboy before he became a cowboy artist. When he lamented the end of the West, he mourned a world where work in nature defined manhood. Machines that didn't need real men, which could be run by women, had broken the tie between labor and nature:.

"Invention has made it easy for man kind, but it has made him no better. Machinery has no branes. A lady with manicured fingers can drive an automobile with out maring her polished nails. But sit behind six range bred horses with both hands full of ribbons these are God made animals and have branes. To drive these over a mountain rode takes both hands feet and head and its no ladys job.[29]"

A man did real work with "God made animals"; a woman could handle machines "with out maring her polished nails." Machines associated with women broke a male connection with female nature, thus creating an almost domestic drama. Clearly for Russell, machines broke the old connections forged by manly labor.

But this division between good work close to nature and bad work, the work of machines that alienated men from nature, doesn't hold up to historical scrutiny. First of all, archaic labor and peasant labor, for

---

27. William G. Robbins, *Hard Times in Paradise: Coos Bay, Oregon, 1850-1986* (Seattle: Univ. of Washington Press, 1988), 122; for a description of work and skill, see Rajala, "Forest as Factory," 81-82.

28. Dietrich, *Final Forest*, 39.

29. Russell to Friend Bob, April 14, 1920, in *Charles Russell, Catalog: C. M. Russell Museum* (Great Falls, Mont.: C. M. Russell Museum, n.d.), 19.

all the knowledge they yielded, were not necessarily kind to the land. Bill deBuys, who works for the Nature Conservancy, deeply admired Jacobo Romero and his work. He was his neighbor and worked beside him. But he has no illusions that such knowledge protected the land from harm. DeBuys has shown how the agriculture of Jacobo and his neighbors took a toll on the land even as his work created knowledge of the natural world and forged a deep connection with it. [30]

A connection with the land through work creates knowledge, but it does not necessarily grant protection to the land itself. There is a modern romanticism of place that says that those who live and depend on a place will not harm it. Its conservative version is wise use. Its environmentalist version appears in bioregionalism or in the work of Wendell Berry. Berry regards his own writing as depending on "work of the body and of the ground."[31] He regards himself as being very much of a place. In part his connection is from deep familiarity, but it also comes from the pleasure he takes in the work of restoring that place by hand. Yet he restores land that others, who were just as fully of this place, destroyed through their work. Berry writes as if working in nature, of being of a place, brought a moral superiority of sorts. Such rootedness supposedly offers a solution to our problematic relationship with the nonhuman world. I do not think this is necessarily true.[32] The choices are neither so simple nor so stark. Both destructive work and constructive work bring a knowledge of nature, and sometimes

30. DeBuys examines this in *River of Traps* and in an earlier book, *Enchantment and Exploitation: The Life and Hard Times of a New Mexico Mountain Range* (Albuquerque: Univ. of New Mexico Press, 1985), 215-34.

31. Wendell Berry, "The Making of a Marginal Farm," in *Recollected Essays*, 336; idem, "The Body and the Earth," ibid., 269-326.

32. Wendell Berry, *The Unsettling of America: Culture and Agriculture* (New York: Avon Books, 1978), 138-40. For romanticism, see, for example, idem, *A Continuous Harmony: Essays Cultural & Agricultural* (New York: Harcourt Brace Jovanovich, 1972), 79.

work is destructive and restorative at the same time, as when we cut or burn a meadow to prevent the encroachment of forest.

The intellectual, social, and political costs of limiting our choice to these two attitudes toward work and nature are immense. Condemning all work in nature marks environmentalists, as the Forks bumper sticker declares, as a privileged leisure class. Approving of archaic work while condemning modern work marks environmentalists as quaint reactionaries; they seem oblivious to the realities of the modern world. Environmentalists appeal to history to maintain these positions, but they turn history into Just-So Stories.

We need to do better. The choice between condemning all work in nature and sentimentalizing vanishing forms of work is simply not an adequate choice. I am not interested in replacing a romanticism of inviolate nature with a romanticism of local work. Nor am I interested in demonizing machines. Environmentalists need to come to terms with modern work. The problem is not that modern work has been defiled by machines. Women who did much of the backbreaking labor on American farms before electricity have never, to the best of my knowledge, grown nostalgic for the work of pumping and carrying water or cleaning clothes on zinc washboards or any of what Senator George Norris of Nebraska called "the unending punishing tasks" of rural life.[33] Anyone in doubt about the hopes for liberation through machines and the kind of labor in nature that prompted those hopes should read the literature surrounding rural electrification; it described the tedium and social cost of this work in graphic detail.[34]

33. Norris, quoted in Craig Wollner, *Electrifying Eden: Portland General Electric, 1889-1965* (Portland, Ore.: Historical Society Press, 1990), 162.

34. See, for example, D. Clayton Brown, *Electricity for Rural America: The Fight for the REA*, Contributions in Economics and Economic History, No. 29 (Westport, Conn.: Greenwood Press, 1980), 115-20.

Coming to terms with modern work and machines involves both more complicated histories and an examination of how all work, and not just the work of loggers, farmers, fishers, and ranchers, intersects with nature. Technology, an artifact of our work, serves to mask these connections. There are clearly better and worse technologies, but there are no technologies that remove us from nature. We cannot reject the demonization of technology as an independent source of harm only to accept a subset of technologies as rescuing us from the necessity of laboring in, and thus harming, nature. We have already been down this road in the twentieth century.

In the twentieth century technology has often become a container for our hopes or our demons. Much of the technology we now condemn once carried human hopes for a closer and more intimate tie to nature. Over time the very same technology has moved from one category to another. Technology that we, with good reason, currently distrust as environmentally harmful—hydroelectric dams, for example—once carried utopian environmental hopes. To Lewis Mumford, for instance, dams and electricity promised an integration of humans and nature. Mumford saw technology as blurring the boundaries between humans and nature. Humans were "formed by nature and [were] inescapably . . . part of the system of nature." He envisioned a Neotechnic world of organic machines and "ecological balance."[35]

In an ironic and revealing shift, Mumford's solution—his liberating technology, his union of humans and nature—has become redefined as a problem. It is not just that dams, for example, kill salmon; they symbolize the presence of our labor in the middle of nature. In much current environmental writing such blurred boundaries are the mark of our fall. Nature, many environmentalists think, should ideally be beyond the reach of our labor. But in taking such a position, environ-

---

35. Lewis Mumford, *Technics and Civilization* (New York: Harcourt, Brace, 1934), 256-57.

mentalists ignore the way some technologies mask the connections between our work and the natural world.

The idea that pure nature, separate from our work, might no longer exist can prompt near hysteria. Bill McKibben fashioned a best-seller, *The End of Nature*, from that possibility. For McKibben, global warming proved the final blow. "We have changed the atmosphere and thus we are changing the weather. By changing the weather, we make every spot on earth man-made and artificial."[36] "We have deprived nature of its independence, and that is fatal to its meaning. Nature's independence is its meaning; without it there is nothing but us."[37]

Now, nature as I have used it in this essay is only an idea. When we use the word "nature," we assert a unity, a set of relations, and a common identity that involves all the things humans have not made. Nature is, in this sense, purely cultural. Different cultures produce different versions of nature. Although nature is only an idea, it is unlike most other ideas in that we claim to see, feel, and touch it. For in everyday speech we use the word not only to describe a unity of all the things we have not made but also to name a common quality—the natural—possessed by seemingly disparate things: for example, sockeye salmon, Douglas fir, and cockroaches. When we see rocks, animals, or rivers in certain settings, we say we are seeing nature.

McKibben admits that his nature is only an idea, but that only raises the question of why he is so upset over the end of an idea. The answer is, I think, that McKibben, like the rest of us, doesn't really carry the distinction between nature as an idea and nature as the living, breathing world around us over into daily life or practice.[38] It is hard to read his *The End of Nature* without thinking that he considers our modern, Western construction of nature to be largely congruent

---

36. McKibben, 58.

37. Ibid.

38. Ibid., 47-49.

with a real world that is also ending. Most human beings can, after all, easily accommodate a change in the meaning of a word. We all change our minds. We don't often pine for old definitions and ideas. What we miss more are people, animals, landscapes that have vanished. And if all McKibben is lamenting is the loss of an idea, then he is a man who lives far more deeply in his head than in the natural world he writes about. It is as if, all the while insisting on the distinction between mothers and motherhood, he mourned the death of his mother, not, so he claimed, for her own sake, but because the idea of motherhood has for him died with her.

To the extent to which McKibben is upset and not merely being histrionic, it is hard not to suspect that it is the end of what he regards as the natural world itself that upsets him. Thunderstorms, mountain ranges, and bears persist, but without the ability to draw a clear line between weather, mountains, animals, and plants and the consequences of our labor, they have ceased for McKibben to be natural, and we have become unable to "imagine that we are part of something larger than ourselves."[39]

If McKibben's angst is widely shared, then the issue of our contamination of nature is a serious one indeed. For while it is in part the deleterious effects of our labor that McKibben objects to, it is ultimately the ability of our labor to touch all aspects of the natural world, even the climate, that dismays him. The popularity of McKibben's book indicates that for many of us the meaning of the world depends on clear boundaries, pure categories, and the separation of nature out there from us, our bodies, and our work in here. This is, I think, a common American reaction to the modern world, and it is worth some notice. This fixation on purity and this distrust of our own labor—along with our casual, everyday ahistoricism that robs us of any sense of how our current dilemmas developed—explain at least some

---

39. Ibid., 64-65, 83.

of our own inability to deal with mounting environmental problems, bitter social divisions, and increasing despair about our relations with the rest of the planet.

When McKibben writes about his work, he comments that his office and the mountain he views from it are separate parts of his life. They are unconnected. In the office he is in control; outside he is not. Beyond his office window is nature, separate and independent. This is a clean division. Work and nature stand segregated and clearly distinguished.

I, like McKibben, type at a keyboard. On this clear June day I can see the Olympic Mountains in the distance. Like McKibben, I do modem work. I sort, compile, analyze, and organize. My bodily movement becomes electrical signals where my fingers intersect with a machine. Lights flicker on a screen. I expend little energy; I don't sweat, or ache, or grow physically tired. I produce at the end of this day no tangible product; there are only stored memories encoded when my fingers touched keys. There is no dirt or death or even consciousness of bodily labor when I am done. Trees still grow, animals still graze, fish still swim.

But, unlike McKibben, I cannot see my labor as separate from the mountains, and I know that my labor is not truly disembodied. If I sat and typed here day after day, as clerical workers type, without frequent breaks to wander and to look at the mountains, I would become achingly aware of my body. I might develop carpal tunnel syndrome. My body, the nature in me, would rebel. The lights on this screen need electricity, and this particular electricity comes from dams on the Skagit or Columbia. These dams kill fish; they alter the rivers that come from the Rockies, Cascades, and Olympics. The electricity they produce depends on the great seasonal cycles of the planet: on falling snow, melting waters, flowing rivers. In the end, these electrical impulses will take tangible form on paper from trees. Nature, altered and changed, is in this room. But this is masked. I type. I kill nothing. I touch no living thing. I seem to alter nothing but the screen. If I don't think about it, I can seem benign, the mountains separate and safe from me as the Adirondacks seem safe from McKibben as he writes his essays for the *New Yorker*. But, of course, the natural world has changed and continues to change to allow me to sit here, just as it changes to allow McKibben to write. My separation is an illusion. What is disguised is that I—unlike loggers, farmers, fishers, or herders—do not have to face what I alter, and so I learn nothing from it. The connection my labor makes flows in only one direction.

My work, I suspect, is similar to that of most environmentalists. Because it seems so distant from nature, it escapes the condemnation that the work that takes place out there, in "nature," attracts. I regularly read the *High Country News*, and its articles just as regularly denounce mining, ranching, and logging for the very real harm they do. And since the paper's editors have some sympathy for rural people trying to live on the land, letters from readers denounce the paper for not condemning these activities enough. The intention of those who defend old growth or denounce overgrazing is not to denounce hard physical work, but that is, in effect, what the articles do. There are few articles or letters denouncing university professors or computer programmers or accountants or lawyers for sullying the environment, although it is my guess that a single lawyer or accountant could, on a good day, put the efforts of Paul Bunyan to shame.[40]

Most humans must work, and our work—all our work—inevitably embeds us in nature, including what we consider wild and pristine places. Environmentalists have invited the kind of attack contained in the Forks bumper sticker by identifying nature with leisure, by

---

40. The *High Country News* is a superb paper. In general it provides the best view of the West now available, and the views in it are not necessarily those of its editors. I am not seeking to apologize for the real harm done by logging, ranching, and mining, but most reporting on those industries is either implicitly or explicitly a denunciation of the industries themselves and their work and not just the specific harm they do. See, for example, *High Country News*, issue of June 13, 1994.

masking the environmental consequences of their own work. To escape it, and perhaps even to find allies among people unnecessarily made into enemies, there has to be some attempt to come to terms with work. Work does not prevent harm to the natural world—Forks itself is evidence of that—but if work is not perverted into a means of turning place into property, it can teach us how deeply our work and nature's work are intertwined.

And if we do not come to terms with work, if we fail to pursue the implications of our labor and our bodies in the natural world, then we will return to patrolling the borders. We will turn public lands into a public playground; we will equate wild lands with rugged play; we will imagine nature as an escape, a place where we are born again. It will be a paradise where we leave work behind. Nature may turn out to look a lot like an organic Disneyland, except it will be harder to park.

There is, too, an inescapable corollary to this particular piece of self-deception. We will condemn ourselves to spending most of our lives outside of nature, for there can be no permanent place for us inside. Having demonized those whose very lives recognize the tangled complexity of a planet in which we kill, destroy and alter as a condition of living and working, we can claim an innocence that in the end is merely irresponsibility.

If, on the other hand, environmentalism could focus on our work rather than on our leisure, then a whole series of fruitful new angles on the world might be possible. It links us to each other, and it links us to nature. It unites issues as diverse as workplace safety and grazing on public lands; it unites toxic sites and wilderness areas. In taking responsibility for our own lives and work, in unmasking the connections of our labor and nature's labor, in giving up our hopeless fixation on purity, we may ultimately find a way to break the borders that imprison nature as much as ourselves. Work, then, is where we should begin.

About the Editors

Finn Wilcox worked in the woods of the Olympic and Cascade Mountains with the forest workers' cooperative, Olympic Reforestation, for over twenty years. From the early 1980s through the early 90s, he was an editor for Empty Bowl, a writers' cooperative publisher. He is the author of *Here Among the Sacrificed* (Empty Bowl) and *Nine Flower Mountain* (Tangram). He has lived the past 32 years with his family in Port Townsend, Washington.

Jerry Gorsline has resided on the Olympic Peninsula since 1975. He has worked as a tree-climber, bookseller, forestry contractor, and restaurateur, and recently retired from serving as policy analyst and habitat campaign director for the Washington Environmental Council. He has been involved in publishing, writing, and editorial work, including early involvement in the bioregional movement as contributing editor for the San Francisco-based Planet Drum Foundation. His published works include: *Shadows of Our Ancestors: Readings in the History of Klallam-White Relations*, and *Rainshadow: Archibald Menzies and the Botanical Exploration of the Olympic Peninsula*.

The Blossoms are Ghosts at the Wedding
Selected Poems and Essays

by Tom Jay

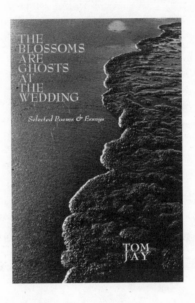

Anyone who reads Tom Jay without being changed
simply isn't reading closely enough.

—Freeman House

301 526 0013

Angel - 206 386 4560